Give

Cognitive Linguistics Research
7

Editors
René Dirven
Ronald W. Langacker
John R. Taylor

Mouton de Gruyter
Berlin · New York

Give

A Cognitive Linguistic Study

John Newman

1996
Mouton de Gruyter
Berlin · New York

Mouton de Gruyter (formerly Mouton, The Hague)
is a Division of Walter de Gruyter & Co., Berlin

P281
.N48
1996

Library of Congress Cataloging-in-Publication Data

Newman, John, 1948–
   Give : a cognitive linguistic study / John Newman.
      p.   cm. – (Cognitive linguistics research ; 7)
   Includes bibliographical references (p.) and indexes.
   ISBN 3-11-014894-3 (alk. paper)
   1. Grammar, Comparative and general–Verb. 2. Gram-
mar, Comparative and general–Syntax. 3. Semantics. 4.
Generosity. 5. Cognitive grammar. I. Title. II. Series.
P281.N48   1996
415–dc20   96-11061
                                    CIP

Die Deutsche Bibliothek – Cataloging-in-Publication Data

Newman, John:
Give : a cognitive linguistic study / John Newman. – Berlin ;
New York : Mouton de Gruyter, 1996
   (Cognitive linguistics research ; 7)
   ISBN 3-11-014894-3
NE: GT

Contents

Preface   ix

Abbreviations   xvii

1. General remarks on GIVE verbs   1

  1.1. GIVE as a basic verb   1
    1.1.1. Giving   1
    1.1.2. GIVE words in language acquisition   4
    1.1.3. Core vocabularies   7
      1.1.3.1. The GIVE morpheme in Kalam   8
      1.1.3.2. GIVE in Dyirbal   10
      1.1.3.3. GIVE and Wierzbicka's semantic primitives   12
      1.1.3.4. GIVE in Basic English   13
    1.1.4. Metaphorical extensions of GIVE   15
    1.1.5. Basic forms of GIVE   17

  1.2. The exceptionality of GIVE words   21
    1.2.1. Directionality   22
    1.2.2. Honorific variants   23
    1.2.3. SG vs PL forms of GIVE   27
    1.2.4. Passive   28
    1.2.5. Exceptional verb morphology   29

  1.3. Summary   31

2. The meaning of GIVE   33

  2.1. Preliminaries   33

  2.2. The spatio-temporal domain   37

  2.3. The control domain   46

  2.4. The force-dynamics domain   48

  2.5. The domain of human interest   51

  2.6. The complex matrix of GIVE   53

  2.7. Unfilled elaboration sites   54

2.8. The meaning of TAKE 56

2.9. Summary 59

3. Constructions with literal GIVE 61

3.1. The AGENT-PATIENT model 61
    3.1.1. Verb marking 68
    3.1.2. Two objects 74

3.2. Beyond the object 80
    3.2.1. RECIPIENT as a dative 82
    3.2.2. RECIPIENT as a goal 88
    3.2.3. RECIPIENT as a locative 93
    3.2.4. RECIPIENT as a benefactive 95
    3.2.5. RECIPIENT as a possessor 98
    3.2.6. More complex networks 101
    3.2.7. THING as an instrument 105
    3.2.8. Incorporated object 109
    3.2.9. THING and RECIPIENT both obliques 110

3.3. Constructions with TAKE 115

3.4. The significance of schematic networks 119

3.5. Integrating the morphemes 122

3.6. Summary 130

4. Constructions with figurative GIVE 133

4.1. Figurative GIVE 133

4.2. Interpersonal communication 136

4.3. Emergence/manifestation of entities 144
    4.3.1. Emergence 145
    4.3.2. Manifestation 156
        4.3.2.1. Reflexive GIVE 158
        4.3.2.2. Impersonal GIVE 160
        4.3.2.3. Passive GIVE 166
        4.3.2.4. Intransitive GIVE 168
    4.3.3. GIVE as "become" 168

4.4. Causative/purposive 171
    4.4.1. GIVE as "have someone do something" 173

4.4.2. GIVE as "cause" — 175
4.4.3. GIVE as a purposive marker — 180

4.5. Permission/enablement — 181
4.5.1. "Give permission" type — 182
4.5.2. "Give someone a book to read" type — 185
4.5.3. "Give someone to think" type — 186
4.5.4. GIVE as "enable" — 188
4.5.5. GIVE as a hortative — 194
4.5.6. Agentive preposition in Mandarin — 196
4.5.7. Mandarin emphatic — 199

4.6. Schematic interaction — 201

4.7. Recipient/benefactive — 211
4.7.1. GIVE as a RECIPIENT marker — 212
4.7.2. GIVE as a benefactive — 217

4.8. Movement — 223
4.8.1. GIVE as "movement away" — 225
4.8.2. GIVE as "movement into" — 227

4.9. Completedness — 228

4.10. Overview of the main categories of extension — 231
4.10.1. The network of GIVE meanings — 232
4.10.2. Motivating semantic extensions — 234

4.11. Miscellaneous extensions — 238
4.11.1. Metonymies — 238
4.11.2. People giving people — 240

4.12. Overview of figurative extensions of GIVE and TAKE — 243

4.13. Summary — 249

5. Conclusion and prospects for future research — 253

5.1. Conclusion — 253
5.1.1. Giving as a basic and complex act — 254
5.1.2. Literal GIVE — 259
5.1.3. Figurative GIVE — 262

5.2. Prospects for future research — 265
5.2.1. Studies of individual languages — 266
5.2.2. Diachronic case studies — 270
5.2.3. Basic vocabulary — 274

Notes   277
Chapter one   277
Chapter two   278
Chapter three   278
Chapter four   281
Chapter five   284

References   285

Index of languages   303

Index of names   307

Index of subjects   311

Preface

This book is an investigation into the properties of "give" verbs across languages, carried out within the framework which has come to be known as *cognitive linguistics*. I use the term *cognitive linguistics* to refer to an approach to the study of language which is guided by certain broad statements of faith concerning the nature of language, by certain research questions which are considered worthwhile and interesting to ask, by research methodologies which are deemed appropriate, and by the writings of those considered to be the major proponents of the approach.

The statements of faith which help to define the kind of cognitive linguistics followed in this book are essentially those identified by Rudzka-Ostyn (1993: 1–2). Rudzka-Ostyn's summing up of the "cognitive paradigm" in linguistics appears as an Introduction to a volume which was based on papers presented at the First International Cognitive Linguistics Conference, which took place between March 28 and April 4 1989, in Duisburg, Germany. Although the intellectual positions identified by Rudzka-Ostyn do not amount to any manifesto as such, they do express the spirit of the cognitive linguistics movement. Some key ideas which permeate the writings of linguists working within this paradigm are: (a) there are important links between linguistic structure and human cognition, making it imperative to acknowledge the role of human cognition and human experience in motivating and explicating linguistic structure; (b) a language community imposes its own categorizations upon the entities which constitute reality and such categorizations may differ considerably from one language community to another; (c) most of the categories relevant to linguistics are viewed as having central and less central members rather than being criterially defined; (d) where the meaning of a form needs to be elaborated, then a larger context or "frame" needs to be invoked in order to properly describe the meaning. When it comes to investigating clause structure, these same key ideas guide the analysis. Consistent with the ideas (a) - (d), an account of clause structure in a language will be informed by considerations of human cognition, perception, and experience, rather than relying exclusively on concepts and principles which have no justification outside the realm of linguistic analysis. So, for example, concepts such as "figure" and "ground" which have significance in human cognition generally may well appear in a cognitive linguistic account of clause structure, whereas concepts like "c-command", "the subjacency parameter", and the "empty category principle", which have no relevance outside of a particular theory of linguistic structure, would be distinctly out of place in a cognitive linguistic approach.

Given some of the key ideas which find favour within the cognitive linguistics movement, as briefly described above, it should not be surprising that the label *cognitive linguistics* was chosen as a way of characterizing this movement. It is interesting, therefore, to note that the name has occasioned some heated debate within linguistics. Rather than being confined to the rushed exchanges at coffee-breaks during conferences or the somewhat lengthier exchanges in pizzerias and pancake parlours in the evenings during conferences, the debate over the name *cognitive linguistics* is preserved for all to behold in the form of a string of e-mail exchanges conducted over the electronic LINGUIST list in February-April 1991. There is, I believe, a feeling that the linguists who refer to themselves as cognitive linguists have appropriated for themselves a label which they have no special right to. There are, after all, linguists who are not part of the cognitive linguistics movement who nevertheless feel that they are in some sense contributing to a better understanding of language and its relation to human cognition. I acknowledge that there may be many linguists outside of the cognitive linguistics movement, as characterized above, who have some right to call themselves cognitive linguists. The kind of cognitive linguistics which forms the backdrop to the present book is naturally called cognitive linguistics in the light of its deep and ever-present interest in cognition, but I accept that it is not the only kind of approach one might label cognitive. For example, one might wish to pursue a more uncompromisingly autonomous approach to the study of syntax relying heavily on syntax-internal principles, but, ultimately aiming to discover ways in which syntactic principles and cognitive principles connect or appear similar. A research programme of this sort might well be labelled cognitive in a larger sense, even if the more immediate goals appear unrelated to cognitive concerns.

The questions raised within a theory contribute also to a full description of the theory. A theory leads to certain specific questions, or at least permits a researcher to ask certain questions. Conversely, there are questions which are not raised in a particular theory, either because such questions make unacceptable assumptions about the nature of the object being investigated or because the questions deal with matters which are simply beyond the scope of the theory. There are some questions which are considered interesting and answerable within cognitive linguistics and which help to define the nature of cognitive linguistics. The questions favoured by cognitive linguists tend to revolve around themes such as the following: lexical and constructional polysemy; mechanisms of semantic change, especially metonymy and metaphor; grammaticalization; the conceptualization of space and time as reflected in language structure; the cognitive basis of a linguistic category; language as a reflection of our experiential reality. This is by no means an exhaustive list, but it serves to give some idea of the research questions being investigated within the cognitive linguistics movement. Researchers drawn to cognitive linguistics would usually find these interesting areas to explore and would usually consider that generative theories of linguistics do not adequately cater to such interests. At the same time, there are questions about language which fail to be asked in this approach. Within the generative approach to syntactic theorizing, for example, numerous questions arise which are only understandable in terms of the quite specific assumptions inherent in the theory. When the assumptions are unacceptable to begin with, then the questions which are formulated within the theory become pseudo-questions without any real import. To the extent that cognitive linguists find the basic assumptions of generative syntax unacceptable, they will also find the questions that these assumptions lead to uninteresting and irrelevant.

As for a characteristic research methodology, I do not believe cognitive linguistics has any one methodology which it can call its own. Instead, there is quite a variation in the ways in which data are collected and investigated. So, for example, the data which figure in cognitive linguistic analyses might be drawn from published grammars, historical texts, original field work, dictionary entries, psycholinguistic experiments, questionnaires, introspection etc., just as one finds with virtually every other linguistic theory. In the analysis of data, too, there is considerable variation regarding such points as whether or not unacceptable sentences figure in the discussion, how much the linguist relies on notation to support the discussion etc. One can expect a considerable amount of talk about cognition, perception, and human experience as part of the process of analysis, as follows from what was said above. There is probably a more modest approach to argumentation than is current in some linguistic theorizing, though, as in any academic discipline, rigour and honesty in argumentation are essential. As might be inferred from what has already been said, the overriding goal in cognitive linguistics is not to construct a formal system in which theorems are proved, but rather to better understand the cognitive basis of language. Consistent with this orientation, the more typical kind of article or presentation in cognitive linguistics aims to persuade by means such as: drawing analogies between language structure and cognitive structure; demonstrating how cognitive, perceptual, or experiential facts constrain or otherwise determine the linguistic facts; establishing the reasonableness of considering two or more meanings to be related etc. Often, these are not the kinds of claims which can be proved in any strict sense in the way one proves a theorem in, say, trigonometry.

There are many important voices which have contributed to the development of the cognitive linguistics movement. There is no one linguist who has set the agenda for other cognitive linguists. This state of affairs inevitably spawns some alternative approaches and methodologies, even when the researchers involved might agree on the basic tenets of the cognitive paradigm. This situation is neither uncommon nor unhealthy and from my own discussions with university colleagues in other disciplines, I have no reason to think that the situation is significantly different in other disciplines. If I were asked to name some of the more influential figures in the specific cognitive linguistics movement alluded to by Rudzka-Ostyn above, then I would certainly put forward the names René Dirven, Dirk Geeraerts, George Lakoff, Ronald Langacker, Eve Sweetser, and Leonard Talmy. It is rather arbitrary to restrict the list to just the ones named, however, and I could easily add to this list names of other linguists who have had some influence on my own thinking about cognitive linguistics.

It is against the background of the cognitive linguistics movement, as I have just sketched it, that the present work took shape. For some years, I had been impressed by the complexity of the morphology and syntax which accompanied "give" verbs across languages. This might be an appropriate place to acknowledge an intellectual debt I owe to a decidedly uncognitive theory of syntax, namely Relational Grammar, and to one of its main proponents, if not its main proponent, David Perlmutter. It was through David Perlmutter's stimulating courses on Relational Grammar at the University of California at San Diego in the late 1970s that I first gained an appreciation of the complexity of "give" clauses and the variation one finds cross-linguistically in the syntactic patterning of such clauses. I may have been unconvinced that "1", "2", and "3" held the key to a complete understanding of "give", but I was sufficiently impressed by the Relational Grammar analyses of "give" clauses to want to explore the topic further.

My own interest in a more cognitive linguistic approach to the study of language dates back to the lectures of Ronald Langacker in 1976, also at the University of California at San Diego. These were the lectures which, refined and honed over the years, eventually gave rise to *Foundations of Cognitive Grammar* Volumes I (1987) and II (1991). In these lectures, we heard about signs, imaging, figure and ground, perspective, lexical networks, prototypes, the rule versus list fallacy, summary versus sequential scanning etc. The double blackboards in the classroom would be covered with roughly drawn rectangles and squares, surrounded by larger rectangles and squares, which in turn were surrounded by even larger rectangles and squares, all connected with squiggly lines in red and yellow and green chalk. It was fascinating, disturbing, refreshing, stimulating, disappointing, lucid, obscure, avant-garde, and strangely pre-modern. And in the end, it won me over.

The fact that I could have been attending lectures of two such opposite linguists such as Ronald Langacker and David Perlmutter and that, furthermore, I was enjoying the courses both of them offered might seem rather strange. I admit there was something slightly bizarre about the situation, but I was not the only one in those days who was able to profit from the lectures of both of these linguists. A fellow student of mine at the time, David Tuggy, was another person who could feel stimulated in these two different ways and it was David who once made the remark which seemed to so neatly sum up the situation as he and I found it at the time: "What Ron [Langacker] says is obviously true, but it's not acceptable, whereas what Dave [Perlmutter] says is very acceptable, but is it true?" Things have changed somewhat over the years and what once seemed unacceptable is more accepted now and what once seemed so acceptable is less so now.

My first attempt at rethinking "give" in terms of cognitive linguistics was an account of Mandarin *gěi*, presented as a paper at the First International Cognitive Linguistics Conference, 1989, referred to above, and published as Newman (1993a). It seemed a natural progression to extend the study of "give" to other languages and the result is the present monograph.

Chapters 1 and 2, I hope, go some way towards establishing why it is worthwhile devoting some time to the study of the one verb "give". In Chapter 1, I detail some of the reasons why "give" is a relatively basic kind of verb. There are various ways in which lexical items might function as basic, but it would seem that "give" is basic in just about any of the ways one wishes to understand *basic*. To begin a study of what might be called the syntax and semantics of "give" with a discussion of giving and its role in human affairs must appear strange to linguists accustomed to the methodology of autonomous syntax. And, indeed, it would be inappropriate in such a context. In a cognitive linguistic approach, however, it is both appropriate and desirable to commence a study of "give" with some reflection on the experiential reality of the act of giving and the status of verbs meaning "give". Chapter 2 tries to unravel the meaning of "give". Giving invokes a scene involving a giver, a thing being passed, and a recipient. Spelling out these components and the additional characteristics of the entities which comprise the giving scene is a necessary piece of groundwork. The components of meaning which are identified in this chapter are relevant to many of the points which are made in the later chapters. The material in Chapters 1 and 2 *motivate* the facts discussed in Chapters 3 and 4.

Chapter 3 deals with the constructions that "give" verbs enter into, where the verb has the sense of "transferring control over something to someone". Quite a variety of case-marking and adpositions is to be found in these constructions cross-linguistically. In cognitive linguistics, case endings and adpositions bear meanings which are susceptible to the same kind of semantic analysis as lexical morphemes. In particular, one may proceed to document the polysemy which is to be found with such morphemes. The variation which is found in the construction types is not a crazy type of variation, but rather is seen to be motivated by facts about the meaning of the predicate "give".

The meanings which interest cognitive linguists are by no means restricted to those one might call *literal* meanings. On the contrary, the full range of meanings of a morpheme or construction, including *figurative* meanings, is seen as a proper and rewarding research area. Hence, Chapter 4 documents the vast range of figurative meanings which may attach to "give" verbs. Once again, the material in Chapters 1 and 2 is relevant, in so far as that material helps us to appreciate why there should be such a proliferation of extensions in the meaning of "give" verbs. The basicness of giving as a common, gestalt-like act between humans and the semantic complexity inherent within the meaning of "give" are both relevant to understanding this state of affairs. Included in this chapter are those constructions in which a "give" verb has become grammaticalized, and here, too, there is a considerable number of such cases.

Chapter 5 is a conclusion to the present study as well as an attempt to identify the ways in which this study leads to future research. Since a study devoted to the concept of "give" might appear very specific and narrow in its focus, I believe it is important to indicate how it does naturally connect with, and lead to, other areas of research.

Throughout the book, I have tried to write in a style which makes the ideas understandable to a wider range of readers than just linguists. One of the pleasant surprises about doing cognitive linguistics is that colleagues from various other disciplines can be interested in what you are saying and are able to participate in a mutually beneficial dialogue about language with you. I would like to think that it is true of the present study, too, that there may be something of interest in it to readers who are not professional linguists.

As one might infer from what I said above, my thinking about linguistic problems owes most to Ronald Langacker and his influence will be evident on most pages of this book and I take this opportunity to express my gratitude to him for his encouragement and support over the years. I am grateful to those linguists who kindly provided me with material on "give" verbs: Barbara Dancygier, Yukio Hirose, Tania Kuteva, Jon Patrick, Robert Petterson, Sally Rice, Noel Rude, and Donna Starks. I am grateful to many others, too, for sharing their knowledge about "give" verbs with me. I am particularly grateful to Sally Rice for feedback on an early draft of this work and her encouragement at the times when some encouragement was needed. The meetings of the International Cognitive Linguistics Asssociation have been particularly valuable to me in providing the setting to air my ideas amongst other cognitively oriented linguists. So, too, the conferences of the Linguistic Society of New Zealand and the seminar series at Otago University and my own university, Massey University, have provided congenial and supportive settings for me to test out my ideas on audiences with diverse linguistic and non-linguistic backgrounds. A grant from the Massey University Research Fund, A90/F/131, enabled me to employ a research assistant during the summer of 1990–1991 and it was with the help of my research assistant, Amanda Keogh, that a considerable amount of data was collected. I thank Amanda for her diligence and good-humoured co-operation at a time when the aims and scope of the project were still only vaguely defined. Massey University also made it possible for me to spend a four-month sabbatical period at the University of California, Berkeley, in 1992–1993, which proved to be a most stimulating, if all too brief, visit. I am especially grateful to Bill Wang at Berkeley for creating the opportunity for me to present some of my work on "give" at a seminar there. The reviewers of an earlier draft of this book are also to be thanked for their extensive and valuable comments.

On another level altogether, I would like to express my deep gratitude to Kathleen for the emotional support and understanding which helped me to continue with this project. I never promised that sharing her life with a linguist would be easy.

Abbreviations

ABL	ablative		INST	instrumental
ABS	absolutive		IO	indirect object
ACC	accusative			
ALL	allative		LINK	linking word
ANIM	animate		LM	landmark
ART	article			
ASP	aspect		MASC	masculine
AUX	auxiliary		NEG	negative
			NOM	nominative
BEN	benefactive			
			OBJ	object
CL	classifier		OBL	oblique
COMP	complementizer			
			PASS	passive
DAT	dative		PERF	perfective
DO	direct object		PL	plural
DU	dual		POSS	possessive
			PRE	prefix
ERG	ergative		PRED	predicate
EXCL	exclusive		PREP	preposition
			PRES	present
FEM	feminine			
FUT	future		REFL	reflexive
GEN	genitive		SG	singular
			SUBJ	subject
IMP	imperative		SUF	suffix
IMPERF	imperfective			
INAN	inanimate		TNS	tense
INCL	inclusive		TR	trajector
INF	infinitive		TRANS	transitive

Chapter 1. General remarks on GIVE verbs

1.1. GIVE as a basic verb

1.1.1. Giving

In referring to an act of giving, I will mean, in the typical case, an act whereby a person (the GIVER) passes with the hands control over an object (THING) to another person (the RECIPIENT).[1] Specific acts of giving may well have additional features. Giving birthday presents, giving "red-packets" containing money in Chinese culture, giving prizes in competitions etc. are types of giving which have their own particular rituals associated with them and are certainly more elaborate than my characterization of giving above. There are types of giving which call for reciprocity so that when X gives something to Y, Y is thereby put in debt to X, and so Y must in turn give something back to X. Some version of this principle of reciprocity is evident in many cultures. It is present as part of commercial transactions which constitute a large class of acts of giving in many societies. Japanese culture is often cited as one where reciprocity of this sort is deeply entrenched (cf. the discussion of gift-exchange practices in Hijirida—Yoshikawa 1987: 46–50). As another example of culture-specific practices relating to giving, consider Dixon's description of Dyirbal society (which may be applicable to other non-monetary societies as well): "there is very little spontaneous non-necessary giving, but a great deal of necessary giving, according to the people's habits of sharing most things with their relatives" (Dixon 1972: 237). As further evidence of the different cultural role of giving in Dyirbal and modern Western societies, Dixon (1973: 206–207, 210) mentions the different range of meanings of the various GIVE-type verbs in Dyirbal compared with English. In Dyirbal, there are GIVE-type verbs which are differentiated in terms of position and movement, and kinship obligation. For example, *wugan* involves giving where there is no significant movement by the participants. It would be used for handing an object to someone nearby. *Bilan* is used when there is significant movement, such as when the giver walks some distance to pass over the object. *Yuṛan* is used when the giving occurs through something else, such as passing an object through a window. *Gibin* means "to provide food for relatives". In English, on the other hand, there are specialized GIVE-type verbs involving money and contracts, like *donate, present, award, pay, lend, sell, rent* etc. These linguistic differences are quite reasonably seen as reflecting the different role of giving in the two societies. So, a full account of giving must take larger social practices into account. There is much that could be said about all the manifestations of giving acts and even what constitutes typical giving in specific cultures. Here I am attempting to do no more than characterize what appears to me to constitute the essence of a giving act in any culture.

Considering the diversity of acts which might all be classed as giving of some kind, one may well wonder why it is that I single out the particular kind of interaction between persons sketched above as a starting point for a discussion of giving. Even if we just limit ourselves to English, for example, there is an impressive variety of uses of the verb *give*, illustrated in (1), all of which are arguably classifiable as some kind of giving:

(1)   a.   *Kim gave Lee a nice birthday present.* (where Kim actually handed over her birthday present to Lee)
      b.   *Kim gave Lee a nice birthday present.* (where Kim arranged for some money to be deposited in Lee's bank account)
      c.   *Kim gave Lee emotional support.*
      d.   *Kim gave Lee a kiss.*
      e.   *Kim gave in to Lee.*

In taking a transfer of control over a thing as a typical instance of giving, I am giving some priority to the use of *give* illustrated in (1a) over the other uses illustrated in (1). One reason for proceeding in this way has to do with a certain cognitive priority of concrete, easily visualizable entities over more abstract and less easily visualizable entities. This priority is evident in the way that we understand abstract notions metaphorically in terms of more concrete things, rather than the other way around. More specifically, when it comes to analyzing and motivating the range of uses associated with words meaning GIVE in languages, it is more intuitive to motivate these uses as extensions, ultimately, from the "transfer of control" sense of the word than from some other sense. Furthermore, to the extent that this is really verifiable, the "transfer of control" sense would appear to be a very common sense found with *give*. West's list (West 1953: 208–209) conveniently provides frequencies of the senses of words and, in the case of *give,* the "transfer of ownership" sense constitutes 35% of all instances of the verb, this being the single most frequent category of all the sense categories associated with the verb. The statistics in West's list can certainly not be taken as definitive statistics relating to all styles of English, but it does give some indication of the centrality of the "transfer of possession" sense. It may be that a GIVE word in some other languages does not have the same high frequency of this sense. In traditional Dyirbal society, for example, there does not appear to have been any transfer of ownership in the sense we are talking about. Nevertheless, the idea of a transfer of "control" over the thing (understood broadly as involving access to the thing and the freedom to do with the thing what one likes) is presumably still part of the core meaning of the GIVE word.

Acts of giving in societies I know about (and I cannot easily imagine a society where this would be different) have considerable functional importance, in terms of the role they play in ordinary human interaction. Acts of giving involve not just human interaction but are also frequent and generally highly purposeful. It would appear, then, that the act of giving is basic and central to human experience. Such reflections lead one to consider the act of giving as a "basic level category", a concept which has been investigated by many researchers, particularly Roger Brown, Brent Berlin, and Eleanor Rosch. Lakoff (1987: 31–38, 46–54) reviews the history of this research and summarizes the main contributions that these researchers have made. Some of the properties which characterize this level of category are: it is the level of distinctive actions (where actions are relevant to the category); it is the level which is learned earliest; categories at this level have greater cultural significance; at this level things are perceived holistically, as a single gestalt. So, for example, "dog" and "chair" have been advanced as basic level categories, while the superordinate categories of "animal" and "furniture" as well as the subordinate categories "rottweiler" and "armchair" do not have the same basic level status. Within a taxonomy of possible action-type categories, it seems to me that the act of giving is a good candidate for a basic level category. The functional significance of acts of giving seems undeniable; it is easy to conceive of an act of giving as a whole; acts of giving occupy a middle-level position between some superordinate categories like "acts" and "events" and some subordinate categories like "donate" and "bribe". All these observations lend support to categorizing an act of giving as a basic-level category in Lakoff's terms.

In the following sections, I will present a variety of linguistic facts which may be seen as reflecting the basic level nature of the act of giving.[2] The intention behind presenting this material is to establish that there is a variety of ways in which GIVE morphemes are noteworthy with respect to what we might call their "basicness" in language. These superficially disparate facts all seem to point to a kind of basicness about the use of GIVE morphemes which would not be recognized in most current approaches to linguistics. Proceeding as we have done from various observations about the central role of the act of giving in human experience, however, we are led naturally to seek out facts about the role of GIVE morphemes in natural languages.

1.1.2. GIVE words in language acquisition

Not surprisingly, the *give me...* construction in English is one of the earliest constructions to be understood by a child acquiring English as a first language.[3] A number of studies testify to the ability of children to understand *give* early on in the child's development of language. Of particular interest is the work by Benedict (1979). Benedict studied the comprehension of words in a group of eight children over a period of a year, from when the children were nine months old to one year nine months. By the end of the observation period, all the children understood at least 50 words and it is this group of words which is relevant here. Verbs like *give* fall into Benedict's class of "action words". These are words that elicit specific actions from the child or that accompany actions of the child (this class makes up 36% of the first 50 words comprehended). The following table shows the action words understood by more than half of the sample population (by the time each child understood 50 words), together with the number of children who understood them.

(2)   *give* (8), *where's* (8), *bye-bye* (7), *pat-a-cake* (7), *get* (7), *come here* (7), *look at* (6), *dance* (5), *peek-a-boo* (5), *do nice* (5), *kiss* (5), *put in* (5)

Interestingly, *give* is one of only two action words included in each child's first 50 words understood. The study thus shows that language acquisition is one area where GIVE words and the constructions they enter into play an exceptionally important role.

Similar results on children's comprehension can be found in Chapman (1981), summarized in Ingram (1989: 166–168). This research investigated the comprehension of various grammatical constructions by children between the ages of 10 months and 21 months. The *give me X* construction (where *X* stands for some object name) was one of the items used by Chapman to test comprehension. In response to the stimulus *Give me the book*, the child was supposed to select the correct object and give it to the researcher. The researchers did not set out to investigate the comprehension of the specific verb *give* as such but, rather, the comprehension of requests involving names of objects, such as *Where's X*, *Go get X*. Consequently, the results of the comprehension of the *Give me X*, *Where's X*, and *Go get X* constructions were all grouped together as the "Object name" item. It is interesting to note that in the age bracket 13–15 months, all twelve children in the group being studied passed the comprehension test of this item (by getting or giving etc. the appropriate item). The only other item for which all twelve children passed at that age was the "Person name" item, where the child had to indicate the correct person in response to a question such as *Where's Mama*. (This is consistent with Benedict's findings which showed that *Where's X* was one of the most frequent early items understood, irrespective of whether *X* referred to a person or an object.) Some of the other items tested for comprehension included: carrying out an action on an object in response to stimuli such as *Kiss the shoe* (only one child passed this test); making some other agent perform an action as in *Make the doggie kiss* (no child passed this test); and making some other agent perform an action on a named object as in *Horsey kiss the ball* (no child passed this test). Notice that there are in fact more arguments of the predicate *give* in *Give me the ball* (consisting of three logical arguments *you*, *me*, *the ball*) than we find with *kiss* in *Horsey kiss the ball* (consisting of two arguments). If the logical structure were any guide to the children's ability to process such utterances, then we would expect the *kiss* sentence to be more easily comprehended, but this was not the case. The results suggest rather that *Give me* constructions reflect a basicness about the giving act in human (or at least in the child's) experience, which of course is not incorporated into a representation of the logical structure. As noted above, however, Chapman did not isolate the *Give me* construction as an item in its own right, but tested it only as part of the larger "Object name" item. Consequently, there are no statistics in Chapman's study specifically on the *give* construction.

The early words produced by children have also been studied. The study by Benedict referred to above, in fact, investigated not only comprehension, but also production. Her results for the production of *give* are quite different from the results on comprehension. None of her subjects produced *give* as one of their first 50 words produced, though five had produced the action words *see* and *byebye* in their first 50 words, for example. The explanation for this state of affairs can be found in Benedict's discussion of her findings, which indicated that action words in general, not just *give*, are relatively rare amongst the early words produced. As Benedict (1979: 198) points out, actions done by the child such as throwing and giving are typically accompanied by a nominal type of word (*ball*, for example) rather than the action word. Presumably, then, virtually any of the nominals which are produced as early words can be used in this way. Thus, although *give*, or a form corresponding to it, does not appear early in a child's speech, acts of giving may still be amongst the earliest acts to be commented on by the child or reflected in some way in the child's speech. Benedict's research does not yield conclusive results on this specific point, but it would be consistent with her general observations. It would also be consistent with observations about the overgeneralizations of words in children's speech (see Ingram 1989: 149–160 for an overview of the research). So, for example, Braunwald (1978) notes the following referential and functional uses of her daughter's word *ball* at age one year four months: (i) a ball, (ii) round objects, and (iii) request for the first and second servings of liquid in a cup. In the request use the word *ball* is functioning to help bring about an act of giving. In so far as the "request" meaning intended by the use of nouns like *ball* is an instance of the meaning GIVE, one can see that the concept of "give me" is expressed very early on by children even if it is not encoded in the adult way.

A similar result may be found in Tomasello (1992: 77–79), who observes that *give* was never frequent in the speech of the child he observed between sixteen and twenty-four months. *Gimme me* occurs as a request in the nineteenth month, *Give it pencil* in the twentieth month, and *Give it to me* at age twenty-three months. Nevertheless, the idea of requesting someone to give her something was possible in this period through the use of other verbs, specifically *get*, *hold*, and *have*. So, for example, *Hold Weezer* was used when she wanted to hold the cat a parent was holding (Tomasello 1992: 76). While the actual form *give* may not have been frequent, the expressions with the implied sense of "give me" were again comparable to the results of Chapman's study. (In fact, the child Tomasello observed also produced utterances with *gave*, reporting on other people giving things, as in *Laura gave that for me*.)

1.1.3. Core vocabularies

There are some language systems serving multifarious communicative functions which rely on extremely meagre basic vocabularies. Such systems may be artificially constructed or may occur as natural language phenomena, as discussed below. The significance of these minimal or "core" vocabularies is that they can be seen as reflecting some of the most basic and versatile concepts relevant to human communication. Some notion of a core vocabulary is relevant to the concerns of language teaching, and it is works such as Stubbs (1986, especially Chapter 6 on "Language development, lexical competence and nuclear vocabulary") and Carter (1987), written with the task of language teaching in mind, which perhaps provide the best overview of attempts to define a core vocabulary. As is very clear from these overviews, there are many different ways in which one might identify minimal sets of words (or morphemes) and different criteria yield, naturally, different results. Almost invariably, a morpheme meaning GIVE appears in these sets of minimal vocabularies, consistent with our view of giving as a basic level category.

The core vocabularies I am mainly interested in are ones which are used, or intended to be used, as the basis for communication between speakers. One might mention, however, that the Swadesh Word List could also be thought of as a kind of core vocabulary. This is the list of words which forms the basis for one approach to determining the time-depth of the separation of languages from a parent language, as described in Bynon (1977: 266–272). As Bynon (1977: 267) describes the list, it comprises items which deal with "elements of universal experience which exist irrespective of the speakers' culture". The list (in both its 200 items and 100 items versions) contains GIVE, alongside items for other activities such as eating, sleeping, and giving birth. Although the Swadesh Word List is not meant to function as a self-contained language system, it does represent one attempt to identify a core of basic concepts and the inclusion of GIVE in the list is worth noting.

1.1.3.1. The GIVE morpheme in Kalam

Papuan languages provide support for the basicness of a GIVE morpheme. As discussed in Foley (1986: 113 ff), there is often a small set of basic, or "generic", verb stems in Papuan languages which enter into combinations with other morphemes to yield the full range of verbal forms. Presumably all languages have verb stems which can be combined with other morphemes to form more complex verbs. (Consider, for example, the verb stem *mit* in English, which can be found in *commit, remit, submit, permit, transmit* etc.) In the Papuan languages discussed by Foley, the number of such basic verb stems is extremely small. According to Foley (1986: 119), the core meanings of the most common of such basic verbs are: "do/make", "say", "hit", "put", and, significantly, "give". This is like a naturally occurring Basic English-type of language, as discussed below.

Kalam, spoken in the central highlands of New Guinea, is one such language. As documented first by Pawley (1966), and summarized in Foley (1986: 114–119), Kalam has a very limited number of verb stems. Only about twenty-five verb stems are in common use, representing a kind of basic vocabulary with which one can build up a more complex vocabulary. One of these basic verbs, *ñ-*, has as one of its meanings GIVE. Although the meaning of the morpheme cannot simply be equated with the meaning GIVE, GIVE is apparently a central meaning. So, for example, "give" is shown as the gloss of the morpheme in Kalam sentences used by Pawley to illustrate these verbs in a presentation to the New Zealand Linguistic Society in 1987. Foley (1986: 119), too, despite characterizing the schematic meaning of the morpheme as "transfer control/position of something" glosses it simply as "give" in examples. I think we are justified, then, in taking GIVE to be a salient meaning of this morpheme. Relevant examples are given in (3).

(3)   a.   *mnm*   *ag*   *ñ-*
           speech   sound   give
           'confide'   (Kalam, Foley 1986: 119)

      b.   *wsym*   *ñ-*
           smoothing instrument   give
           'smooth by grinding'   (Kalam, Foley 1986: 119)

      c.   *ywg*   *ñ-*
           lid   give
           'put a lid on'   (Kalam, Foley 1986: 119)

      d.   *mnan*   *pwŋy*   *ñ-*
           bribe   force   give
           'bribe'   (Kalam, Foley 1986: 119)

e.   *bag*   *ñ-*
     signal give
     'signal'   (Kalam, Foley 1986: 119)

When one tries to assign "schematic" meanings to such verb stems, covering all possible uses of the stems either by themselves or in combination with other morphemes, then the meanings naturally will be extremely general. This is comparable to giving a broad, schematic meaning ("send"?) for a stem like *mit* in English, covering its meanings in all of its uses (in *permit, transmit, remit, admit* etc.). But the existence of such schematic meanings does not invalidate the observation that GIVE is a core meaning of the morpheme.

What we find in Kalam, then, is something like what we find in Ogden's Basic English: an extremely small number of verb morphemes exist, but these enter productively into combination with other morphemes to form more complex verbal units corresponding to the large set of verbs in ordinary English. The same principle is operative in all languages, but Kalam makes extreme use of the principle, allowing these systems to get by with an exceptionally small number of basic verb morphemes. And in both cases, a morpheme meaning GIVE turns up in the minimal verb set.[4]

1.1.3.2.   GIVE in Dyirbal

Another example of the special status of the GIVE morpheme comes from the taboo language described by Dixon (1971). Speakers of the North Queensland language Dyirbal made use of two varieties of the language: the normal or "everyday" variety and a taboo variety used in the presence of certain taboo relatives. In the case of a woman, the taboo relative is the father-in-law; in the case of a man, it is the mother-in-law and some others. These two varieties have no lexical words in common, but they have an identical phonology and a similar grammar. The vocabularies of the two varieties are, however, related in a special way. The vocabulary of the taboo variety is considerably smaller than that of the normal variety with a one-to-many correspondence between the taboo variety and the normal variety. In describing the vocabularies of these languages, Dixon draws a distinction between what he calls "nuclear" and "non-nuclear" verbs. The former can be defined in terms of "primitive semantic features" but not in terms of other verbs, whereas the non-nuclear verbs can be so defined (by referring either to nuclear verbs or other non-nuclear verbs). Dixon describes the two varieties using the following analogy:

> Suppose that there were a language which had the requirement that its lexicon contain an absolute minimum number of verbs. Such a language need not contain any non-nuclear verbs. In place of a putative non-nuclear verb it could simply use a "definition": thus instead of *stare* it could have *look hard*. The language would, however, have to contain a full set of nuclear verbs, since nuclear items cannot be replaced by definitions as can non-nuclear verbs. Dyalŋuy [the taboo variety of Dyirbal] behaves almost exactly like this. (Dixon 1971: 441)

The GIVE morpheme, *wugan* in the normal variety and *dʸayman* in the taboo variety, functions as a nuclear verb in Dixon's terms. Thus, *dʸayman* is the verb used in the taboo variety which corresponds to *wugan* and seven other non-nuclear terms of the normal variety. As an example of how the GIVE morpheme is used in the taboo variety, consider the normal verb *munʸdʸan* 'to divide'. According to Dixon (1971: 458), this concept is expressed in the taboo variety by *dʸymaldʸaymal-barinʸu* which literally means "give to each other" containing a reduplication of the one verb in the taboo variety meaning GIVE. Once again, we see that the GIVE morpheme functions as one of the basic set of verbs.

1.1.3.3.   GIVE and Wierzbicka's semantic primitives

In a number of works, most recently Wierzbicka (1992, 1993), Anna Wierzbicka has explored the notion of semantic primitives, which represent yet another kind of minimal vocabulary. The semantic primitives which Wierzbicka seeks are based on the following criteria, taken from Wierzbicka (1993: 28–29): (1) the concepts must be intuitively clear and self-explanatory; (2) the concepts must be impossible to define; (3) the concepts must be demonstrably active as building blocks in the construction of other concepts; (4) the concepts should "prove themselves" in extensive descriptive work involving many different languages; and (5) the concepts should be lexical universals, having their own "names" in all languages of the world. Although some aspects of these requirements may not be entirely self-explanatory, it is clear that Wierzbicka is aiming to identify a set of relatively basic concepts to which other concepts can be reduced. The set of these "semantic primitives" has been revised over the years, but as of Wierzbicka (1992) the ideal set of primitives appears to contain the following thirty-two elements: *I, you, someone, something, this, the same, two, all, much, know, want, think, feel, say, do, happen, good, bad, big, small, very, can, if, because, no (not), when, where, after (before), under (above), kind of, part of, like* (Wierzbicka 1992: 223–224). This represents a much more expanded list of primitives than the thirteen or so proposed in her earlier works, such as Wierzbicka (1972) and Wierzbicka (1993, but written for a conference in 1989). Three elements which had earlier been proposed but have since been discarded are *imagine, become,* and *world.*

As can be seen, GIVE is absent from the 1992 list of thirty-two and, as far as I can ascertain, has never been included in any of Wierzbicka's lists. Its omission may appear surprising in the light of the other examples of core vocabularies discussed here, but it is understandable if we consider Wierzbicka's criteria more carefully. Note in particular the importance Wierzbicka places on the *indefinability* of the semantic primitives (her second criterion). The semantic primitives by this criterion will necessarily be ones which are not further decomposable into more elementary meanings. Given this requirement for the semantic primitives, the omission of GIVE from the list of primitives is understandable, indeed it is thoroughly justified. Although I have postponed a detailed description of the semantics of GIVE until the next chapter, it should be apparent that GIVE is not an irreducible concept. GIVE is easily understood as the transference of a thing from the control of one person to the control of another. Location of the thing at some point, the movement of the thing to a new point, and causation are all components of the meaning of GIVE. Indeed, in some languages, the verb corresponding to GIVE is morphologically complex, combining morphemes corresponding to some of these component meanings. In Ainu (Shibatani 1990: 48), for example, GIVE is literally a causative of a verb of possession (*kor-e* 'have-causative'). So, as long as one insists on semantic primitives being not further definable, then GIVE should not be considered a semantic primitive.

The omission of GIVE from Wierzbicka's semantic primitives highlights an important difference in ways to conceive of core vocabularies. Wierzbicka's semantic primitives are motivated in part by their metalinguistic usefulness, that is how useful or, indeed, indispensable they are to linguists or language philosophers in paraphrasing the meanings of words or expressions in a language. As illuminating as this approach is, it fails to do justice to the experiential and cognitive reality involving the way humans conceptualize certain events. In particular, it ignores the cognitive reality that internally complex events, like giving, can be construed as single gestalts and can be seen as basic in terms of human interaction. The basicness of the concept of GIVE in the context of actual human experience is presumably what leads to its inclusion in most core vocabularies. Whether it is definitionally "basic" or "derived" in some semantic account of words is quite separate from its centrality in human experience.

1.1.3.4. GIVE in Basic English

Another example of a core vocabulary is Basic English. Basic English refers to the simplified form of English first proposed in the 1930's by C. K. Ogden and later published in a revised and expanded form as Ogden (1968). Like Wierzbicka's semantic primitives, Basic English is a set of primitive terms which may be combined to express any thought, though Ogden did not consider the universal validity of the individual primitives (cf. Wierzbicka's criteria (4) and (5) in the list of criteria given in the preceding section). Ogden's primitives were justified according to whether or not they could effectively be used in place of other English words. Furthermore, Basic English was designed to serve as an international auxiliary language, as well as an introduction to English for learners of English as a second language. The vocabulary was limited to 850 words (this was increased to 1,000 words for specific scientific purposes), which according to Ogden could be used in place of 20,000. So, for example, *coffin* could be replaced by *box for a dead body*, *coin* by *(bit of) metal money* etc. The movement to popularize Basic English did not enjoy the support necessary to make it the kind of *lingua franca* which Ogden had hoped for and it has not been adopted as an international language. Nevertheless, the system itself is of some linguistic interest in so far as it represents a serious and extensive attempt to reduce a language to its bare minimum. Indeed, some modern dictionaries for learners of English as a second language do, in fact, utilize their own versions of a Basic English.

Interestingly, while there were hundreds of nouns in the vocabulary of Basic English, there were very few verbs or "operation-words". Ogden admitted less than twenty verbs in his system: *make, have, put, take, keep, let, give, get, go, come, be, seem, do, say, see, send* and the auxiliaries *may* and *will*. Significantly, *give* features in this list. Ogden proposed that *give* replace a number of distinct verbs. So, for example, *move* was seen as equivalent to *give (a thing) a move*, *push* was seen as equivalent to *give a push to (a thing)*, and *pull* as equivalent to *give a pull to (a thing)*. These particular circumlocutions may not be as "basic" as one might wish, since *push* and *pull* in their nominal uses would appear to be derived from the corresponding verbs. (*Push* and *pull* are given as "things" rather than "operations" in the Basic English list.) While one may have doubts about some aspects of the paraphrases provided by Ogden, it is still of interest to note that *give* was deemed to be one of the Basic English words, functioning as a building-block to help create larger semantic units.

1.1.4. *Metaphorical extensions of GIVE*

The GIVE morpheme is a rich source of metaphorical extensions in languages. I refer here not to poetic or literary metaphor, but to the metaphorical extensions which underlie ordinary usage in language along the lines of Lakoff—Johnson (1980). The abundance of non-literal uses of GIVE morphemes (where the morpheme is used to mean something other than "to pass control over some object to someone with the hand") testifies to the centrality of the giving act in our everyday experiences. The GIVE morpheme, being a salient and easily understood component of human experience, is quite naturally employed to help conceptualize various acts or events. For a more extensive discussion of metaphorical extensions of GIVE predicates, the reader is referred to Chapter 4. Here, I will just briefly give some indication of the variety of the semantic extensions which are found with GIVE morphemes.

One class of extensions involves the use of the GIVE morpheme with non-prototypical entities functioning as the THING, but still involving a person in a RECIPIENT-like role. Among the many such semantic extensions in English, for example, we find:

(4) a. *give (advice, opinion etc.)* = 'to express (advice, opinion etc.) to someone'
     b. *give one's word* = 'to promise'
     c. *give permission, consent etc.* = 'to permit'
     d. *give a hand* = 'to help'
     e. *give a push* = 'to push'
     f. *give a punch* = 'to punch'

One also finds the GIVE morpheme occurring with various types of complement phrases which are not so easily construed as either the THING phrase or the RECIPIENT phrase, as in (5).

(5)   a.   GIVE + person + to know, understand etc. = 'to inform person'
English: *I was given to understand.*
Malay: *mem-beri-tahu* 'TRANS-give-know' = 'to inform'

   b.   GIVE + person + to do something = 'to allow person to do something'
Russian: *dat'* 'give; permit'
Finnish: *antaa* 'give; permit'

   c.   GIVE + person + to do something = 'to do something for a person'
Mandarin: *gěi* 'give; for, on behalf of'

   d.   Reflexive GIVE = 'to happen, yield, result in'
Spanish: *dar-se* 'give-REFL' = 'to happen, exist'
German: *sich ergeben* 'REFL prefix-give' = 'result in; arise'

   e.   Impersonal GIVE + X = 'there are X's'
German: *es gibt* = 'there is/are'

   f.   GIVE + in some direction = 'to face some direction'
Spanish: *dar al Norte* 'to face the north'
Finnish: *antaa pohjoiseen* 'to face the north'

These are no more than a few of the many examples of such extensions. Nevertheless, they give some idea of the productivity of GIVE as a source of metaphorical extension and grammaticalization in English and other languages.

The productivity of a word/morpheme is also one of the criteria of core vocabulary discussed by Stubbs (1986: 109), who suggests, as a (very!) simple measure of the metaphorical productivity, counting the number of related but different senses recognized for a word in a dictionary. *Give*, in fact, is one of the words Stubbs includes some figures for, and comparison of the *give* figures with those for the other words studied would indicate that *give* does indeed belong to the core vocabulary by this criterion.

1.1.5. Basic forms of GIVE

It is not surprising in the light of the basic nature of the act of giving that the form of the GIVE predicate in some languages is also "basic" in the sense of being simple in form or structure. Underlying this observation is the idea that linguistic form can be, but need not be, iconic for the meaning carried by the form. More specifically, the structural complexity of a form tends to reflect conceptual or experiential complexity. It should be said that this is nothing more than a tendency and counter-examples are not hard to find. In the case of GIVE and its formal realization in languages, there is evidence of a tendency to relatively simple forms.

The structure of verbal roots in the reconstruction of Proto–Australian (pA), as described in Dixon (1980: 408–421), is relevant here. pA had a number of monosyllabic verbal roots, alongside polysyllabic verbal roots. Dixon (1980: 415) refers to "the most common verbs" as being monosyllabic, consistent with Zipf's Law. The monosyllabic roots which Dixon posits for pA include the reconstruction of the root GIVE as well as roots meaning: to see, look at; carry, bring, take; give; hit; cry, sob, weep; go; put; fall; eat. Dixon is undoubtedly correct in describing these as common verbs — a situation which is matched in an iconic way by the shortness of the form of these words.

Amele, a Papuan language spoken near Madang in Papuan New Guinea, and described in Roberts (1987), has a particularly interesting way of encoding the concept of GIVE, namely as a zero morph. Affixes which normally attach to verb stems marking tense and agreement appear instead as a string of affixes in the position where one would normally expect the verb. (Amele has a rich set of affixes including eight sets of subject agreement affixes and a number of portmanteau affixes which combine agreement and tense/aspect marking.) Examples of the Amele encoding of GIVE are shown in (6).

(6)   a.   *Naus   Dege   ho   Ø-ut-en.*
                Naus   Dege pig   give-3SG:OBJ-3SG:SUBJ:PAST
                'Naus gave Dege the pig.'   (Amele, Roberts 1987: 34)

  b. *Ija   dana leis sab   Ø-al-ig-a.*
      I   man   two   food give-3DU:OBJ-1SG:SUBJ-PAST
      'I gave the two men food.'   (Amele, Roberts 1987: 316)

  c. *Uqa   sab   Ø-i-te-i-a.*
      he   food give-PRED-1SG:OBJ-3SG:SUBJ-PAST
      'He gave me food.'   (Amele, Roberts 1987: 281)

"PRED" in (6c) refers to a predicate marker -*i*, which must occur between the verb stem (zero in this case) and the affix marking the RECIPIENT (*te* in this case) in certain constructions. Compare these sentences with a normal three-place predicate like *ihac* 'show' in (7).

(7)   *Jo   eu   ihac-i-ad-ig-en.*
        house that show-PRED-2PL:OBJ-1SG:SUBJ-FUT
        'I will show that house to you (plural).'
                                        (Amele, Roberts 1987: 69)

In (7) the verbal affixes are attached to a verb stem and the predicate marker appears between this stem and the affix indicating the RECIPIENT.

It should be pointed out that a string of verbal affixes unattached to a verb stem does appear in another construction in Amele, namely an impersonal or dative subject construction, illustrated below:

(8) a. *Ija   wen   te-i-na.*
         I   hunger 1SG:OBJ-3SG:SUBJ-PAST
         'I was hungry.'   (Amele, Roberts 1987: 281)

     b. *Ija   nu-ug-a   te-Ø-na.*
         I   go-2SG-IMP   1SG:OBJ-3SG:SUBJ-PRES
         'I want to go.'   (Amele, Roberts 1987: 264)

In this impersonal construction, the zero-marked subject affix is always understood as 3SG, unlike the GIVE construction, where it can be any person and number. Furthermore, it is only the GIVE sense which can be rendered in this way, i.e. a zero morph with any person and number occurring as a subject affix.

Amele offers, therefore, a striking example of the uniqueness of the GIVE morpheme. Where the clause already contains the morphemes marking the GIVER, the RECIPIENT, and the THING passed, Amele "assumes" the sense of GIVE will be understood without any need for an overt realization of GIVE. This way of realizing GIVE is entirely consistent with the observations made at the beginning of this chapter to the effect that the act of giving is a common and fundamental aspect of normal human interaction.

A similar situation holds in the Amerindian language Koasati (Louisiana). Kimball (1991: 102) notes that the verb GIVE in Koasati is irregular since it has no overt realization, being made up only of affixes which indicate the GIVER and the RECIPIENT. Although there are various kinds of irregularities in the Koasati verb system, as discussed by Kimball, this is the only verb which is irregular in lacking any overt realization.

Chamorro (Guam, Austronesian) deserves to be mentioned in this connection too. Chamorro *na'i* 'give' must be recognized as a word in its own right, but it can be decomposed etymologically into a sequence of two derivational affixes. Indeed, this is how the form is described in the dictionary entry in Topping—Ogo—Dungca (1975: 149). The two affixes are: a prefix *na'-* 'causative' and a suffix *-i*, described as a referential focus in Topping (1973: 249–251) or as the marker of 3-2 Advancement in Gibson (1980: 34). These affixes are quite productive in Chamorro and are exemplified in (9) and (10).

(9)   Causative *na'-*:
    a. *bubu*   'angry'   *na'-bubu*   'to anger'
    b. *la'la'*   'living'   *na'-la'la'*   'to activate'
    c. *poddung*   'to fall'   *na'-poddung*   'to drop'
    d. *taitai*   'to read'   *na'-taitai*   'cause to read'

(10)   Referential *-i*:
    a. *Hu   tugi' i   kätta pära i   che'lu-hu.*
       I   write the   letter to   the sibling-my
       'I wrote the letter to my brother/sister.'
                                (Chamorro, Gibson 1980: 34)

b. *Hu   tugi'-i   i   che'lu-hu   nu   i   kätta.*
I   write-SUF   the   sibling-my   OBL   the   letter
'I wrote my brother/sister the letter.'

(Chamorro, Gibson 1980: 34)

In Chamorro, the GIVE construction with *na'i* requires the same kind of syntax as one finds in the *tugi'-i* sentence above, i.e. the RECIPIENT functions as the object of the verb. Compare examples (11a) and (11b).

(11) a. *In   nä'i   si   tata-n-mama*
we:EXCL   give   the   father-LINK-our
nu   i   bäbui.
OBL   the   pig
'We gave our father the pig.'

(Chamorro, Gibson 1980: 153)

b. **In   nä'i   i   bäbui*
we:EXCL   give   the   pig
pära   si   tata-n-mama.
to   the   father-LINK-our
'We gave the pig to our father.'

(Chamorro, Gibson 1980: 153)

In these two sentences, *tatanmama* 'our father' contains an *n* linking the head noun *tata* to its modifier *mama*. The first vowel of *nä'i*, which is stressed, is umlauted on account of the preceding *in* form. Notice that the RECIPIENT and THING transferred are encoded in the same way as for the recipient and the letter in the *tugi'-i* sentence above. From this point of view, it is as though the *i* at the end of *na'i* is functioning like the referential marker *-i*. This would be consistent, too, with the fact that *na'i* does not add the *-i* suffix, the *-i* suffix already being present in the basic form of the verb. The other verbs mentioned in Topping (1973: 250–251) as not permitting the addition of the *-i* suffix can also be analyzed as containing a final *i* (which alternates in a rule-governed way with *e* in word final position).

GIVE, then, is construed in Chamorro as making something happen involving a RECIPIENT.[5] It has the shape of a causative formation plus referential marking, except that the stem to which the causative and referential marking are attached is missing. It is not clear whether this interpretation is merely a product of speculation on the part of the linguist or whether it is something which native speakers feel. The Chamorro dictionary entry referred to above, which mentions this decomposition of *na'i*, suggests that it is a fairly obvious decomposition, since the entries in the dictionary are not otherwise abstract in any particular way.

1.2. The exceptionality of GIVE words

We have seen in the preceding sections how there are special facts about GIVE words in languages which may be seen to reflect the basic category status of the act of giving. There are other ways in which GIVE words may be seen as "special" in a language without necessarily reflecting anything "basic" about the act of giving. It may be that the GIVE word has properties (apart from phonological shape) which are unique to that word or which are evidenced in a very restricted number of forms. In some cases, one might still be able to argue that these properties reflect, or are motivated by, some aspect of the structure of the giving act.

Borg and Comrie offer, in fact, a warning to linguists collecting data on ditransitive verbs, which is worth quoting in full:

> ...in many languages... "give" is syntactically a very atypical ditransitive verb. This is not particularly surprising: items from the most basic vocabulary are more likely to be anomalous morphologically and syntactically. But this does demonstrate that more care needs to be taken in the choice of the most typical ditransitive verb [i.e. "give"], selection of "give" always requiring crosschecking with a variety of other verbs of similar valency. (Borg—Comrie 1984: 123)

1.2.1.   Directionality

There is inherent in the notion of giving a strong sense of directionality, with a THING proceeding from one person to another. As discussed in later chapters, a number of the uses of GIVE predicates, understood both literally and figuratively, are motivated by this component of the meaning of GIVE. Not surprisingly, GIVE predicates collocate easily with directional adverbs/particles, as in English: *give something away, give something out, give something to somebody.* In German, the separable prefixes *hin-* and *her-* occur with *geben* as *hingeben* 'give away from speaker' and *hergeben* 'give to speaker', as happens with other verbal predicates involving physical motion.

In Māori, directional morphemes *mai* 'hither' and *atu* 'thither' have become integrated with a GIVE verb stem *hō*, resulting in the two verbs *hōmai* 'give to speaker' and *hōatu* 'give away from speaker'. *Hō* in Māori is not an independently occurring free morpheme anymore. Thus we find contrasts as in (12a) and (12b).

(12) a.   *Kua   hōmai   ia   i   te   pukapuka ki   ahau.*
           PAST give   he/she OBJ   ART   book   to   me
           'She/he gave the book to me.'   (Māori)
     b.   *Kua   hōatu   au   i   te   pukapuka ki   ā   ia.*
           PAST give   I   OBJ ART   book   to   ART   him/her
           'I gave the book to him/her.'   (Māori)

The *hōmai* form is also appropriate where the RECIPIENT is a group with which the speaker identifies closely. So, for example, Foster (1991: vi, ix) has *hōmai* in sentences describing God's gift of languages to various races and the giving of the Māori language to the Māori people. The speaker in such cases identifies with the RECIPIENT rather than with God. The GIVE verbs in Māori are unusual in not having a separate suffixed form for the passive.[6] Instead, the active forms function also as passive. The directional morphemes *mai* and *atu* are quite common morphemes in Māori which never take passive endings and presumably this fact is connected to the lack of distinct passive endings for the GIVE verbs.

In Ik (Kuliak family, Uganda), directional affixes attach to verbs in interesting ways (cf. Serzisko 1988: 432–436). With some verbs in Ik it is possible to affix either the *-et* 'hither' or *-uk'ot* 'thither' forms to the verb stem (*k'* represents an ejective), with an appropriate modification of meaning. So, for example, with the verb stem *n'at* 'run', we have both *n'at-et* 'run hither' and *n'at-uk'ot* 'run thither' (*n'* represents an ejective). The addition of the affix is necessary here to indicate the directionality (or perfectivity) of the motion. There are other verbs, however, which must be thought of as being inherently specified for directionality. The verbs "come" and "go" are two such verbs which have the concept of directionality implicit in their meaning, the former being "source-oriented" and the latter "goal-oriented". Neither of these two verbs ever appears with a directionality affix. With the GIVE stem *ma*, directionality away from is optionally expressed by the "thither" affix, while directionality towards must be expressed by the "hither" affix. Adding the "thither" affix to the GIVE verb expresses only a certain emphasis; it does not impose a particular directionality onto the verb meaning. The GIVE verb functions, therefore, like the goal-oriented verb "go", as though it has as part of its meaning the notion "away from". (The TAKE verb functions in the opposite way, behaving like the source-oriented verb "come".)

1.2.2. Honorific variants

In Japanese, a number of GIVE verbs are available with the choice between them determined by two main factors: (a) whether the speaker identifies with the GIVER or the RECIPIENT, and (b) the relative status of the GIVER and RECIPIENT with respect to each other. The reader is referred to Loveday (1986: 57–78) for a full discussion of the options in expressing GIVE. Tables 1–3, adapted from Loveday (1986), summarize the basic set of choices for GIVE verbs.

Table 1.
Japanese GIVE verbs used when Speaker identifies with GIVER

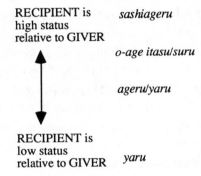

RECIPIENT is
high status
relative to GIVER   *sashiageru*

o-age itasu/suru

ageru/yaru

RECIPIENT is
low status
relative to GIVER   *yaru*

Table 2.
Japanese GIVE verbs used when Speaker identifies with RECIPIENT

GIVER is
high status
relative to
RECIPIENT   *kudasaru*

kudasaru/kureru

GIVER is
low status
relative to
RECIPIENT   *kureru*

Table 3.

Japanese GIVE verbs used when Speaker identifies with
neither GIVER nor RECIPIENT

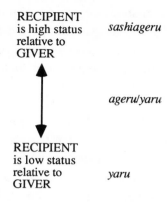

RECIPIENT
is high status   *sashiageru*
relative to
GIVER

                          ageru/yaru

RECIPIENT
is low status
relative to   *yaru*
GIVER

The verbs in Table 1 are the appropriate ones to be used when the
Speaker identifies with GIVER, as in *My daughter gave the university
lecturer a camera*, where *my daughter* is the participant with whom I
identify. Table 2 verbs are used when the Speaker identifies with the
RECIPIENT, as in *The university lecturer gave my daughter a camera*.
Table 3 verbs are used when the Speaker identifies with neither of the
participants, as in *The student gave the university lecturer a camera*.
There is some overlap between the verbs in Tables 1 and 3, which is to
say that the "default" set of verbs, used when there is no Speaker identification with the participants in the act of giving, is based on the set
used when the Speaker identifies with the GIVER. The concepts of
"identification with GIVER" and "identification with RECIPIENT" in
this context are by no means simple, and various discourse and pragmatic factors may influence a decision to adopt one of these three per-
spectives. Within each of these three sets, further decisions are needed
to determine which of the verbs is appropriate and this depends on the
relative status of the GIVER and RECIPIENT, as perceived by the
Speaker. So, for example, among the verbs in Table 1, *sashiageru* is the
appropriate one in translating a sentence such as *I gave the teacher a
book* (the teacher being of higher status than the GIVER), but only *yaru*
may be used in translating *I gave the dog a bone* (the dog being of lower

status than the GIVER).[7] The pair of sentences in (13) illustrates some of these points. In (13a), the Speaker identifies with, indeed *is* the subject referent, and so the appropriate verb set is that in Table 1. Since the RECIPIENT has high status compared with the GIVER, *sashiageru* is appropriate. In (13b), on the other hand, the Speaker identifies with the RECIPIENT, so one must choose amongst the set of verbs in Table 2. Again, since the teacher has higher status than I have, the appropriate verb to use is *kudasaru*.

(13) a.   *Watashi wa   sensei   ni   hon   o   sashiage-mashita.*
           I   TOPIC teacher DAT camera ACC give-PAST
           'I gave the teacher a book.'   (Japanese)

     b.   *Sensei   ga   watashi ni   hon   o   kudasai-mashita.*
           teacher NOM me   DAT camera ACC give-PAST
           'The teacher gave me a book.'   (Japanese)

As in Māori, there is a choice of GIVE verbs in Japanese involving considerations of directionality. In Māori, the directionality is encoded by morphemes *mai* and *atu*, which are basically spatial in reference meaning "hither, towards speaker" and "thither, away from speaker". In Japanese, on the other hand, the directionality encoded in the verbs is based on a concept of social verticality, where the speaker would normally present himself/herself as lower in status than others. Giving to other humans would normally involve giving "upwards" and receiving from others would normally involve giving "downwards" to the speaker. It is significant that the first syllable of *ageru* (which also appears in *sashiageru*), used when the Speaker gives to others, is written with the Kanji character 上 'up', while the first syllable of *kudasaru*, used when others give to the Speaker, is written with 下 'down'. While these verbs are native Japanese words and not derived from Chinese, the choice of these particular Kanji characters in these instances may be seen as reflecting a consciousness about a vertical orientation in the society.

Although only the most important aspects of GIVE verbs in Japanese have been dealt with here, it is clear that the encoding of GIVE in Japanese is a complex matter. Indeed, the GIVE verbs in Japanese are unique in showing this degree of complexity. Verbal concepts in Japanese are not generally expressed by different verb stems depending on whether the Speaker is the doer or receiver of an action. *I kissed Mary* and *Mary kissed me*, for example, both translate into Japanese with the one verb *kisu-suru* (literally, 'kiss-do'). There are not alternative forms of the verb depending on whether the Speaker is the kisser or kissee:

(14) a.   *Watashi wa   Meri   ni   kisu-shi-mashita.*
       I   TOPIC Mary DAT kiss-do-PAST
       'I kissed Mary.'   (Japanese)

     b.   *Meri wa   watashi ni   kisu-shi-mashita.*
       Mary TOPIC I   DAT kiss-do-PAST
       'Mary kissed me.'   (Japanese)

1.2.3.   SG vs PL forms of GIVE

The GIVE sense may be realized as two forms, depending on whether or not the object of the verb is singular or plural number. In the Papuan language Barai there is a small set of verbs which have distinct singular and plural forms. The phenomenon appears to be restricted to just the verbs "take", "give", "sit", and "stand", as shown in (15).

(15) a.   *abe* 'take one'   *ke* 'take many'
     b.   *m-* 'give one'   *vaj* 'give many'
     c.   *fi* 'one sits'   *kari* 'many sit'
     d.   *mani* 'one stands'   *ire* 'many stand'
                             (Barai, Foley 1986: 129)

One might see in this set a kind of "basic" vocabulary, though I will not attempt to explain away their unusual behaviour as being a reflection of this. My point here is merely that the meaning of GIVE is expressed by a doublet, a phenomenon which is restricted to just a handful of verbs in this language.

1.2.4. Passive

Borg—Comrie (1984: 114–6) discuss ways in which constructions based on the verbs *ta* 'give' and *wera* 'show' in Maltese differ from constructions normally associated with ditransitive verbs. One striking way in which the constructions differ concerns the passivizabilty of the indirect objects using *gie* (literally 'come') as the passive auxiliary. Normally, only the direct object may be passivized in Maltese in this way, as illustrated in (16).

(16) a.   *Pawlu   kiteb   l-ittra   lil   Marija.*
          Paul   wrote-he   the-letter to   Mary
          'Paul wrote the letter to Mary.'
                          (Maltese, Borg—Comrie 1984: 115)
    b.   *L-ittra   gie-t   m-iktub-a   lil   Marija.*
          the-letter   came-she   written-FEM to   Mary
          'The letter was written to Mary.'
                          (Maltese, Borg—Comrie 1984: 115)
    c.   **Marija   gie-t   m-iktub-a   l-ittra.*
          Mary   came-she   written-FEM the-letter
                          (Maltese, Borg—Comrie 1984: 115)

With *ta* 'give' (and *wera* 'show'), on the other hand, it is possible to passivize either the direct or indirect object, as shown in (17).

(17) a.   *Marija   ta-t   l-ittra   lil   Pawlu.*
          Mary   gave-she   the-letter to   Paul
          'Mary gave the letter to Paul.'
                          (Maltese, Borg—Comrie 1984: 117)
    b.   *L-ittra   gie-t   moghtij-a   lil Pawlu.*
          the-letter came-she   given-FEM   to Paul
          'The letter was given to Paul.'
                          (Maltese, Borg—Comrie 1984: 118)

c. *Pawlu ġie   moġħti   l-ittra.*
   Paul   came-he given-he the-letter
   'Paul was given the letter.'

                                 (Maltese, Borg—Comrie 1984: 118)

(A similar pattern exists with the morphological passive.) Perhaps the RECIPIENT has a special salience in the giving frame which is absent in the case of other three-place predicates such as "write". This may help explain why the RECIPIENT seems to act like a typical object with respect to the passive construction (likewise the indirect object with "show"). In any case, GIVE is one of just a couple of three-place predicates in Maltese which behave in this way, showing once again the special place of the GIVE predicate in this language.

1.2.5. *Exceptional verb morphology*

There are cases where the GIVE verb in a language is exceptional in its morphology when compared with other comparable predicates involving RECIPIENTS or recipient-like roles in its frame. It can happen that the morphology associated with GIVE is formally simpler than with other three-place predicates. Consider, for example, the following facts from Woods Cree (Donna Starks, personal communication). Three-place predicates in Woods Cree appear in verb forms with a number of suffixes with various functions, including one which specifies the transitivity of the verb. We see this in the "send" example below, where *am* and *aw* specify the objects of a transitive verb. The particular forms of the morphemes indicate that the RECIPIENT morpheme functions as the primary object. There is also an obligatory *ah* morpheme present indicating an instrumental component of meaning:

(18)   *Itis-ah-am-aw-iːw.*
         send-by instrument-INAN:OBJ-recipient:OBJ- 3SUBJ:3OBJ
         'She/he sends it to her/him.'   (Woods Cree)

Typically, then, three-place predicates have considerable internal complexity. A striking exception to this pattern is GIVE which does not occur with such suffixes except for the final person marking:

(19)   *Mi:th-i:w.*
         give-3SUBJ:3OBJ
         'She/he gives it to her/him.'   (Woods Cree)

The exceptionally meagre structure associated with *mi:th* in Woods Cree is surely not unrelated to some of the properties of the act of giving itself, as discussed earlier. The minimal formal shape of the GIVE construction might well be seen as a reflection of the basic nature of the act of giving.[8] The kind of iconicity involved in the construction is then: the more "basic" the act in terms of human behaviour, the "simpler" the formal expression of the act.

The GIVE verb in Kanuri (northeastern Nigeria) is exceptional with respect to the kind of verb morphology it occasions. In Kanuri, the applicative form of the verb correlates with certain semantic and syntactic changes. These changes are varied and include: converting an intransitive verb into a transitive verb, preserving the intransitivity of a verb but enabling that verb to occur with an oblique benefactive/dative, keeping a transitive verb transitive but enabling it to occur with a benefactive/dative phrase. The applicative form is typically marked by the presence of a derivational morpheme *ke/ge*. Some examples of these changes are given below:

(20)   1st SG Imperfect Basic   1st SG Imperfect Applicative

         a. *hâmngìn* 'I lift'   *hápkə̀kìn* 'I lift for someone, I
                                             help someone lift'
         b. *bàyènngîn* 'I explain'   *bàyèngə́kìn* 'I explain to someone'
         c. *gŭlngîn* 'I say'   *gùlə́gə́kìn* 'I say to someone, I
                                             teach someone'
                                     (Kanuri, Hutchison 1981: 141–142)

One might expect the presence of a RECIPIENT in a GIVE clause would trigger similar changes. However, as Hutchison (1981: 136) notes, the GIVE verb is "a bit irregular" in this respect. Exceptionally, the presence of the RECIPIENT in the GIVE clause does not occasion the use of an applicative form of the verb *yí* 'give'. Instead, the basic form of the verb is maintained and the RECIPIENT phrase is indexed on the verb in the same way as direct objects of ordinary transitive verbs are (with zero morph for 3rd person forms).

In Bahasa Indonesia a verb generally adds a suffix *-kan* when a benefactive or recipient type of phrase functions as the direct object of the verb. This is illustrated in (21).

(21) a. *Mereka   mem-bawa   daging   itu   kepada dia.*
         they   TRANS-bring   meat   the   to   him/her.
         'They brought the meat to him/her.'
                                              (Indonesian, Chung 1976: 54)

   b. *Mereka   mem-bawa-kan   dia   daging   itu.*
       they   TRANS-bring-SUF   him/her   meat   the
       'They brought him/her the meat.'
                                              (Indonesian, Chung 1976: 54)

As noted by Chung, there are just a few verbs that do not add any suffix or mark the RECIPIENT phrase as an object. At least in the speech of younger speakers, as described by Chung (1976: 55), these verbs include *beri* 'give', *kasih* 'give', *bajar* 'pay'. These are the only verbs cited by Chung (1976: 55) which lack the suffix in the (21b) type of construction. It is not clear how many other verbs are like this, but in any case it is a small group. Notice that the GIVE verbs belong to this very exceptional group.

1.3.   Summary

The act of giving is arguably one of the more significant interpersonal acts which humans perform. It has a functional importance in our normal, everyday lives which is reflected in the way in which GIVE morphemes are part of basic vocabularies. While there are many definitions one might propose for the term *basic vocabulary*, a GIVE morpheme is typically part of any basic vocabulary. So, for example, GIVE expressions are among the first expressions to be comprehended as part of first language acquisition. A GIVE morpheme is one of the small set of morphemes found in the restricted core vocabularies of Kalam and the Dyirbal taboo language. Ogden found it desirable to include GIVE as one of the few verbal predicates which formed part of his Basic English. The expression of GIVE in Amele, involving a lexically empty verb with affixes attached, is particularly interesting as a further manifestation of the basicness of GIVE.

A common feature of GIVE verbs in languages is their special status in terms of their shape, morphology, or syntax, as observed by Borg— Comrie (1984: 123). While it would be clearly too strong to claim that a GIVE verb is always irregular in one of these respects, there nevertheless is a tendency for a GIVE verb to be atypical in some way. There is a good deal of semantic complexity in a GIVE predicate, discussed more fully in Chapter 2, and to some extent this semantic complexity may motivate some atypical properties of GIVE. So, for example, prototypical GIVE makes reference to two human participants engaging with each other in a unique way. This interpersonal aspect of GIVE, involving the relevant status of the participants, is relevant to understanding the choices which need to be made in expressing GIVE in Japanese.

Chapter 2. The meaning of GIVE

2.1. Preliminaries

The act of giving has a relatively rich structure in so far as it involves (typically) three easily distinguishable entities: the GIVER, the RECIPIENT, and the THING being transferred. Admittedly, there are acts involving fewer obvious entities which nevertheless can be quite complex. Take the act of laughing, for example. There is no obvious interaction between people or things in the case of laughing and in English *laugh* functions as an intransitive verb and does not require a syntactic object. Nevertheless, there are various conditions which are typically present when someone laughs which all contribute to a certain complexity in a full description of laughing. For example, one does not normally laugh for no reason. Usually, there is an external cause, something heard or seen. If there is no external cause, then there would normally be some internal cause, such as visualizing or recalling something humorous. Thus, although laughing describes something one person does by oneself, it would normally be associated with some other entity which brings on the laughing. Laughing also involves very specific kinds of facial movements, usually centred on the mouth and cheeks, accompanied by characteristic laughing noises. I think one would have to acknowledge that the combination of all these facets of laughing amounts to a relatively complex act. Laughing is not unusual in its complexity and there are many acts involving just one person which have a comparable complexity to them. The typical act of giving something to someone is additionally complex in so far as three very distinct entities are involved and interact in particular ways. In addition to the interaction between the GIVER and the THING transferred, there is also an interaction between the THING and the RECIPIENT. There is also an interaction between the GIVER and the RECIPIENT (mediated by the THING transferred). Thus, when we turn to acts of giving, we are considering acts which are not only salient in human interactional terms but also relatively elaborate in their structure.

It may appear odd that the act of giving should have considerable internal complexity and yet at the same time be analyzed as a basic category, as argued in Chapter 1. There is, however, no contradiction here. The basicness of the act of giving derives not from properties relating to the internal structure of the act (whether it has one, two, or three participants etc.) but rather from the way in which the act is perceived and the functions and effects of the act in human interactional terms. In particular, the task of determining what constitutes basic categories is not reducible to any simple inspection of the components of the act in isolation from these social, functional considerations. One must remember, too, that we are able to assign gestalt status to certain complexes of entities and relationships, permitting us to deal with these complexes conceptually as single wholes. The act of giving is easily construed as a single, unitary event of this type. This duality about giving — a basic interpersonal act, but at the same time having considerable internal complexity — is reflected in forms for the concept of giving in languages. The form of the morpheme GIVE may be relatively simple, even to the point of being a zero morph, reflecting the conceptual basicness of GIVE, as discussed in Chapter 1. Alternatively, the GIVE word may be morphologically complex, as in Ainu, where it may be decomposed morphologically into "cause to have", reflecting some of the internal conceptual complexity of GIVE.

The relatively rich structure of the act of giving suggests an examination of GIVE constructions across languages as a useful way of exploring the diversity in the conceptualizations of an event (even though it must be seen as a rather indirect way of learning something about the working of the mind). In other words, what are the linguistic properties of the clausal structures which are employed in languages to describe acts of giving? How do languages integrate references to the GIVER, the RECIPIENT, and the THING into a clause in describing an act of giving? The fact that the act of giving is such a basic category is some reason to be optimistic that we will find relatively well established organizational patterns to encode GIVE in different languages. These questions will be pursued further in Chapter 3.

The focus in this chapter is to provide an account of the meaning of GIVE, understood in its basic prototypical sense of passing an object from one person to another person. My account will draw in part upon concepts and styles of representation developed by Langacker in publications extending over a number of years, but which appear in perhaps their most definitive and comprehensive form in Langacker (1987, 1991). It is this work which I will rely on most in my attempts to articulate semantic structure. As suggested by the name given to this approach, i.e. "Cognitive Grammar", this framework makes a serious attempt to understand linguistic structure as far as possible in terms which have general cognitive significance. In Cognitive Grammar, the task of carrying out an analysis of linguistic structure is seen as part of the larger enterprise of characterizing cognitive events and recognition is given to our general cognitive and perceptual experience in describing the functioning of language. While an appreciation of the cognitive basis of language is valuable in analyzing most aspects of grammar, it appears to be quite indispensable when one is dealing with polysemy. It is of some interest to note that it is a problem of polysemy (in this case, the various meanings of the verb *keep*) which Jackendoff (1983: ix) uses to illustrate the need for a more cognitively based approach which seeks to understand the structure of the concepts. (Jackendoff's further comment (p. ix) is also apropos: "...I found myself frustrated at every turn trying to incorporate my findings into existing theories of semantics.") As examples of the cognitive orientation in Langacker's approach, one can cite the reliance on notiohs of imagery, modes of scanning objects in space, and figure vs. ground, all of which are key concepts in this approach. This is contrasted with an approach which posits (and proliferates) entities which are unique to linguistic theory and which have no counterparts in cognition.

A strong theme running throughout Cognitive Grammar is the desire to provide an integrated account of language phenomena. Any sharp dichotomy between, say, syntax and semantics is rejected in favour of an approach in which language structures from the smallest morpheme to the largest grammatical construction are all viewed as symbolic units of varying complexity. Since meaning is crucial to the characterization of all symbolic units, an account of syntactic phenomena in autonomous syntax terms, independent of semantic description, would be seen as largely misguided.

In Cognitive Grammar there is a serious interest in capturing the relationships which hold between different senses of a morpheme. This interest can be seen in two relatively early works within the cognitive linguistics movement, Lindner (1981) and Brugman (1981), where the full range of senses of a lexical item (literal and figurative) is explored by carefully analyzing the nature of the relations between these senses. These two works are all the more interesting because the lexical items investigated (*out, up, over*) have important syntactic significance. What at first sight may appear to be merely a study in lexical semantics or metaphor turns out, upon closer study, to have ramifications for the analysis of sentence structure. Here, too, this approach contrasts sharply with the dominant view, summed up neatly in an introductory textbook on semantics in the following way: "In this area, as indeed everywhere where one is dealing with the notion of sense, one has to ignore metaphorical and figurative interpretations of sentences. We are dealing with the strictly literal meanings of predicates." (Hurford—Heasley 1983: 191)

It should not be thought that the neglect of metaphor and figurative language is merely an omission on the part of introductory textbooks (such as Hurford—Heasley 1983), since neither of these areas receives any attention in a more definitive work such as Katz (1972), in which there is no reference to either of them in the subject index. Nor is there any reference to metaphor and figurative language amongst the fifteen phenomena identified in Katz (1972: 4–6) as characterizing, even at a pretheoretical level, the field of semantics. Metaphor and, more generally, figurative language of all kinds are given due recognition in Cognitive Grammar as reflecting important and fundamental characteristics of language use. Studies such as Lakoff—Johnson (1980) and Lakoff—Turner (1989) have been important contributions to a better understanding of these areas.

2.2. The spatio-temporal domain

A natural starting point for an analysis of GIVE structures is to picture the typical scenario involving the act of giving, along the lines discussed in Chapter 1: there is a person who has some thing and this person passes over the thing with his/her hands to another person who receives it with his/her hands. Routines of this sort have been labelled in many ways in recent literature: *frame, scene, schema, script, idealized cognitive model.* Here I will simply refer to it as (a part of) the *frame* invoked by GIVE in its basic sense. I have qualified my description as only "a part" of a larger frame, since there are many ways in which the frame could be further elaborated — persons function in many related routines and typically act for certain reasons with certain goals in mind; acts of giving may be part of established rituals (birthdays, Mother's Day etc.), possibly accompanied by ritualistic speech acts and involving presents of a certain type wrapped in a certain way etc. The existence of such interconnections, though virtually impossible to document fully, is real and in the "encyclopedic" approach adopted here contribute to the meaning of GIVE-type verbs. A frame, then, is made up of numerous domains (spatial, temporal, sensory, causal, socio-historical etc.), though for convenience some of these can be backgrounded at different points in the discussion. For the purposes of this study, it is convenient to distinguish the following domains: the spatio-temporal domain, the control domain, the force-dynamics domain, and the domain of human interest. I will begin with the spatio-temporal domain, this being the domain which explicates the physical dimension. It is the domain in which the relevant facts about the shape of the participating entities are expressed, together with changes affecting the spatial relationships amongst these entities through time.

The frame shown in Figure 1 constitutes the spatio-temporal *base* of many common GIVE-type predicates involving a transference of a thing, including English predicates such as *give, donate, award, present, bestow upon,* and *hand over.* By base, I mean that it is the context within which particular GIVE senses are defined, though it cannot simply be equated with any one specific GIVE verb. It necessarily involves a time dimension with the location of the THING (indicated by a small shape in the hand of the stick person in Figure 1 changing through time, from being in one person's hand to being in another person's hand. A particular GIVE verb will impose additional structure on this base. This will include a profile, referring to selected parts (either things or the interconnections between things) of the base which are designated by the *predicate* (here used to refer to the semantic pole of any morpheme). In the case of simple nouns like *dog, house, skin* etc., the profile will be some thing, whereas for relational predicates like verbs the profile may include things and the relations between these things. For the GIVE predicate, the profile will include the GIVER, THING, RECIPIENT, and the relations which hold between them. Furthermore, within the profile of a relational predicate, there will be one or more instances of *trajector-landmark* organization. These terms capture a cognitively based asymmetry in relations between profiled entities, a special case of which is the distinction between syntactic subject (one type of trajector) and object (one type of landmark). The notions of trajector and landmark are most easily appreciated in the case of predicates referring to a single entity moving with respect to a fixed point, where the moving entity functions as the trajector and the fixed point as the landmark. Other scenes in which there is more than one moving entity or in which there is no moving entity may not have such obvious asymmetries, though all verbal predicates in a language are analyzed as involving some trajector-landmark asymmetry in Cognitive Grammar. The trajector-landmark distinction can be understood as a manifestation of the *figure-ground* relationship fundamental to perception and cognition generally. Following Langacker (1987: 120): "Impression-istically, the figure within a scene is a substructure perceived as 'standing out' from the remainder (the ground) and accorded special prominence as the pivotal entity around which the scene is organized and for which it provides a setting." It is important to note that the organization of a scene into figure-ground, or trajector-landmark, is not something automatically provided by the scene, although there are scenes in which there is a strong tendency for relations to be construed in particular ways. It is a feature of human cognition that one and the same scene can be construed with different figure-ground relationships, or different *images*. The reader is referred to Langacker (1987: 120–

Figure 1. The base of GIVE-type predicates

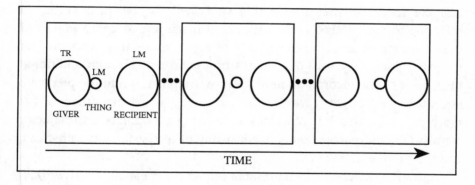

Figure 2. The spatio-temporal domain of GIVE

122, 217–222) for further discussion of this generalized interpretation of the figure-ground distinction. (Cf. also a more restricted application of the figure-ground distinction in Talmy 1975, 1985).

Any one of the three most salient entities in the GIVE base may function as the trajector, or in more syntactic terms the subject, with particular predicates. Examples showing each of the three salient entities functioning as subject are:

(1) a. *The teacher gave the girl a book.*
     b. *The leaked document changed hands.*
     c. *The students got the answers from the lecturer.*

In (1a) the GIVER functions as the trajector; in (1b) it is the THING; in (1c) it is the RECIPIENT. Of the three verbs used in (1), only *give* is appropriate when the GIVER is construed as the trajector, as in (1a), and the focus of attention in this study will be on such verbs. In referring to the GIVER as the trajector, I mean this to apply as part of the definition of *give*, independently of any additional restructuring of the basic image by way of changes brought about through additional morphemes. The incorporation of passive morphemes into the predicate structure will affect *give* in the same way it affects other verbal predicates with which it combines, converting a landmark into trajector status in the morpheme complex consisting of the basic verbal predicate and the passive morpheme.

Figure 2 is a schematic representation of the meaning of *give* illustrated in (1a). This diagram utilizes a more streamlined and more abstract form of notation compared with Figure 1, with the participating entities of the frame all represented by circles. The profiled portion of the base includes the circles representing the GIVER, the THING, and the RECIPIENT. To simplify the metalanguage used in talking about these diagrams, I will refer to the circle representing the person who is doing the giving as the GIVER, the circle representing the object passed as the THING, and the circle representing the receiver as the RECIPIENT. Since this predicate designates a sequence of distinct configurations which evolve through time, rather than being simply a static unchanging spatial configuration, the time dimension of the meaning of the predicate will also be included in the overall profile.

The trajector-landmark relationships in a clause such as (1a) call for some comment. As mentioned above, there is a very basic manifestation of the trajector-landmark relationship where there is a moving figure which moves with respect to a stationary ground. This is the most literal interpretation of a trajector and its landmark. In the GIVE clause (1a), we may identify the moving entity, a book, as a trajector in this sense, and the girl as the landmark. Some part of the girl who is the RECIPIENT may be moving, such as her arm and hands. However, the girl is viewed as a single entity at one location for the purposes of the GIVE construction in (1a) and the book moves to the girl at this location. There is, in addition, another layer of the trajector-landmark asymmetry superimposed on this scene and that is the trajector-landmark relationship understood at the level of subject and object. As mentioned earlier, Cognitive Grammar understands the subject-object asymmetry as yet another manifestation of figure and ground, even when there may be no physical movement. The agentive GIVER, the teacher, is the entity controlling the movement of the book and functions as the trajector with respect to the landmark, a book, at the level of clause structure. These two layers of trajector (TR) and landmark (LM) may be visualized as in (2), where TR_1 represents the "agentive" trajector and TR_2 represents the "moving-figure" trajector:[1]

(2)

$$LM_2 \quad TR_2$$

The teacher gave the girl a book.

$$TR_1 \qquad\qquad LM_1$$

In the diagrams in this chapter, I will only indicate the trajector and landmark entities in the sense of the subject versus object(s). Thus, in Figure 2, we label the GIVER entity TR and both the THING and the RECIPIENT as LMs. In discussing particular GIVE constructions, as in Chapters 3 and 4, it may be useful to consider the fact that the THING is a moving entity with respect to the RECIPIENT, but at this point in the discussion, it is convenient to rely on just this one higher-level sense of trajector versus landmark. To simplify matters, detailed information about what kinds of entities can elaborate these positions has been omitted from the diagram. An alternative representation of the spatio-temporal domain is shown in Figure 3, where the movement of the THING through time is indicated by the arrow.

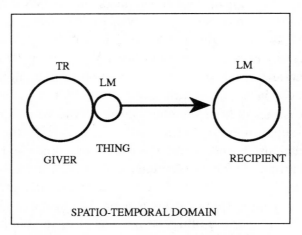

Figure 3. The spatio-temporal domain of GIVE
(alternative representation)

Sentence (1a) represents but one of a number of possible GIVE constructions in English which construe the GIVER as the trajector. Another possibility is the construction *give a book to the girl*. There are more possibilities in other languages, too, which treat the THING and the RECIPIENT in quite different ways. I will postpone discussion of this to Chapter 3.

Figures 2 and 3 fail to express a fairly salient aspect of the scene connoted by GIVE predicates, namely the obvious role of the hands in the typical giving act. The hands are not referred to as such in *The teacher gave the girl a book*, although one could build more structure spelling out the role of the hands as in *The teacher gave the girl a book with her own hands*. Even when it is not spelled out in overt linguistic form, though, the hands of the GIVER and the RECIPIENT are parts of these entities which play a crucial role. It is similar to the role of eyelids with the predicate *blink*, or the role of the foot and leg with *kick*. Such components of entities which are directly involved in the interaction are called *active zones* in Langacker (1987: 271–274). While it is not always necessary to indicate such active zones in the representations of meaning, it is sometimes helpful to do so. Consider, for example, the pair of sentences in (3).

(3)   a.   *Tom gave Mary the ball.*
      b.   *Tom threw Mary the ball.*

Both *give* and *throw* as used in these sentences involve transfer of things, but the active zones of the human participants are slightly different with these two verbs. With *give*, it is the hands (one or both) of the GIVER and RECIPIENT which constitute the most obvious active zone. With *throw*, on the other hand, it would appear to be the movement of the whole arm of the thrower which seems the more salient body part relevant to the throwing. Of course, in so far as the hand is part of the arm and the part in contact with the thing thrown, the hand is also to some extent an active zone. Nevertheless, the arm seems the more appropriate unit to take as the relevant active zone. Undeniably, the arm is involved in the act of giving, but in a less conspicuous way than in the act of throwing. In part, this may derive from the fact that the larger, more energetic action of the arm in throwing makes the role of the hand appear minimal. (3b) strongly implies that the ball was intended to be caught (more so than, say, *Tom threw the ball at Mary*) and so it is appropriate to include the catcher of the ball in the profile of this version of *throw*. The person catching the thing thrown typically receives the thing in the hands with a less conspicuous arm action, so the active zone in the case of the person catching the ball is more appropriately identified as the hands. In other words, one throws (mainly) with the arm and catches (mainly) with the hands. These differences between (3a) and (3b) are shown in Figures 4 and 5. The active zone (AZ) for each person, the hands, is shown in a lighter outline. In the case of *throw*, it seems relevant only to the thrower at the time of releasing the thing and relevant only to the catcher at the point where the thing is caught. Figure 5 shows a greater distance between the two persons involved compared with Figure 4, reflecting a further point of difference

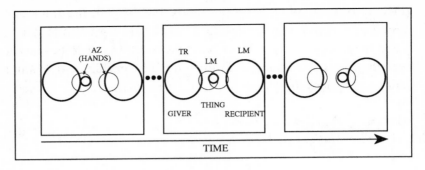

Figure 4. The spatio-temporal domain of GIVE showing Active Zones

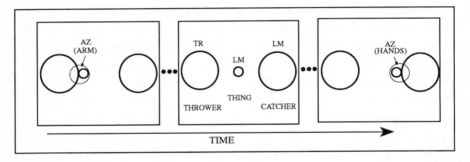

Figure 5. The spatio-temporal domain of THROW

between *give* and *throw*. The concept of an active zone is directly relevant to bringing out some of the crucial semantic differences in these
cases.

As a way of further illustrating the relevance of the active zones in
these representations, consider again sentence (1b): *The leaked document changed hands.* The scene depicted by this sentence involves the
same kind of base described above for *give.* Specifically, it implies a
GIVER who passes a THING to a RECIPIENT. There are some differences in the frames of *give* and *change hands.* So, for example, the sentence lacks the weak implication which often attaches to *give* sentences
of the THING being intended as a gift. (Cf. *The house changed hands*
and *X gave the house to Y*, where the latter more strongly suggests that
the house was transferred as a gift.) Concentrating just on the spatio-
temporal domain, though, the frame in Figure 1 would appear appropriate also in the case of *change hands.* The profile imposed on this
frame is quite different in the two cases, however, and Figure 6 shows
the profile imposed on the GIVE scene in the case of *change hands.*

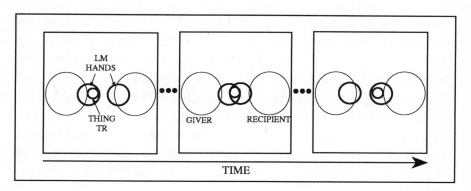

Figure 6. The spatio-temporal domain of CHANGE HANDS

In sentence (1b), the trajector is *the leaked document* with *hands* functioning as the landmark. The unprofiled active zones (in a light outline) of *give* in Figure 4 appear as the profiled landmarks (in a darker outline) in the expression *change hands*, as diagrammed in Figure 6. Conversely, the circles representing the GIVER and RECIPIENT appear unprofiled and in a lighter outline in Figure 6, but profiled and in a darker outline in Figure 4.

The significance of the hands in characterizing the meaning of GIVE predicates is reflected in the way in which a morpheme meaning "hand", "palm" etc. may be incorporated into the GIVE construction. English *hand* and *hand over*, which are partially synonymous with *give*, are examples of this. Chipewyan (Amerindian)[2] provides a further example in its basic GIVE construction, illustrated in (4).

(4)   *Kɛni   ɛritɬ'istil   aniyɛs   tɬ'a-ɣĩ-tã.*
         Kenny box   Agnes   palm-PERF-CL
         'Kenny gave Agnes the box.'   (Chipewyan)

In (4) the verbal complex contains a morpheme recognizable as a variant of the morpheme *tɬ'aɛ* 'palm'. As with other verbs of transfer and manipulation, the Chipewyan GIVE construction employs an object-classifier which classifies the THING transferred in terms of its shape or, one could say, its *handleability*. So, for example, there are distinct classifiers appropriate for round, animate, stiff/sticklike, flat/flexible, liquid, open container, closed container, and granular objects. Thus, not only is the GIVE word based upon the morpheme closely related to the concept of "hand", but the object-classifier system is also based upon the different ways in which the hands take hold of and interact with the THING.

2.3.   The control domain

In Section 2.2, we concentrated on the spatio-temporal aspects of GIVE predicates. Another significant aspect of GIVE predicates concerns the change in control over the thing which is typically involved in giving

acts. I use the term control here in order to allow for the range of situations associated even with prototypical GIVE predicates. It can
include, for example, strict legal possession (*Tom gave his children
their inheritance money before he died*), ordinary types of possession
removed from legal contexts (*Tom gave his boss one of his sandwiches
for lunch*), access to a thing without any implication that the GIVER
owns the THING any more than the RECIPIENT. So, for example, *The
secretary gave me a set of felt pens at the beginning of the semester*
might be said when neither the GIVER nor the RECIPIENT actually
owns the pens which strictly speaking belong to the institution. It may
be that the notion of possession has a privileged status within the range
of meanings possible, being a kind of prototype from which the other
meanings are extensions. It is not necessary to insist on any strong sense
of possession as the prototypical sense connected with most GIVE
predicates, however, and I am not aware of any compelling reason to
proceed in this way, at least for English *give*. It suffices to describe this
aspect in terms of a change in the location of the THING with respect to
the "sphere of control" of the GIVER and RECIPIENT. This is
diagrammed in Figure 7.

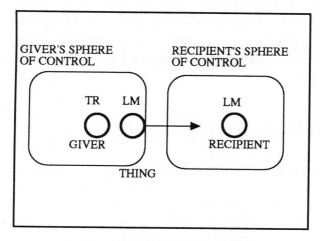

Figure 7. The control domain of GIVE

For simplicity's sake, the two spheres of control have been drawn as distinct and non-overlapping. For some of the instantiations of the notion of sphere of control, there may be quite clear physical boundaries between the two or there may be definite points in time when the object is deemed to have changed from one sphere of control to another. In determining legal ownership over a thing, for example, one must accept legal definitions of such boundaries. In ordinary contexts of interpersonal interaction, however, there may be considerable fuzziness about the boundaries and there may be some overlap between the two spheres of control. The diagram makes no attempt to express all these possibilities. I have shown the THING as proceeding to a location in the vicinity of the RECIPIENT within the RECIPIENT's sphere of control. Typically, the giving act will involve the RECIPIENT actually coming to hold the THING, but there can be some vagueness about the final phase of the act. Often the GIVE predicate can refer to an act of giving which transfers the THING into the immediate vicinity of a RECIPIENT without the eventual RECIPIENT actually taking hold of the THING. So, for example, *We gave our neighbours a bag of apples* could be used to describe taking apples over to a neighbour and leaving them on the doorstep, although it is not the most precise way of describing such an act. The notion of "recipient's sphere of control" is a useful way of describing the endpoint of the giving act in such cases. It represents a kind of semantic extension of the prototypical meaning, though a rather more subtle extension than we find with the figurative meanings discussed in Chapter 4.[3]

2.4.   The force-dynamics domain

The domains considered so far have not said anything directly about the various ways in which the participants contribute to the interaction. Implied in the discussion of the control domain is the conception of the GIVER and RECIPIENT as controlling entities whereas the THING is a controlled entity. It is useful to state more explicitly some of the different contributions made by these entities to the complex relation described by GIVE predicates. We will refer to these aspects as force-dynamics.

It is attractive to think of actions like giving in terms of energy flow, involving an initial "energy source" and a final "energy sink", to borrow Langacker's terms (Langacker 1991: 292–293). Giving is easily construed as a flow of energy from the GIVER to the RECIPIENT. The "energy" in this case is made up of physical movement of all three entities participating in the giving event, together with mental activity on the part of the GIVER and RECIPIENT. The event begins with the GIVER — it is the GIVER who is understood as the initiator of the event, as the initial controller of the thing transferred, and as the locus of the physical region in which the thing is initially situated. It ends with the RECIPIENT, who, by accepting the thing, completes the act of giving, is the final controller of the thing transferred, and is the locus of the physical region in which the movement of the thing comes to a halt. There are numerous alternative ways in which the whole event may be more precisely construed (whether the interaction is basically between GIVER and THING, or GIVER and RECIPIENT; whether the concept of a path is incorporated into the image etc.), but I believe the flow of energy as described in these broad terms is a highly natural way of understanding the act of giving, regardless of how one chooses to integrate the individual parts of the scene into one larger image. It qualifies as a *natural path* (Langacker 1991: 293). Figure 8 is an attempt to represent these aspects of the meaning of GIVE predicates by depicting the flow of energy as an arrow from the GIVER to the RECIPIENT. The vertical lines are appropriate as a way of suggesting the starting and end points of this energy flow. The THING is positioned on this arrow at an intermediate point indicating that it is somehow involved in this flow of energy. The broken lines from the GIVER and the RECIPIENT express a further aspect concerning the active participation of these two entities in the event. A double broken line is used to represent the wilful initiation of the event on the part of the GIVER. The single broken line represents the lesser degree of initiation involved on the part of the RECIPIENT in accepting the THING.

We may compare the force-dynamics of GIVE predicates in Figure 8 with that of RECEIVE-type predicates, in particular *receive,* in Figure

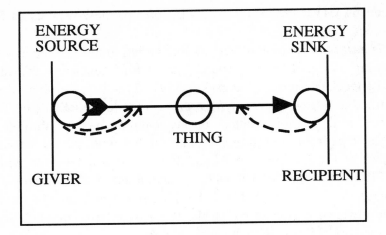

Figure 8. The force-dynamics of GIVE

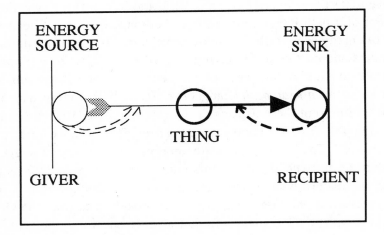

Figure 9. The force-dynamics of RECEIVE

9. *Receive* suggests itself as a kind of converse of *give*, which it is in some ways, although there are special uses of *receive* which one would not expect simply on the basis that it is a converse of *give*. So, for example, the sense of "receive through the mail" frequently attaches to *receive* (but not *give*), though it also occurs as part of the phrase *receive presents* (for a birthday), which does not imply that the THING was sent through the mail. Ignoring these special characteristics of *receive*, we can assume an identical base for both *receive* and *give*. With *receive*, however, only part of that base is profiled: the part involving the interaction of the RECIPIENT and THING. This is indicated by the darker outline for just this part of the base in Figure 9. It is still the case that the GIVER initiates the whole process, of course.

2.5. The domain of human interest

There is a further dimension of meaning to GIVE predicates which needs to be recognized and that is the dimension of meaning which has to do with the ways in which the participants are advantaged or disadvantaged by the event. This is the domain I have called "human interest". The focus on advantages and disadvantages may seem too limited in scope to be of much relevance in describing meanings. Why not posit also a dimension of meaning relating to the colour of the participants' hair or clothes etc.? The reason for recognizing a domain of human interest as opposed to a domain of hair or clothes etc. is that humans and their involvement in acts and the way they are affected by acts are typically crucial components in the overall meaning of a predicate. The way in which humans are advantaged or disadvantaged by acts is something a speaker will often wish to include in a message. There are special benefactive and adversative constructions (case marking etc.) in languages which serve to integrate these aspects into a larger message.

Figure 10 represents part of the human interest domain of GIVE. It shows a schematic scale of effects on the RECIPIENT, from benefactive effects at one end to adversative effects at the other end. The act of giving is shown as being located towards the benefactive end of this scale. This reflects the fact that the THING is typically passed to the

RECIPIENT for the benefit of the RECIPIENT. It is not hard to imagine how one might give things which harm RECIPIENTs (exploding bombs, for example), but this is not the way humans normally interact (fortunately). My representation of the domain of human interest reflects the typical scenario, not the atypical. One could add information, too, about the effect of the act on the GIVER to make the representation more complete, but in the case of GIVE there seems to be little one can say about the effect of the act on the GIVER. The GIVER ends up with less than what he/she started out with, but that does not mean the GIVER is necessarily disadvantaged in any way.

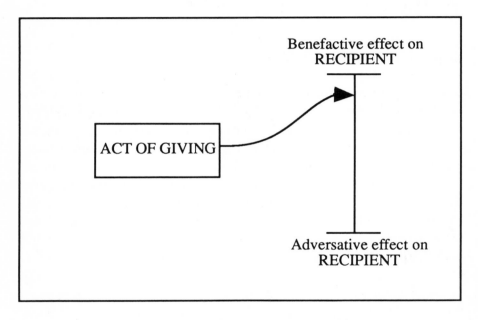

Figure 10. The human interest domain of GIVE

2.6.   The complex matrix of GIVE

Each of the domains singled out in the preceding sections throws light
on some aspect of the event described by GIVE predicates. All these
domains are simultaneously present in the meaning of GIVE. They are
separated out in our discussion only to make the analysis more manage-
able. In other chapters, too, it will be convenient to be able to refer
back to just one of these domains in order to better understand some
point about a particular use of GIVE. Taken together, these domains
make up a *complex matrix* containing each of these domains and others
which are of less relevance to the present discussion. One could think of
all the domains as cards all stacked together, with each card having
something more to say about the nature of the predicate. An even more
appropriate metaphor might be to think of them as a stack of transparencies such that one can make out all the properties of each entity in
the frame by looking through all the transparencies at once.
Alternatively, one can remove one of the transparent sheets to inspect
the properties of the entities in relation to one domain only.

There are other aspects of the complex matrix of GIVE predicates
which may be noted. Often, for example, there is a later act involving
the RECIPIENT and the THING. That is to say, we normally give
things to a RECIPIENT so that the RECIPIENT can make some use of
the object. Any consequential interaction between the RECIPIENT and
the THING is not included in the profile of GIVE predicates but it is a
typical part of the base when viewed in an expanded way. This aspect of
the complex matrix is relevant when it comes to understanding some of
the extensions of meaning which we see with GIVE predicates, as discussed in Chapter 4. Here, we may just note in passing how common it
is for GIVE predicates to appear as part of a larger construction in
which some interaction between the THING and the RECIPIENT is indicated, as in *I gave Kim the book to read*. The additional verbal predicate *to read* is here understood as referring to an activity involving the
RECIPIENT (rather than the GIVER) and the THING. This way of interpreting the infinitival expansion of the basic GIVE clause should not
be thought of as a semantic quirk about English. Rather, it reflects a
basic feature associated with the act of giving, namely that the

RECIPIENT would normally proceed to do something with the THING transferred.

2.7. Unfilled elaboration sites

In the examples of GIVE predicates discussed so far each of the entities GIVER, THING, and RECIPIENT, has been encoded in the GIVE clause. It is possible, though, for one or more of these entities to have no realization in a clause. Like many other verbal predicates in English, the usual way of forming the imperative, without any overt second-person subject, is also relevant to GIVE predicates, as in *Give me the book*. Besides this, however, it is possible for GIVE clauses to lack any overt reference to either the THING or the RECIPIENT. This is possible with certain choices of lexical items, as in the following examples:

(5) THING is unspecified:
    a. *Haven't we given to the Red Cross already this year?*
    b. *I like to give to the church.*
    c. *I gave to the Red Cross collector when she called at our house.*
    d. *We always give to the needy.*
(6) RECIPIENT is unspecified:
    a. *I never give sweets as presents.*
    b. *I like to give presents.*
    c. *The teacher gave the answers before the test.*
    d. *The police here give tickets for parking offences.*

In (5), the THING is left unspecified. As far as I am aware, this requires a *to* + RECIPIENT phrase in English, rather than a RECIPIENT in the immediate postverbal position (cf. **I like to give the church*). The most felicitous contexts are ones which strongly suggest a particular type of THING. So, for example, one normally gives money to the church and charities, so (5a) and (5b) are easily interpreted in that way. Having a context of habitual giving further supports such interpretations, forcing one to construe the THING as the usual THING associated with that act of giving. Even single, isolated events of giving, as in (5c), may still allow lack of overt reference to THING if there is a strong association with a particular THING. Similar remarks apply to the sentences in (6) where the context supplies enough clues to interpreting the RECIPIENT in an appropriate way even where there is no overt reference to such. It is even possible to leave both the THING and RECIPIENT unspecified in the actual GIVE clause. A possible way of advertising, say, a door-to-door appeal for money by the Red Cross might be along the lines: *The Red Cross appeal for funds on Saturday 15th May: Give generously!* Or to cite an actual example from a sign outside a mobile blood-transfusion centre: *Blood-donors: Please give here*. In this case, of course, we are no longer dealing with literal GIVE, but an extension of the basic, literal meaning. It must be recognized, however, that the omission of a THING or RECIPIENT is constrained and to some extent a matter of collocation in certain phrases. It is not in general possible to omit one of these entities simply because it is retrievable from contextual clues. So, for example, in the context of a conversation having as its topic a certain gardening tool and where it is presently located, I cannot say in English *Oh, I remember now, I gave to the neighbours last week.*

Some languages, such as Cantonese and other Chinese dialects[4], tolerate more extensive omission of THING and RECIPIENT phrases in GIVE clauses than does English. Compare, for example, the English sentence (7a) with the Cantonese equivalent in (7b), the THING being inferrable from context:

(7) a. *?Give (to) me!*
  b. *Béi   ngoh!*
    'Give me!'

The English sentence is incomplete even when the THING is interpretable from context. As observed above, the omission of the THING phrase elsewhere in English requires the *to* + RECIPIENT construction. But even inserting the *to* here barely improves the sentence. At best, it could be called abrupt, but it is really not a structure which is sanctioned for either formal or informal styles of English. The Cantonese equivalent, on the other hand, is a perfectly natural and common phrase which is complete in itself.

The possibility of having one or more of GIVER, THING, and RECIPIENT missing in a clause leads to the necessity of recognizing sub-parts of the semantic structure as *elaboration sites* (*e-sites*). These are the parts of the base which are filled in an actual construction. In the discussion so far we did not have any reason to insist on a distinction between profiled entities and e-sites. In the discussion in preceding sections, the examples were such that each profiled entity in the base was also an e-site and was filled by a lexical item. But the examples in (5)–(6) above require that we now take heed of this distinction. Thus, we say that in the sentences (5)–(6) the GIVER, THING, and RECIPIENT are all part of the profile, but only two of these entities constitute e-sites. One might question whether it is right to say that these covert entities are even profiled in such cases, taking them instead to be present in the base but not part of the profile. In the case of GIVE predicates, however, I regard all three entities as playing a salient role in the semantic structure, with the GIVER functioning as the trajector and the other entities as landmarks. Consistent with this view, I will treat all three entities as part of the profile. In order to represent e-sites where it is relevant to do so, I will follow the practice of Cognitive Grammar and use shading for an entity functioning as an e-site. (All the profiled entities in the diagrams above could thus be redrawn with shading in the circles if one wished.) GIVE clauses lacking any overt reference to a RECIPIENT, such as *The teacher gave the answers*, may therefore be diagrammed schematically as in Figure 11 (ignoring the additional grammatical structure present in the clause).

2.8. The meaning of TAKE

We may compare GIVE and TAKE, understood as the basic meaning of English *take*. It is useful to distinguish similarities and differences between these predicates. The similarities between the two predicates include: the movement of a thing, typically involving the hands of a

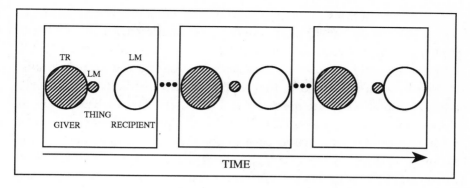

Figure 11. The spatio-temporal domain of GIVE with RECIPIENT unspecified

person; the movement is initiated by a person; the thing ends up in the sphere of control of a person. A striking difference between the two predicates, on the other hand, is the fact that the two predicates involve different directions of movement of a thing with respect to the subject referent. In the case of GIVE, the movement of the thing is away from the subject referent, while in the case of TAKE, the movement is toward the subject referent. It must be noted, however, that it is not simply a matter of different direction of movement within an otherwise identical base. There is no GIVER necessarily present in the base of *take*, whereas a GIVER must be present as part of the base of GIVE. So, for example, *The teacher took the pen* is complete, without any specification of a GIVER or indeed the original location of the thing being taken. One may specify the original location of the thing taken, as in *The teacher took the book from the table, The teacher took the book from the student* etc. Even when one chooses to elaborate a TAKE clause in this way, however, there is still no GIVER necessarily implied by the structure. There is only one person necessarily involved in the characterization of the basic meaning of TAKE, whereas there are two distinct persons involved in the case of GIVE.

Figure 12 attempts to capture the force-dynamics of TAKE. The direction of the energy-flow is shown as originating with the TAKER, flowing to the THING, and returning to the TAKER. Since the TAKER initiates the action, I have included a double-dash arrow to reflect this, similar to what was done in Figure 8. It is also instructive to compare the representation of the meaning of TAKE with that of RECEIVE, as shown above in Figure 9. RECEIVE highlights a different portion of what is essentially the same base as for GIVE, with the focus of the meaning shifting to the terminal part of the giving act. With TAKE, however, there is an entirely different force-dynamic structure which constitutes the base for the meaning. Because the person who comes to have the thing is the initiator of the act with TAKE, TAKE is a more obvious converse to GIVE than is RECEIVE. TAKE is a natural converse of GIVE, whereas RECEIVE is simply GIVE viewed from a different perspective.

Despite the semantic differences between GIVE and TAKE, there are the similarities mentioned above. It is presumably these similarities which are part of the reason why one of these predicates may influence the other in the course of development of a language. This has been noted for various phenomena in unrelated languages.[5] The (unexpected) stem vowel of the GIVE word in some Germanic languages, for example, is claimed to be a result of analogy with the stem vowel of the TAKE word. So, for example, the *e* in Old High German *geban* GIVE (where one would have expected a stem vowel *a* on historical grounds) is presumed to be influenced by the stem vowel of Old High German *neman* TAKE. The *n* in the stem of French *rendre* /Italian *rendere* 'give back' (from Latin *reddere*) is claimed to be due to the influence of the *n* in French *prendre*/ Italian *prendere* TAKE (Latin *prehendere*). German *geben* GIVE is cognate with Old Irish *gabim* which means TAKE, suggesting some kind of semantic connection between the two senses. A number of additional examples like these are cited in Kretschmer—Wahrmann (1931: 207–208).

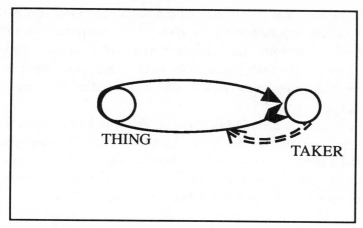

Figure 12. The force-dynamics of TAKE

2.9. Summary

In discussing the meaning of a morpheme, it is convenient to employ the ideas and notation proposed in Langacker (1987, 1991). As a first step, one needs to distinguish the different domains which all contribute to a full characterization of the meaning. In the case of GIVE, we distinguish the spatio-temporal domain, the control domain, the force-dynamics domain, and the domain of human interest. Each of these domains draws attention to some aspect of the meaning of GIVE. Taken together, they constitute a relatively complete statement of the meaning of GIVE. This totality of the components of meaning of a morpheme is referred to as a complex matrix.

The GIVER, THING, and RECIPIENT entities are salient or "profiled" parts of the meaning of GIVE and appear in each of the domain-specific characterizations of GIVE. While these three entities are always present as part of the meaning of GIVE, different versions of GIVE have different kinds of additional structure associated with them. For one thing, there can be different choices of imagery underlying various GIVE constructions. These different choices correlate with the range of construction types found with GIVE verbs across languages, explored more fully in Chapter 3. Furthermore, the

GIVER, THING, and RECIPIENT need not all be overtly present, even though they are implicit in the meaning of the morpheme. In the terms of Cognitive Grammar, these implicit participants in the meaning are referred to as unfilled elaboration sites. Here, too, there is some variation cross-linguistically as to which elaboration sites may be left unfilled.

Spelling out the meaning of GIVE in the way I have done here is a useful starting point for the discussions in Chapter 3, dealing with literal GIVE, and Chapter 4, dealing with figurative GIVE. Regardless of whether we discuss literal or figurative GIVE constructions, there is a constant need to refer back to the basic meaning of GIVE.

Chapter 3. Constructions with literal GIVE

3.1. The AGENT-PATIENT model

In this chapter I will document some of the diversity which presents it-self in languages relating mainly to the expression of literal GIVE. By "literal GIVE" I mean the use of a GIVE verb in the sense elaborated upon in Chapter 2. That is to say, I will be discussing GIVE construc-tions which involve the transference of a THING (and the control over the THING) from one person to another. Often, the THING is some-thing which can be passed by hand. These uses of GIVE verbs are opposed to "figurative GIVE" which will refer to other meanings which may be associated with GIVE verbs and these meanings are discussed in Chapter 4. The literal GIVE constructions which I will focus on in this chapter are the types where the GIVER appears as the subject of an ac-tive clause, such as *I gave Tom the money, I gave the money to Tom*, rather than constructions where one of the other entities functions as the subject, such as *The money changed hands* and *Tom received the money*.

In discussing the syntactic devices appropriate for encoding GIVE scenes, we can find some motivation for the form such clauses take by considering a basic cognitive tendency which is evident in language: the imposition of an AGENT-PATIENT model (or metaphor) of interac-tion on actions and, even more broadly, events (cf. Langacker 1991: 282ff.). This inclines us to identify entities in a scene which can be con-strued as instances of an AGENT interacting with a PATIENT. These terms are understood as referring prototypically to a volitional, human instigator of an action (AGENT), acting upon a relatively inert, affected inanimate entity (PATIENT). This characterization of the AGENT-PATIENT model of interaction holds for the prototype of this model and serves as the cognitive basis of the subject-direct object organization of clause structure. It is important to note that many kinds of events are treated, for the purposes of linguistic encoding, as though they are in-stances of an AGENT-PATIENT model of interaction, even though they do not fit the literal description of this model. Here, as is always the case when dealing with human categorization of the world around us, we must acknowledge that there will be central and less central members of a category. The AGENT-PATIENT model, as described above, is frequently extended to events and situations giving rise to syntactic subjects and objects which may be associated with many diverse semantic roles.

Since we are focusing on GIVE constructions in which the GIVER is functioning as the subject of an active clause, a question immediately arises as to which other entity may function as an object. When one compares structures across languages one finds that either the THING or the RECIPIENT in the GIVE scene may be encoded as the object. In the Russian example (1a), the THING functions just like the object in a prototypical transitive construction appearing in the accusative case; in example (1b) from Mandak (Austronesian, Papua New Guinea), the RECIPIENT appears as a direct object of the verb, just like an object in any transitive clause. The Mandak GIVE construction is similar to what is found with English *present*, as in *They presented him with a gift.*

(1)   a.   *Ya   dal   knig-u   uchitel-yu.*
           I   gave   book-ACC   teacher-DAT
           'I gave the book to the teacher.'   (Russian)
      b.   *Di   ga   raba   i   mi   la-mani.*
           they PAST give   him   with the-money
           'They gave him the money.'   (Mandak, Blansitt 1984: 141)

It may happen that a language conventionalizes one or the other of these two ways of conceptualizing giving. Dryer (1986) gives explicit recognition to the frequency of the structure in which the RECIPIENT is treated just like a prototypical object by proposing a category called "primary object" which includes the object (direct object) in a mono-transitive clause and the RECIPIENT in a ditransitive clause where the RECIPIENT functions like a direct object. This leads Dryer to a distinction between the two types of encoding GIVE-type events as "direct objectivity" and "primary objectivity":

(2) a. *Direct objectivity* refers to the structural pattern whereby the phrase referring to the THING in a GIVE-type clause is encoded in the same way as the single object of a monotransitive clause.

   b. *Primary objectivity* refers to the structural pattern whereby the phrase referring to the RECIPIENT in a GIVE-type clause is encoded in the same way as the single object of a monotransitive clause.

There are plenty of examples of both construction types in the world's languages. Māori and French show only direct objectivity in GIVE constructions, Ojibwa and Ttzotzil show only primary objectivity, while both types are found in Indonesian.

These alternative linguistic encodings of the giving scene reflect alternative ways of extending the AGENT-PATIENT model to one and the same scene. The GIVE scene is indeed a complex assembly of relationships — old and new possessors and a possessed entity, movement away from one entity to another, and there are animate and inanimate contrasts between the entities which make up the scene. Being such a complex interaction of entities, it should be no surprise that the scene may be construed or metaphorized in terms of an AGENT-PATIENT model of interaction in alternative ways. The THING, for example, is a suitable candidate for the object function when we consider its characteristics *vis-à-vis* the GIVER. In so far as an inanimate entity is maximally differentiated from a fully volitional human actor, the GIVER and the THING are easily construed as an extension of the asymmetric relationship of a prototypical AGENT-PATIENT pair. Furthermore, the inanimate entity can be easily construed as an entity which is affected by an action of the AGENT, the location and ownership of the THING being changed by a wilful act on the part of the GIVER. All these considerations can be seen as providing a cognitive basis for "direct objectivity" whereby the THING is construed as the PATIENT in an AGENT-PATIENT kind of interaction. The GIVER and RECIPIENT may also be construed as extensions of prototypical AGENT and PATIENT respectively, though the cognitive basis for this extension is somewhat different. The RECIPIENT is an active participant in the act of giving, but is not the instigator. When one focuses on the human participants in the giving scene, there is an asymmetry with the GIVER the more agent-like and the RECIPIENT the more patient-like. It is this asymmetry which motivates the construal of the GIVER-RECIPIENT pair as a kind of AGENT-PATIENT interaction. It should be clear that neither of these two ways of construing the GIVE scene is more basic than the other. Neither the THING transferred nor the RECIPIENT are examples of prototypical PATIENTs. The THING transferred is not affected or changed in an obvious way by the GIVER as one expects of prototypical PATIENTs. Nor is the RECIPIENT a typical PATIENT, since it is a person rather than an inanimate and there is no direct effect that the GIVER has on the RECIPIENT. Both construals of the GIVE scene represent extensions of the AGENT-PATIENT prototype.

Where there is more than one literal GIVE construction available in a language, a variety of factors may influence a choice of one construction over the other. My aim here is basically to document the range of grammatical possibilities rather than to explore the precise conditions of use of any one of these, but I acknowledge the complexity of the issues involved in accounting for the choice of one alternative over another in any one language. Consider, for example, the alternative construction types in English, the ditransitive and the oblique *to* constructions, exemplified by *I gave Kim the book* and *I gave the book to Kim* respectively. This pair of constructions has been the subject of extensive research (see the references in Thompson 1989) aimed at teasing out the factors (especially discourse factors) which are relevant to a preference for one construction over the other in a certain context. A good example of this kind of research is Thompson (1989), who investigates, amongst other things, the pronominality, specificity, identifiability, length, and "givenness" of the THING and RECIPIENT in the two *give*-type constructions.[1] When both the THING and RECIPIENT are realized as pronouns, then there is no choice. There is no ditransitive possibility with both objects as pronouns (**I gave her it*). Instead, one must use the alternative oblique *to* construction (*I gave it to her*). As with other "heavy" noun phrases, objects with relative clauses as part of their structure will tend to be positioned in a clause-final position, leading to alternative construction types in the sentences in (3).

(3)　a.　*I gave Kim* [NP *a copy of that interesting article that you had lent me*].

　　b.　*I gave the article to* [NP *one of the students who is writing an essay on the topic*].

In ordinary narrative discourse, there seems to be a preference for the ditransitive construction in the case of *give*. My own examination of a contemporary novel written in a very natural style, *Nice Work* by David Lodge, revealed very different frequencies of occurrence of the two *give* constructions (literal and figurative), summarized in (4).

(4)　a.　GIVE THING TO RECIPIENT　　　　18　　22.5 %

　　　　GIVE RECIPIENT THING　　　　　　62　　77.5 %

　　b.　GIVE THING$_{Noun}$TO RECIPIENT$_{Pro}$　　0　　0 %

　　　　GIVE RECIPIENT$_{Pro}$ THING$_{Noun}$　　52　　100 %

(4a) contains the figures for the two GIVE constructions appearing in the book, ignoring for the moment whether the THING and RECIPIENT phrases have pronouns or nouns as their heads. The GIVE RECIPIENT THING construction is far more common, appearing three times more often than its alternative. Most of the GIVE clauses have the RECIPIENT phrase realized as a pronoun, referring to a person already introduced in the discourse, and with such clauses there is a very strong tendency towards the GIVE RECIPIENT THING construction. Indeed, as shown in (4b), when the THING is a noun and RECIPIENT is a pronoun, the ditransitive construction is the *only* construction which was used in this particular novel, even though the alternative is grammatically possible. These results are comparable to the findings of Givón (1984b: 153–157), who found pronouns with a dative/benefactive function appeared *only* as direct objects in a study of actual occurrences in printed narrative. Givón's study included a range of verbs, including *give*, but not restricted to it. My own investigation into *give*, however, proved consistent with his findings. Thompson (1989: 11) found that the RECIPIENT in the direct object position in ditransitive constructions (not just with *give)* was pronominal in 73% of the cases and animate in a full 99% of cases. Thompson (1989) argues that the immediately post-verbal position is the favoured site for "topicworthy" non-subject noun phrases, with "topicworthiness" subsuming "givenness" and pronominality. This is comparable to the findings of Davidse (to appear) who distinguishes the discourse functions of "referring" (i.e. referring to a discourse referent which has already been established) and "introducing" (i.e. introducing a new discourse referent) in GIVE-type clauses in English. She finds that in the ditransitive construction, the post-verbal nominal serves a referring function in 93% of cases. As part of the prepositional phrase in the alternative construction type, the RECIPIENT-type phrase is less strongly referring (only 53%). Without attempting to account for all the factors influencing the choice of one construction over the other in English, it should be clear that the two constructions are not always felt to be equally appropriate stylistically.[2]

The two basic alternatives for extending the AGENT-PATIENT model to the GIVE scene are depicted in Figure 13. Since the notions of AGENT and PATIENT pertain to the nature of the interaction between entities, it is appropriate to view the meanings involved in terms of force-dynamics, as introduced in Chapter 2. The box on the left depicts the most literal kind of AGENT-PATIENT interaction, with the energy flow proceeding from a PERSON to an affected THING. The box has been enclosed in a darker outline to represent the prototypical case from which proceed the extensions to the less prototypical cases. The double dashed arrow emanating from the PERSON in this diagram represents the volitional instigation of the act by the PERSON. Single dashed lines show the extensions (or "mapping") of this model to the GIVE scene. In the top box, I have shown how the categories of AGENT and PATIENT are mapped onto GIVER and RECIPIENT respectively, while in the lower box they are mapped onto AGENT and THING respectively.

The pairing of the AGENT-PATIENT meaning and subject-object syntactic form makes up a construction, parallel to the pairing of form and meaning which is found with morphemes. Constructions are a key component of the grammar of a language in Cognitive Grammar (Langacker 1987: 409–425), as well as Construction Grammar

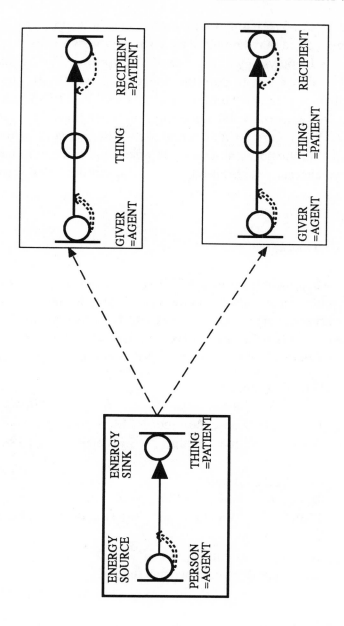

Figure 13. The AGENT-PATIENT model extended to GIVE

(Fillmore 1988). The parallel with morphemes holds in many respects. In particular, there may be polysemy associated with a construction just as there may be polysemy in the case of a morpheme. The extensions of the subject-object construction to interactions which are similar to, though distinct from, the prototypical AGENT-PATIENT interaction give rise to "constructional polysemy" in a language (cf. Goldberg 1992a: 26–33). Figure 13 thus forms part of the network of meanings associated with the polysemous subject-object construction in languages which have alternative subject-object encodings of the GIVE scene.

3.1.1.   Verb marking

Sometimes the occurrence of the THING or RECIPIENT as the direct object requires some marking on the verb. It may happen that a verb is marked with some affix when the RECIPIENT functions as the object, as in Tzotzil, where a *-be* suffix is attached to the verb when a RECIPIENT phrase is present in the GIVE clause :

(5)   THING is object:
   a.   *?a   li   Xun-e,   ba   y- ak'   chitom.*
     TOPIC the Xun-clitic   go   3ERG-give pig
     'Xun went to give the pig.'   (Tzotzil, Aissen 1987: 104)

     RECIPIENT is object:
   b.   *?a   li   Xun-e,   ba   y- ak' -be   chitom*
     TOPIC the Xun-clitic   go   3ERG-give-SUF pig
     li   ?antz-e.
     the   woman-clitic
     'Xun went to give the woman the pig.'
                      (Tzotzil, Aissen 1987: 105)

While *li ?antz* 'the woman' does not appear in the prototypical object position immediately after the verb, there is substantial evidence that the phrase nevertheless functions as the main object for the purposes of syntactic rules (passive and reflexivization). In Tzotzil, the RECIPIENT must function as the object in such sentences and the inclusion of a RECIPIENT object in a GIVE-clause requires that the verb be marked with the *-be* suffix, as in (5b). (5a) illustrates a GIVE clause with unspecified RECIPIENT and in this case there is no *-be* suffix. Bemba, as discussed in Givón (1979: 167–171), provides another example of verb affixation registering a RECIPIENT as the object of the verb. The verb *peele* 'gave' takes no suffix when the THING functions as the object, but it requires the suffix *-ko* when the RECIPIENT functions as such. It is particularly interesting to observe the presence or absence of this suffix in relative clauses:

(6) a. *Naa-laandile ku-muana uko   umukashi àa-peele icitabo.*
         I-spoke   to-child to-whom woman   she-gave book
         'I spoke to the child to whom the woman gave a/the book.'
                                        (Bemba, Givón 1979: 169)
     b. *Naa-mweene umuana uo   umukashi àa-peele-ko   icitabo.*
         I-saw   child whom woman   she-gave-SUF book
         'I saw the child to whom the woman gave a/the book.'
                                        (Bemba, Givón 1979: 170)

The choice between *peele* and *peele-ko* in the relative clause is related to constraints on the formation of relative clauses in Bemba. As noted by Givón (1979: 169–170), the relative pronouns and their antecedent head nouns agree in case, determined by the head noun (unlike, for example, in German where the cases of the relative pronoun and its antecedent are independent of each other). Thus, we see the head noun *(u)muana* 'child' and the relative pronoun both appearing in a dative case in the first sentence, (6a), while they both appear as objects in the second sentence, (6b). The availability of the two ways of structuring GIVE-type clauses in Bemba, with RECIPIENT functioning either as an oblique phrase or as the direct object, enables one to manipulate relative clauses containing verbs like *peele*. It is comparable to the way in which the availability of passive structures enables relativization of certain noun phrases in languages where only the subject phrase is relativizable. In both Tzotzil and Bemba a suffix on the verb indicates the presence of a

RECIPIENT as an object, although they differ in that a RECIPIENT, when present, *must* appear as an object in Tzotzil whereas this is just one of the options available for GIVE clauses in Bemba.

A variation of this pattern is found in languages where only certain types of RECIPIENTs in the object position occasion the appearance of an additional morpheme attached to the GIVE verb. Such is the case in Namakir (Austronesian, Central Vanuatu). In this language a RECIPIENT object requires an *-i* suffix on the verb, but only when "higher level" RECIPIENTs are involved. Humans count as higher level, pigs do not. Hence, we find the *-i* suffix on the GIVE verb in (7a), but not (7b).

(7) a. *Ko   ?or-i   ke-anu   na-tus.*
         2SG   give-SUF   ART-mother   ART-book
         'Give mother the book.'   (Namakir, Sperlich 1993: 202)
     b. *Ri   bi?or   na-bokah   na-human.*
         they   gave   ART-pig   ART-residue
         'They gave the pig the left-overs.'
                                      (Namakir, Sperlich 1993: 340)

The *-i* suffix has a more general role as a marker of certain types of transitive clauses beyond what is suggested just by the GIVE clauses in (7), but the difference between higher and lower types of objects is crucial in all its uses. The Namakir facts are consistent with observations made elsewhere concerning the difference between humans and non-humans with respect to verb marking (see Lichtenberk 1982).

It needs to be noted, however, that the THING phrase is also capable of triggering some additional verbal morphology when it occurs as the object (or primary object, as explained below). In some varieties of Malay/Indonesian, including the prescriptive style, an optional *-kan* suffix on the verb is occasioned by a THING as the object, as in (8a).[3]

(8)   THING is object:

  a. *Saya mem-beri(-Ø, -kan) buku itu kepada Ali.*
     I   TRANS-give   book that to   Ali
     'I gave the book to Ali.'   (Malay/Indonesian)

      RECIPIENT is (main) object:

  b. *Saya mem-beri   Ali   buku itu.*
     I   TRANS-give Ali   book that
     'I gave Ali the book.'   (Malay/Indonesian)

Superficially, at least, it might appear that a similar state of affairs exists in West Greenlandic (cf. Fortescue 1984: 88–89). The verb *tuni* 'give' appears in this form when the RECIPIENT is the object, but with a suffix *-ut* (>*up* before *p*) when the THING functions as the object, as shown in (9).

(9)   THING is the object:

  a. *Aningaasa-t Niisi-mut tunni-up-pai.*
     money-PL   Niisi-ALL give:3SGSUBJ:3PLOBJ-SUF-Indicative
     'He gave the money to Niisi.'
                     (West Greenlandic, Fortescue 1984: 88)

      RECIPIENT is the object:

  b. *Niisi   aningaasa-nik   tuni-vaa.*
     Niisi   money-INST:PL give:3SGSUBJ:3SGOBJ-Indicative
     'He gave Niisi money.'
                     (West Greenlandic, Fortescue1984: 89)

While the *-ut* suffix might appear to be marking the presence of both a THING object and a RECIPIENT as an oblique with GIVE verbs, other facts suggest that it is more correct to associate the presence of the verbal suffix more precisely with the inclusion of the allative phrase into the clausal structure. The discussion of the suffix in Woodbury (1977) is helpful in further understanding the function of this suffix. Although there are many functions of *-ut*, its use in (9) would seem closest to the additional use we see in (10b).

(10) a. *Tuur-paa.*
thrust-Indicative
'He thrusts at it (in the absolutive case) with something (in the instrumental case).'
(Greenlandic Eskimo, Woodbury 1977: 251)

   b. *Tuxx-up-paa.*
press-SUF-Indicative
'He presses it against something (in the allative case).'
(Greenlandic Eskimo, Woodbury 1977: 251)

In (10b), an allative construction is used and it is this construction which necessitates the use of the verbal suffix in question. Thus, it would appear that the inclusion of an allative way of viewing an interaction is what triggers the addition of the extra verbal morpheme in West Greenlandic. This goes hand in hand with the tendency in this family of languages for the instrumental way of viewing interactions as being the more common and relatively unmarked way of encoding such events.

The facts about verb marking and choice of direct object raise problems for approaches which assume one of the two structural types is basic cross-linguistically. In classical Transformational Grammar and Relational Grammar, for example, the THING is analyzed as the direct object in the underlying or initial representation. A transformational rule (Dative Shift) or a relation changing rule (3-2 Advancement) converts this representation into one in which the RECIPIENT takes over the role of direct object. The addition of a verbal affix is seen as a way of registering the application of the rule. That is, a change to the syntax of the clause is parallelled by the addition of an affix to the verb. The fact that affixation on the verb appears when the THING functions as direct object in some languages argues against such an analysis. So, for example, in West Greenlandic Eskimo and Indonesian/Malay, the additional verbal morphology appears only when the THING is the direct object. One could show the verb marking possibilities as in (11).

(11) a.   Bemba, Tzotzil:

GIVE Verb	*Direct object*	*Oblique/indirect object*
V - Ø	THING	RECIPIENT
V - Affix	RECIPIENT	

b.   Greenlandic Eskimo, Indonesian/Malay:

GIVE Verb	*Direct object*	*Oblique/indirect object*
V - Affix	THING	RECIPIENT
V - Ø	RECIPIENT	

One could argue that there is nothing in the theory of Transformational Grammar or Relational Grammar which requires that the underlying structure be relatively unmarked compared with the surface structure. Nevertheless, this is what one typically finds. When one converts an active clause into a passive clause, for example, one typically finds verbal morphology in the derived passive structure.[4] If one insists on Dative Shift or 3-2 Advancement as the only means by which a RECIPIENT comes to function as a direct object, then there will be cases where the derived structure appears with the relatively unmarked verbal morphology. We have then a decidedly odd matching of morphological and syntactic facts.

It happens sometimes that the verbal affix which occurs with the RECIPIENT as the object phrase is etymologically related to an adposition used with the RECIPIENT in the alternative construction. That is, one may find the morphemes in bold in (12) to be cognates.

(12) a.   ... GIVE-**Affix** RECIPIENT$_{DO}$ THING
     b.   ... GIVE   THING$_{DO}$ **Adposition**-RECIPIENT

This is arguably the case in Bemba, for example, where we find a verbal suffix *-ko* and the preposition *ku* 'to'. Parallel facts hold for a verbal suffix *-mo* and a preposition *mu* 'in, at'.[5] Rude (1991: 194–195) discusses a reanalysis of prepositions as verbal affixes, including the preposition identical to the GIVE morpheme, in Sahaptian and Klamath. It is possible to see in these facts one historical source for the emergence of the GIVE-Affix RECIPIENT construction (cf. also Weir 1986 and Craig—Hale 1987). A repositioning of constituents, perhaps related to a choice of focus, leads to the juxtaposition of the verb GIVE and the adposition. A reanalysis of the constituent boundaries then results in the GIVE-Affix construction, as sketched in (13).

(13)   ... GIVE   THING$_{DO}$ **Adposition-RECIPIENT**
  ---->   ... GIVE   **Adposition-RECIPIENT**   THING$_{DO}$
  ---->   ... **GIVE-Adposition**   RECIPIENT$_{DO}$ THING

Where there is a cognate relationship between a verbal affix and an adposition, then it is relevant to seek this kind of connection between the two morphemes.[6] Nevertheless, not all such affixes can be explained away along these lines.

3.1.2. *Two objects*

It is possible to have both THING and RECIPIENT as kinds of objects, as in the ditransitive construction *I gave Harry the book*. In Langacker (1987: 217–220), where the notions of subject and object in clause structure are construed as instantiations of the more general concepts of trajector and landmark, the ditransitive structure would be associated with one trajector and two landmarks at the clausal level. This is similar in some ways to the multiple landmarks observable in *The tree stood behind the fence and in front of the house*, where *the fence* and *the house* both function as landmarks with *the tree* construed as the trajector at the clausal level.

  For English ditransitive structures, it is arguably the case that the *give* construction, as in *I gave Harry the book*, is one of the central members of the ditransitive category. This is the position argued for in Goldberg (1992a: 30, 1992b: 54). *Give*, along with other verbs that inherently refer to the transfer of things, is one of a few classes of verbs which make up the "central sense" of the English ditransitive construction in her analysis. Other senses which are associated with the ditransitive construction are motivated with reference to properties of the central sense. One pertinent piece of evidence which Goldberg uses in support of the centrality of giving in the network of meanings of the ditransitive is the way in which nonsense forms of ditransitive verbs are interpreted. Thus, in the sentence *She topamased him something*, the nonsense form *topamased* was understood as referring to giving, indicating a close relationship between the sense of giving and the construction.

Often, there is some basis for considering one of the objects in the ditransitive construction more object-like than the other. So, for example, Comrie (1982) speaks of "prime objects", Lichtenberk (1982) distinguishes "primary" and "secondary" objects, and Kisseberth—Abasheikh (1977) distinguish "principal" and "subsidiary" objects. Each one of these works appeals to specific linguistic criteria in the languages under discussion as a basis for distinguishing one of the objects as the main object and none of them proposes universal criteria for identifying a main object. Nevertheless, it happens that in all three of these approaches, it is the RECIPIENT in the case of ditransitive GIVE clauses which functions as the main object (Comrie 1982: 107–108, Lichtenberk 1982: 264–266, Kisseberth—Abasheikh 1977: 186).

It would also appear possible for the THING to function as a main object in ditransitive GIVE clauses. Consider in this respect the double object construction with *béi* 'give' in Cantonese, illustrated in (14).

(14)   A-Sām   béi   fóng-jō   kéuih.
           A-Sām   give   room-charge   him/her
           'A-Sām gave him/her money for the room.'   (Cantonese)

The lack of any preposition, as found with typical oblique phrases in Cantonese, makes it natural to consider *fóng-jō* 'room-charge' and *kéuih* 'him/her' as object phrases, and this, I believe, is appropriate for this construction. Nevertheless, one can also consider *fóng-jō* as the primary object on the basis that it occurs in the immediate post-verbal position typical of object phrases in simple transitive clauses.[7] Word-order facts like this are relevant, but other syntactic facts need to be considered too. In the case of Cantonese, one can consider correspond-ing passive sentences. With simple transitive clauses, the object in the active can appear as the subject of the passive, with a preposition-like morpheme *yàuh* introducing the equivalent of the *by*-phrase:

(15) a. *Ngóh sé   ni   fūng wù:ih-sūn.*
       I   write this CL   reply
       'I wrote this reply.'   (Cantonese)
    b. *Ni   fūng wù:ih-sūn yàuh ngóh sé.*
       this CL   reply   PASS me   write
       'This reply was written by me.'   (Cantonese)

The native speakers I consulted agreed that in the case of *béi* 'give', the THING phrase could appear to the left of *yàuh*. Attempts to position the RECIPIENT phrase to the left of *yàuh*, however, were rejected or con-sidered questionable at best:

(16) a. *Fóng-jō   yàuh A-Sām béi   kéuih.*
       room-charge PASS A-Sām give him
       'The money for the room was given to him by A-Sām.'
                               (Cantonese)
    b. **/? Kéuih   yàuh   A-Sām   béi   fóng-jō.*
       he   PASS   A-Sām give room-charge
       'He was given money for the room by A-Sām.'
                                (Cantonese)

One speaker offered the opinion that he thought the passive with RECIPIENT in initial position would be more acceptable in writing than in speech. Judgements, therefore, are not as straightforward as the */? suggest. Nevertheless, to the extent that the *yàuh* construction can differentiate the behaviour of THING and RECIPIENT, the evidence points to the THING as behaving more like a prototypical object than the RECIPIENT.[8]

The "passive test", as applied in the Cantonese example, is a favourite way of identifying the more prototypical object (i.e. syntactic object) but it is only one means of distinguishing roles of objects. Languages may lack a passive construction altogether, in which case there is no possibility of applying a passive test. Or, even where there is a passive construction in a language, the passive test may not identify either of the THING or the RECIPIENT as functioning unambiguously as the direct object.[9] Apart from the passive construction, there may be other syntactic phenomena affecting a syntactic object which treat the two objects differently. In Sochiapan Chinantec (Amerindian, Mexico), a test for distinguishing the grammatical status of the two objects in a double object construction involves the presence or absence of nasalization of the verb. In this language, animate subjects of intransitive verbs, as well as third-person direct objects, trigger a kind of agreement on the verb which has its vowel nasalized (as described in Foris 1993: 389–393). An example of a transitive construction with animate third-person direct object is shown below (nasalization is indicated by an *n* after the vowel nucleus):

(17) a. *Súh³*   *tsú²*   *hiúh²*   *hën².*
      cause fall:PL:INAN:OBJ:FUT:3SUBJ   3   seed   chili
      'S/he will shake off (the) chili seeds.'
                              (Chinantec, Foris 1993: 391)

     b. *Sunh³*   *tsú²*   *chi³mah².*
      cause fall:PL:ANIM:OBJ:FUT:3SUBJ   3   ant
      'S/he will shake off (the) ants.'
                              (Chinantec, Foris 1993: 391)

Turning to the GIVE clauses in (18), note the absence of any nasalization in the verb when "money" is the direct object and the recipient is part of an oblique phrase. Note also that the double object construction with GIVE in (18b) employs a verb form lacking any nasalization, indicating that "money" must still be construed as the direct object (according to this test).

(18) a.   *Cué³²*   *tsú² quie³ ñí¹con² jon²*
          give:INAN:OBJ:FUT:3SUBJ   3   money to   child:3
          tsa³háu².
          tomorrow
          'S/he will give money to her/his child tomorrow.'
                                                       (Chinantec, Foris 1993: 378)

      b.   *Cuéh³²*   *tsú² jon²   quie³ tsa³ háu².*
          give:INAN:OBJ:FUT:3SUBJ   3   child:3 money tomorrow
          'S/he will give her/his child money tomorrow.'
                                                       (Chinantec, Foris 1993: 378)

It is possible to have a nasalized form of the verb GIVE. This happens
when the direct object is animate. So, for example, replacing "money"
with "cat" as the thing given in an example like the one above requires
accompanying nasalization. It is the second noun phrase (the THING
given) which functions as the direct object in the double object construction.

(19) a.   *Cuen³*   *tsú² jon²   jan² mí¹ tiei²¹.*
          give:ANIM:OBJ:FUT:3SUBJ   3   child:3 one cat
          'S/he will give her/his child a cat.'
                                                       (Chinantec, Foris 1993: 378)

An impressive demonstration of how the two objects in a double object construction may be differentiated in a language is Chung's (1976)
discussion of direct objects in Indonesian. As an example of this approach, consider Chung's sentences (written here in a more modern
spelling) which illustrate a rule commonly referred to by its transformational name Quantifier Shift:

(20) a.   *Saya beri-kan   semua barang   saya   kepada Hasan.*
          I   give-BEN all   thing   my   to   Hasan
          'I gave all of my things to Hasan.'
                                                       (Indonesian, Chung 1976: 82)

b. *Saya   beri-kan   barang   saya   semua-nya   kepada Hasan.*
  I   give-BEN   thing   my   all-Pronoun   to   Hasan
  'I gave all of my things to Hasan.'

(Indonesian, Chung 1976: 82)

Chung shows that Quantifier Shift (moving the quantifier *semua* 'all' away from its position next to the noun *barang*) applies to the object phrase, as above, as well as to phrases with any one of a variety of roles. The rule does not apply, however, to the second of two objects in the case of a double object construction:

(21) a. *Saya   beri   saudara   perempuan   saya   semua   barang   saya.*
     I   give   sibling   female   my   all   thing   my
     'I gave my sister all my things.'

(Indonesian, Chung 1976: 84)

  b. *?* Saya   beri   saudara   perempuan   saya   barang*
     I   give   sibling   female   my   thing
     saya   semua-nya.
     my   all-Pronoun

(Indonesian, Chung 1976: 84)

In the case of Indonesian, one is able to show that there is a congruence between many different syntactic phenomena differentiating the two object phrases, as illustrated here in the case of Quantifier Shift. All the syntactic phenomena which Chung discusses point to the RECIPIENT in the double object construction as being the primary object. Sometimes, however, there may be conflicting results from different kinds of tests. Consider the English double object construction with *give: I gave Tom the book.* The passive test points to *Tom*, the RECIPIENT, as the primary object on the basis of the following comparison:

(22) a. *I gave Tom the book.*
  b. *Tom was given the book.*
  c. OK/? *The book was given Tom.*

The lesser acceptability of (22c) and sentences like it is often taken as a basis for claiming that it is the RECIPIENT, rather than the THING, in the English double object construction which functions as the primary object. Compare this, however, with the formation of *wh*-questions in English. Corresponding to the declarative (23a), one finds an interrogative (23b) in which the *wh*-word functions as the object of the verb:

(23) a. *Mary contacted Tom.*
      b. *Who did Mary contact?*

In the case of double object constructions with *give*, it is the second object, the THING, which behaves as the primary object:

(24) a. *I gave Tom the book.*
      b. *What did I give Tom?*
      c. *?/* Who did I give the book?*

Hudson (1992), in an insightful discussion of the English double object construction, assembles a variety of evidence relating to the objecthood of the two object-like phrases. The weight of evidence which he produces points clearly to the THING phrase as behaving more like the object of a monotransitive clause.[10] This state of affairs, where the THING functions more like a prototypical object for some rules while for others the RECIPIENT functions in this way, can be found in a number of languages (cf. Kisseberth—Abasheikh's (1977) discussion of this situation in a Bantu language).

3.2. Beyond the object

In the previous section we looked at how either the THING or the RECIPIENT (in some cases both) can function as an object. In what follows, I will review a selection of ways in which languages codify the THING and RECIPIENT in ways other than the double object construction.

When it comes to integrating a RECIPIENT phrase into a structure already containing the GIVER as a subject and the THING as a direct object, the following possibilities would appear to be the main ones which occur: marking the RECIPIENT as a dative, a goal, a locative, a benefactive, and a possessor. Although "dative" is a label which may cover very many semantic roles, I will be concerned with those instances of dative cases where RECIPIENT-marking is a central meaning. As explained below, this is a very common basis for employing the label "dative".

In examining these different possibilities, we will be exploring the semantics of the syntactic categories (cases and adpositions), which are employed in the various constructions. Typically, the syntactic category marking the RECIPIENT will also be associated with other semantic roles, giving rise to a multiplicity of polysemous meanings for any one syntactic category. For each of the formal categories involved (dative case, allative case etc.), then, we will posit a network of related meanings, referred to as "schematic networks" in Cognitive Grammar (Langacker 1987: 369–386). Each schematic network represents a set of meanings associated with the category, structured so that submeanings which are held to be more closely related to one another appear under the same node in the network. Schematic networks are relevant to the description of all kinds of linguistic categories, including syntactic constructions and morphemes. Figure 13 above, for example, would form part of the schematic network of the meanings of the subject-object construction in languages where that construction is extended to the relationship between GIVER and THING, as well as GIVER and RECIPIENT. In the following sections the schematic networks relate to the meanings carried by cases and adpositions.

I have not found it possible to fully specify all the detail which properly belongs in the schematic networks which follow. Langacker's schematic networks include two broad kinds of relationships between submeanings. One is the relationship of a schematic meaning to its more specific instantiations, reflecting the extraction of a commonality amongst other submeanings. The other is the relationship of an extension from a more central submeaning to a less central submeaning.[11] Incorporating these relationships into schematic networks is not always a simple matter. To quote Langacker (1987: 377):

> We are...not without potential resources for elucidating the structure of a complex category. Seldom, though, can we expect a clear-cut basis for determining all the specific features of a schematic network; in practice many points of detail are bound to remain uncertain if not indeterminate. (Langacker 1987: 377)

My schematic networks in the following sections reflect my judgements of commonality between the submeanings and the schematic meanings are shown with an arrow leading down to their specific instantiations. I make no claim that a particular native speaker must necessarily see the same higher-level schematic meanings which I have proposed. Speakers may assign more or less schematic structure than what I have proposed, though I suggest that my proposals are reasonably self-evident. While acknowledging the reality of native speakers' own judgements about semantic extensions, I have nevertheless refrained from incorporating this aspect into the schematic networks. The reason for this is the un-availability to me of reliable judgements by native speakers about such things. Relying, as I have, on published grammars and dictionaries of the languages concerned for much of the data I have collected, I do not feel confident in pinpointing prototypes and extensions in the networks (though see my comments in Section 3.4 below). One can gain some sense of the direction of extensions from some dictionaries, grammars etc., but only in a very crude way. In proceeding in this way, I have also taken seriously the criticisms of network analyses of meanings made by Sandra—Rice (1995: 98–104), particularly their cautionary warning about the limits of what can be claimed to be psychologically real in such analyses.

3.2.1. *RECIPIENT as a dative*

In this section we discuss one of the most common ways of case-marking the RECIPIENT, namely by means of a case labelled "dative". One speaks of a dative case where the case is used prototypically to mark a RECIPIENT phrase in GIVE constructions, as in Russian:

(25) *Ya   dal   knig-u   uchitel-yu.*
      I   gave   book-ACC teacher-DAT
      'I gave the book to the teacher.'   (Russian)

It is true that the dative case in Russian has more extensive use than just
marking the RECIPIENT in a GIVE construction. It is used, for example, to mark the objects of numerous verbs. These include *verit'* 'to believe (someone)', *pomogat'* 'to help', *sluzhit'* 'to serve (someone)',
sovetovat' 'to advise', *meshat'* 'to disturb', *grozit'* 'to threaten', and *iz-
menyat'* 'to betray'.[12] As has often been observed, however, it is possible to construe the role of the dative nominal with some of these verbs
as a kind of RECIPIENT, though admittedly not all of these verbs are
equally amenable to such an analysis. If one considers the English
counterparts to these verbs, there are *give* paraphrases with some of
them, suggesting a kind of RECIPIENT semantically (*give help to
someone, give service to someone, give advice to someone*), but not
others (**give betrayal to someone, *give disturbance to someone*). It is
difficult, then, to assign one schematic meaning to all these uses of the
dative case in Russian. Nevertheless, the RECIPIENT meaning is quite
salient within the range of meanings evident in the use of the case. It
appears in its most literal sense, of course, with verbs meaning "give"
and "send" in Russian. In a slightly extended sense it appears with verbs
meaning "show", "write", and "tell", and in an even more extended
sense with the verbs mentioned above, such as "to help" and "to serve".
It seems reasonable, then, to consider the RECIPIENT meaning to be a
relatively central meaning of the dative case in Russian. This is also
claimed to be so in an analysis of the Russian and Czech dative cases in
Janda (1993a: 536, 1993b: 47, 113).

Figure 14 sketches a small part of the schematic network associated
with the dative case in Russian. It indicates a selection of the more
specific meanings which the dative case carries, as well as indicating
some of the commonality which holds between meanings. This
commonality is a relatively schematic type of meaning, representing
what is common to the particular instantiations of it. Following
Langacker, the instantiation of a schematic meaning is represented by a

downward arrow to the specific instantiation. Speakers will extract different schematic meanings, depending on the extent to which they see commonalities between the particular meanings. The schematic meanings indicated in Figure 14 reflect commonalities which occur to me most readily in reflecting on the (limited!) range of meanings shown. A particular speaker of Russian may have more or less in the way of schematic meanings. While a speaker of Russian may be expected to feel a commonality within some pairs of meanings, like "to give someone something" and "to help someone", it is less likely that a speaker would feel a commonality between all these meanings. In other words, it may be only the intermediate level schemata in the network which have much reality to them (from the point of view of speakers' intuitions). If a higher-level schematic meaning can be extracted, it would be along the lines of "an active experiencer who, though not the instigator of an action, is nevertheless affected by it". This is similar to Langacker's (1991: 327) characterization of an indirect object as an "active experiencer in the target domain". As a schematic meaning of the Polish dative, based on the range of uses discussed, Wierzbicka (1988: 427) suggests that it "implies a situation which is not controlled by a person Z, but which is likely (though not certain) to have an effect on Z" and this may be relevant to the Russian dative as well.

The dative in other Indo-European languages may be described along similar lines, with the RECIPIENT sense relatively prominent. As in Russian, so also in German, other uses of the dative present themselves which might be relatable in varying degrees to the role of the RECIPIENT in a GIVE scene. The act of giving and speaking can be thought of as happening within the sphere of interest of the recipient/addressee, leading to the additional use in German in which the dative marks the person in whose sphere of interest an event takes place. This is the "dative of interest", as in German *Fahr mir nicht zu schnell!* 'Don't drive too fast' where the dative *mir* adds a sense of concern or involvement on the part of the speaker. This is just one of many typical extensions of the dative case in Indo-European languages. Wierzbicka (1988: 391–433) and Rudzka-Ostyn (to appear, a) provide insightful accounts of the many uses of the dative in one such language, Polish. The various uses of the Polish dative constitute an extremely large network

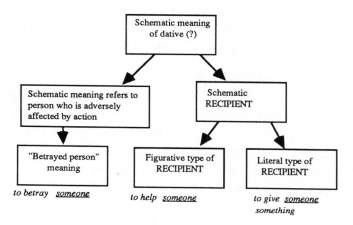

Figure 14. Russian dative case

. of related meanings, including meanings which appear, at first, quite far removed from the RECIPIENT meaning. Rudzka-Ostyn's account also includes a fairly comprehensive schematic network for the Polish dative which gives some indication of the complexity of the dative category in Polish. Smith (1987, 1993) also considers a number of extensions of the German dative case, as part of a Cognitive Grammar account of both accusative and dative cases in German.

Where the dative is used to refer to the RECIPIENT in an act of giving, there may be some vagueness as to whether the THING is transferred specifically to the RECIPIENT or whether the THING is transferred to the vicinity of the RECIPIENT. For example, one might say *I gave the handouts to the students during the lecture* to mean that I handed each student a handout individually, or that I gave a bunch of handouts to just one student who passed them around to the other students in the class, or even that I just placed the whole pile of handouts on a desk in the room and students helped themselves to them. While such vagueness is common with a GIVE morpheme, languages may also keep such meanings distinct. Crowley (1982: 197) notes a distinction of this sort in Paamese (Oceanic, Vanuatu). A "punctual" dative preposition is used when the RECIPIENT physically receives the object of transfer, while an "areal" dative is used when the THING is transferred merely to some physical domain pertaining to the RECIPIENT. The contrast is illustrated in (26a) and (26b).

(26) a. *Inau   nesa:n   ratio   onak   mini.*
      inau   na-sa:ni   ratio: ona-ku   mini-e (Underlying)
      I   1SG-give radio   POSS-1SG   punctual DAT-3SG
      'I gave him my radio.'   (Paamese, Crowley 1982: 197)

    b. *Onom   vilmemun   nesa:ni*
      ono-mo   vilme-mune   na-sa:ni-e
      POSS-2SG   film-additional   1SG-give-3SG
      ven   Rei Kalimo.
      veni   rei kalimo: (Underlying)
      areal DAT Ray Gillmore
      'I delivered your film to Ray Gillmore's too (though I didn't give it to him personally).' (Paamese, Crowley 1982: 197)

It would be mistaken to assume that the RECIPIENT role must be a prototypical meaning of a dative case wherever a dative case has been proposed. Nevertheless, I think it may well be true that the most common criterion for calling a particular case dative in a language is RECIPIENT marking, consistent with the centrality of that function of the dative cases of the major Indo-European languages. It is significant that the Greek term for the case, as well as the Latin *dative*, are both etymologically related to GIVE morphemes (cf. Blake 1994: 144). As noted already, Janda (1993a, 1993b) describes the range of functions of the dative case in Czech and Russian, proceeding from its use to mark the RECIPIENT in a GIVE clause as its central meaning. Wierzbicka (1988: 391) identifies the dative as the case-marking of the RECIPIENT in GIVE clauses in languages such as Latin, Russian, and German (though she goes on to discuss many uses of the Polish dative which could not be so described). Rudzka-Ostyn (to appear, a) takes the RECIPIENT-marking of the Polish dative to be the most central meaning. Smith (1987: 363) uses a GIVE sentence to illustrate the prototypical dative indirect object in German.The reference to GIVE predicates is also quite explicit in the following justifications for the label dative:

> ...Between these two rather clearcut categories [actor and under-goer] there is an indistinct middle ground: the typically animate, intended goal of an action, i.e. its beneficiary or the recipient of verbs like "give". I will refer to these as dative nominals, adopting the usual name for the corresponding case in Indo-European languages. (Foley 1986: 96)

> The recipient in the prototypic bitransitive is the prototypic dative. In English, the prototypic bitransitive verb is *give*. (Blansitt 1988: 186)

Where a dative case is illustrated in a grammar of a non-Indo-European language, it is not at all uncommon to find an example clause containing a GIVE predicate. Nevertheless, linguists might choose a label "dative" for reasons other than its use with the RECIPIENT in a GIVE clause. A case which marks beneficiaries and goals, for example, may well be called a dative even if it does not mark the RECIPIENT. The name of a case which appears in the published grammar of a formerly undescribed language will have been chosen (presumably) on the basis of some per-ceived similarity between its functions and the functions of some gram-matical case as used in grammars that the author is familiar with. In the end, one has to acknowledge that the basis for naming a case "dative" in a particular language is subject to some variability.[13] Nevertheless, in the major Indo-European languages which have a distinct dative case, a prototypical meaning of that case (though not necessarily its only proto-typical meaning) is to mark the RECIPIENT in a GIVE clause.

The basicness of GIVE, as discussed in Chapter 1, is surely relevant to understanding why the semantic role of RECIPIENT should be such a prominent meaning within the category of a grammatical case. Just as the act of giving can be considered as a basic type of act of considerable functional importance, so too the role of RECIPIENT within the GIVE schema can be considered as a basic role, alongside the AGENT and PATIENT roles. Within the category of the dative, RECIPIENT typically forms a relatively central meaning with other submeanings of the case interpreted as metaphorical extensions of the RECIPIENT role. Again, this parallels the way that the concept of GIVE itself is a natural source for metaphorical understandings of many other complex concepts, as discussed in Chapter 4.[14]

3.2.2. RECIPIENT as a goal

Another common way in which a RECIPIENT phrase is integrated into a GIVE clause is through treating the RECIPIENT as a goal. A prototypical goal is to be understood here as the stationary entity located at the end of a well-defined path along which some other entity moves. The giving scene does not include within it any entity which fits this prototypical goal function. So, for example, in the prototypical GIVE scene, where the THING is being transferred with the hands, it is always touching either the GIVER or the RECIPIENT, so that there is no well-defined path which the THING traverses independent of a source and a goal. One can imagine acts of giving where this is not so, when, for example, a hot face-towel is passed to someone with a pair of tongs. But in this case, too, the THING is attached to an extension of the GIVER up to the point where it passes to the RECIPIENT. Also, there is no completely stationary entity to which the THING moves, since the RECIPIENT typically moves a hand to meet the object being passed. Despite these considerations, there is a sufficient match of cognitive topologies involving goal and RECIPIENT to support categorizing the RECIPIENT as a goal. A match in the cognitive topologies is helped by considering the THING and RECIPIENT abstracted away from the busy movement of hands which accompanies the act of giving. The fact that the RECIPIENT (understood now as a single large entity) is typically stationary and relatively passive in the act of giving presumably encourages a construal of it as a goal. Abstracting away from the function of the hands, one can also think of the object as moving to the RECIPIENT and stopping at the RECIPIENT, parallel to what happens when an object moves along a path to a goal. Considered in this way, the GIVING scene may be understood as including a RECIPIENT functioning as a goal parallel to the typical encoding of a meaning such as "X hit the ball to Y".

The concept of a goal may be encoded in many different ways, including prepositions, postpositions, case marking etc. A very clear illustration of the goal image can be found in Finnish, where RECIPIENT appears with a suffix marking allative case:

(27)   *Annan*   *kirja-n*   *tei-lle.*
        give:PRES:1SG book-ACC   youSG/PL-ALL
        'I (will) give the book to you.'   (Finnish)

The allative case marks motion to something or onto something (though not actually into something, for which the illative case is used) or where some event is construed in this way. Thus, the allative case appears on the nouns indicating destinations in Finnish equivalents for "put it on the table", "go to the church", "go to the market" etc. The allative in Finnish takes its place alongside other "local" cases which together form a nicely symmetrical system of oppositions. The relevant cases and their main functions are:

(28)   *inessive* 'location inside'   *adessive* 'location at/on'
        elative 'movement out of'   *ablative* 'movement from'
        illative 'movement into'   *allative* 'movement to'

Each of the cases has additional functions which may be rather more abstract than the glosses suggest. From the point of view of systematizing the case system, however, it is convenient to contrast them in terms of their basic spatial meanings. The names given to the cases reflect this. The RECIPIENT marking function of the allative in Finnish must be understood as an extension of the more basic function of marking the goal or destination. This is quite different from the dative case in Russian which, by itself, is incapable of marking the goal or destination.

The Papuan language Iatmul (as discussed in Foley 1986: 96–97) offers another example of a broad "movement to" function of a case being extended to include RECIPIENT marking:

(29) a. *Ntɨw   waalə-ŋkət   yɨ -nti.*
       man   dog-ALL   go-3SG:MASC
       'The man went to the dog.'   (Iatmul, Foley 1986: 96)
  b. *Ntɨw   waalə   wɨ-ŋkət   kwɨy-nti.*
       man   dog   1SG-ALL give-3SG:MASC
       'The man gave the dog to me.' (Iatmul, Foley 1986: 96)

Figure 15 illustrates the kind of schematic network one finds in languages which mark the RECIPIENT as an allative case, that is, in the same way as a goal. It represents some of the meanings associated with the goal-marking morpheme *to* in English. Specific meanings of this morpheme are: designating the spatial path leading to a landmark entity, as in *the road to Auckland*; a stretch of time leading up to a particular point in time, as in *five minutes to three*; movement along a spatial path over a stretch of time, as in *She walked to the store*; the RECIPIENT in an act of giving, as in *She gave the book to me*. All of them are instantiations of the notion of a path, leading to a goal as landmark. Hence, I have shown this as the schematic meaning underlying all the other meanings indicated. (Again, I have taken only a selection of all the possible meanings of the morpheme.) Furthermore, there is a similarity in the two meanings represented in *She walked to town* and *He gave the book to Mary*, as explained above. Both these uses of *to* relate to the movement of some entity through time along a path to a goal. Consequently, I have shown this commonality as a schematic meaning involving movement along a path in a spatio-temporal domain.

Sometimes the allative marker used in a GIVE construction is related to, or even identical with, a verb meaning "come" or "go". In Iban (Austronesian, Sarawak), for example, the form *gagay* can appear as a full verb meaning "chase", or as a motion verbal predicate translatable as "come to, go to", or as a preposition meaning "to". In these uses, it appears with nasal replacement of the initial underlying *g*, hence *ŋagay*. As a preposition, it seems to be mainly confined to human landmarks, though the expressions *ari pukul 11 ŋagay 12* 'from 11 to 12 o'clock' and *mulayka diri ŋagay mənoa iya* 'return to her country' are possible (cf. Scott 1956: 53, 120 and Asmah Haji Omar 1981: 49, 114–115, 216). Compare these various uses of *ŋagay* in (30).[15]

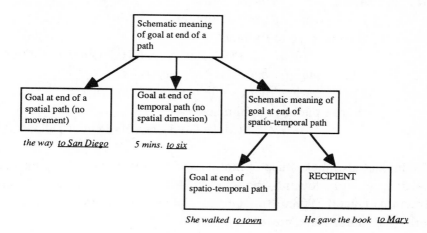

Figure 15. English *to*

(30) a. *Iya ŋagay pənchuri.*
     he/she chased thief
     'He/she chased the thief.'   (Iban, Scott 1956: 53)

   b. *Iya ŋagay aku əmay kəmari?.*
     he/she came-to me evening yesterday
     'He/she came to me last night.'   (Iban, Scott 1956: 53)

   c. *Iya rari ŋagay ini iya.*
     he/she ran to mother his/her
     'He/she ran to his/her mother.'
                 (Iban, Asmah Haji Omar 1981: 115)

   d. *Iya məri? ayam to? ŋagay adi iya.*
     he/she gave toy this to younger sibling his/her
     'He/she gave this toy to his/her younger sibling.'
                 (Iban, Asmah Haji Omar 1981: 115)

Melanau (Austronesian, Sarawak) shows a similar use of the form *mapun* :

(31)　a.　*Akou　gi?　mapun　ba?i.*
　　　　　I　　will　go-to　Bintulu
　　　　　'I want to go to Bintulu.'
　　　　　　　　　　　　　　(Melanau, Asmah Haji Omar 1983: 627)

　　　b.　*Aku　muju?　bup　ya?　mapun　sa.*
　　　　　I　　gave　book　this　to　　him/her
　　　　　'I gave the book to him/her.'
　　　　　　　　　　　　　　(Melanau, Asmah Haji Omar 1983: 627)

Cambodian also makes use of motion verbs ("minor verbs") to express
the directionality towards the RECIPIENT in GIVE (and other) constructions (Jacob 1968: 78). Compare the use of *tr̀u* and *mɔ̀ːk* as full
verbs and minor verbs/prepositions below:

(32)　a.　*Pùː　tr̀u　na?*
　　　　　uncle　go　where
　　　　　'Where is uncle going?'　　(Cambodian, Jacob 1968: 71)

　　　b.　*Nɛ̀ək　mɔ̀ː k　phnùm-pèɲ　pìː　?ɔŋkal?*
　　　　　you　come　Phnom Penh　when
　　　　　'When did you come to Phnom Penh?'
　　　　　　　　　　　　　　(Cambodian, Jacob 1968: 71)

　　　c.　*Khɲom　?aoy　siəuphr̀u　tr̀u　nɛ̀ək.*
　　　　　I　　give　book　　　go　you
　　　　　'I give you the book.'　　(Cambodian, Jacob 1968: 78)

　　　d.　*Nɛ̀ək　?aoy　siəuphr̀u　mɔ̀ːk　khɲom.*
　　　　　you　give　book　　come　me
　　　　　'You give me the book.'　　(Cambodian, Jacob 1968: 78)

　　Given the spatio-temporal realities of the giving act, it would be surprising to find a morpheme marking the source of a movement being
extended to mark the RECIPIENT. Nevertheless, it is possible to have
adpositions which indicate the landmark of motion, referring to either
the source from which an entity moves or the goal towards which an
entity moves. In such a case, the goal sense of the morpheme may also
be extended to a RECIPIENT. An example of this kind of polysemy is
found in Sochiapan Chinantec, as discussed in Foris (1993: 352–353,

378). The preposition *ñíˡconˀ* marks an animate noun phrase as either a source or goal, as well as marking a RECIPIENT. The RECIPIENT marking of the preposition is naturally seen as a special instance of the allative sense, rather than as an extension specifically from a source sense.

3.2.3. RECIPIENT as a locative

Languages may incorporate the RECIPIENT into a GIVE clause through the use of a morpheme covering either location at or direction towards, rather than a morpheme where the meaning is restricted to an allative function. I will refer to a morpheme like this as a locative (though sometimes this term is reserved for the "location at" sense alone). Usually the allative sense forms a salient part of the schematic network of general locative-marking morphemes, in which case the RECIPIENT-marking function of the morpheme is still relatable to an allative submeaning. Examples of this include Modern Greek and Māori. Modern Greek employs a preposition *se* (*s* before the definite article) followed by the accusative case to mark the RECIPIENT. The range of meanings of *se* includes "in, at, to, on" and could simply be described, at the most schematic level, as marking location. The use of this preposition is illustrated in (33).

(33) a. *O   Tákis   píje   s   to   nosokomío.*
     ART Takis:NOM   went:3SG   to   ART   hospital:ACC
     'Takis went to the hospital.'
          (Greek, Joseph—Philippaki-Warburton 1987: 4)

    b. *Perpatóndas   s   to   ðrómo, ...*
     walk:Gerund on   ART street:ACC
     'While walking on the street, ...'
          (Greek, Joseph—Philippaki-Warburton 1987: 174)

    c. *Éðosa   s   ton   Jáni   to   vivlío.*
     gave:1SG to   ART John:ACC ART book:ACC
     'I gave the book to John.'
          (Greek, Joseph—Philippaki-Warburton 1987: 125)

Māori has a preposition *ki* with a similarly broad range of locative meanings which is used to integrate the RECIPIENT phrase into a GIVE construction:

(34) a. *I   haere au ki   te   whare.*
        PAST go   I to   ART house
        'I went to the house.'   (Māori)

     b. *I   haere au ki   roto i   te   whare.*
        PAST go   I to   in OBJ ART house
        'I went into the house.'   (Māori)

     c. *Ka   noho a   Ani   ki   te   turu.*
        PRES sit   ART Ani   on   ART chair
        'Ani is sitting on the chair.'   (Māori)

     d. *Kei te hōatu a   Pita i   te   wai ki a   Mere.*
        PRES give ART Peter OBJ ART water to ART Mary
        'Peter is giving the water to Mary.'   (Māori)

It appears that in both Greek and Māori, the allative sense is relatively central within the meanings of the locative preposition, in which case the RECIPIENT marking function of the preposition is easily viewed as an instantiation of a schematic allative meaning, similar to English, Finnish etc. In a review of such types of case-marking in languages, Blansitt (1988: 186) arrived at the generalization that if a language contains an adposition marking dative and location (understood as "location at"), then it also marks the allative. This supports the view taken here that it is the allative, rather than a "location at" sense, which is the bridge to the dative sense. Figure 16 sketches part of the schematic network of *ki* in Māori, incorporating my proposals concerning some of the commonalities of meaning.

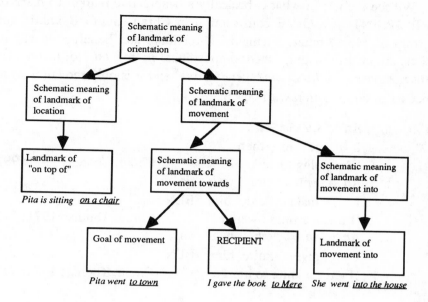

Figure 16. Māori *ki*

3.2.4. *RECIPIENT as a benefactive*

In Chapter 2, we mentioned a feature of typical giving situations: the RECIPIENT usually makes some use of the THING for his/her own benefit. This aspect of giving is present as part of the larger complex matrix associated with GIVE. It relates to a chronologically later part of the act of giving, in so far as the benefit to the RECIPIENT may not be fully enjoyed or expressed until some time after the actual act of giving. Many languages have benefactive morphemes which express a relation between an act and a person for whose benefit or on whose behalf the act was carried out. It may happen that the GIVE construction integrates the RECIPIENT phrase into the clause by marking it in the same way as a benefactive.

We see the use of what is basically a benefactive marker to mark the RECIPIENT in a GIVE construction in Chrau (South Bahnaric subgroup of Mon-Khmer, Vietnam). Directional and benefactive adpositions are clearly distinguished: prepositional *tu* 'to', *tʌt* 'to, arrive' versus postpositional *iin* or *maʔ* 'benefactive' and it is only the latter which occurs in construction with GIVE:

(35) a. *Aɲ   saʔ tu   tǐʔ.*
      I   go to   there
      'I'm going there.'   (Chrau, Thomas 1971: 99)

   b. *Aɲ   op   rʌm něh iin.*
      I   make field him BEN
      'I make a field for him.'   (Chrau, Thomas 1971: 71)

   c. *Aɲ   an   pih něh iin.*
      I   give knife him BEN
      'I gave a knife to him.'   (Chrau, Thomas 1971: 71)

Another example of this can be found in the Sumambuq dialect of Murut (Austronesian, Sarawak), as described by Asmah Haji Omar (1983: 377–378). The benefactive preposition *nu,* distinct from the directional *do,* is the one used in the GIVE construction.[16]

(36) a. *Isô   môy do Kuala Lumpur.*
      he/she goes to   Kuala Lumpur
      'He/she goes to Kuala Lumpur.'
               (Murut, Asmah Haji Omar 1983: 378)

   b. *Tinakan   ku   duit   nu   ulun hiyô.*
      gave   I   money BEN person that
      'I gave the money to that person.'
               (Murut, Asmah Haji Omar 1983: 378)

Figure 17 represents part of the schematic network of the Chrau benefactive marker (as well as the Sumambuq benefactive). One can expect that there will be a range of specific senses which attach to a benefactive marker in a language. Here I have only indicated the benefactive meaning which appears in Thomas (1971: 71). In addition, some languages might have the sense of "on behalf of", which has much in common with the "for the benefit of" meaning. I see a commonality in the specific meanings indicated in Figure 17 ("true" benefactive and RECIPIENT-marking) and I have described this schematic meaning as referring to a person to whom an act is directed.

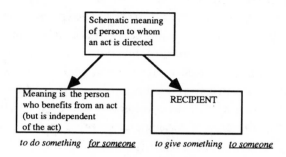

Figure 17. Chrau benefactive marker

One may note here also the use of *for me* to refer to the self as a RECIPIENT in the early utterances of the child observed in Tomasello (1992). At the age of 22 months, the child began to produce utterances like *Laura gave that for me, Tommy gave that necklace for me, Mommy gave that cereal for me to eat* (Tomasello 1992: 78). Here, the preposition marking a benefactive in English is extended to mark the RECIPIENT. In fact, the use of *for* in this sense by the subject predates the use of *to* in the GIVE construction, which does not emerge until 23 months. The sentences where *for* is used are of course ones where the RECIPIENT is clearly the beneficiary of the act of giving and the extension is an easy one to make. Note also the early possibility of expanding the GIVE clause with an infinitival form, referring to what the RECIPIENT is going to do with the THING, as in *Mommy gave that cereal for me to eat*. The infinitival form here elaborates on the way in which the RECIPIENT will benefit from the act of giving.

3.2.5.   *RECIPIENT as a possessor*

Yet another alternative is to highlight the role of the RECIPIENT as the possessor of the THING. In Dyirbal (and in the neighbouring language Warrgamay according to Dixon 1980: 292), GIVE constructions make aspects of possession quite explicit by the use of a genitive case with the RECIPIENT. As Dixon (1972: 109, 237) explains, there are two genitive cases in Dyirbal. The "simple" genitive refers to alienable possession and indicates a relation of present possession. It contrasts with a "general" genitive, which is used for alienable possession involving a past owner, appropriate in sentences like "I picked up the white man's cigarettes (which he had dropped and lost)". Dixon (1972: 109) singles out as one of the uses of the general genitive that it is used "to describe something given by its owner (particularly European-type giving, involving a white man)". As an example of the simple genitive in a GIVE construction, Dixon gives sentence (37).

(37)   *Balam   miraɲ   baŋun   ɖugumbilŋu   baŋgul   yaɽaŋgu*
       ABS   beans:ABS   GEN   woman:GEN   ERG   man:ERG
       wugan.
       gave
       'The man gave the woman beans.'
                                        (Dyirbal, Dixon 1972: 237)

In this case, the RECIPIENT is marked in the same way as a typical present possessor of an object, so the sentence above should be understood as "The man gave the beans to the person to whom they belong" (cf. Dixon 1972: 237, 300). In this case, there is no change in any legal sense of possession, only a change in some accessibility to the THING. (Compare the remarks about possession in Dyirbal in Chapter 1.) The Dyirbal sentence highlights not the "new" possessor of the THING, but the "true" possessor.[17]

Figure 18 sketches part of the schematic network of the simple genitive morpheme in Dyirbal.

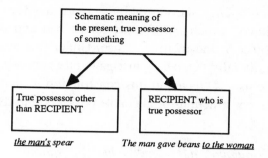

Figure 18. Dyirbal simple genitive

A GIVE construction in Sochiapan Chinantec is also relevant here. Sochiapan Chinantec has three different construction types available for the expression of giving: a ditransitive construction, a transitive construction with the RECIPIENT marked in the same way as a benefactive, and a transitive construction with the RECIPIENT in a subordinate clause containing the verb "have, possess". These three types are illustrated below:

(38) a. *Cuéh³²   tsú²   jon²   quie³   tsa³ háu².*
       give:FUT:3   he/she   child:his/her   money   tomorrow
       'He/she will give his/her child money tomorrow.'
                           (Chinantec, Foris 1993: 378)

    b. *Cuéh³²   tsú²   quie³   ñí¹con² jon²   tsa³ háu².*
       give:FUT:3   he/she   money   to   child   tomorrow
       'He/she will give his/her child money tomorrow.'
                           (Chinantec, Foris 1993: 378)

    c. *Juo¹³   dí²   lí¹   lí²-cué³²   hña³ láu³ héih³²*
       boss:1PL   we:INCL adv   TNS-give:3   hundred   measure
       quie³   hi³   quiú¹³.
       money   COMP   have:1PL
       'Our boss just gave one hundred pesos to us.'
                           (Chinantec, Foris 1993: 280)

The last of these constructions is described as a possessor relative clause in Foris (1993: 279–282), introduced by a complementizer hi^3, followed by the verb "have" which is inflected for person and number of the understood subject of the relative clause. Under this analysis, the example above is literally "Our boss just gave one hundred pesos that we now have". The use of "have" in this construction is comparable to the use of "have" in constructions of alienable possession in the language, as illustrated in (39).

(39)   *Cuá¹-quiaun² nú²   en³   hi³   quion²¹   jná¹³.*
         go-bring:2   2SG   bed   COMP   have:1SG   I
         'Go and bring my bed.'   (Chinantec, Foris 1993: 280)

The complementizer hi^3, however, has a much wider distribution than just introducing relative clauses. It introduces a variety of subordinate clauses, such as clauses functioning as the complement of verbs of saying and thinking. It also introduces purpose clauses as in the example below:

(40)   *Tsanh³²   sú² hñú¹³   hi³   tsá²-jmú³   má³².*
         return-home:3SG 3   house:3 COMP   PRES-make:3   food
         'She/he is returning home to make/prepare the food.' /
         'She/he is returning to make/eat a meal.'
                                           (Chinantec, Foris 1993: 488–489)

In the light of such examples, one might take the hi^3 in the GIVE construction to be more like introducing a purpose clause, meaning literally "Our boss just gave one hundred pesos for us to have/in order that we may have it". Regardless of how one wishes to interpret the exact function of hi^3, however, the notion of possession certainly enters into the construction.

Again, Tomasello's (1992: 77) study of a young child is relevant. *Have*, which has as one of its central meanings "to possess", is used by the child to refer to acts of giving. So, for example, at age 19 months the child produced the utterances *Balloon have-it* and *Have-it cards*, where these utterances were used as requests that the objects named be given to her. *Have* was also used in describing her own acts of giving to others, as in *Daddy have this wallet*, said as she gives it to him. As noted in the previous section, the child also used *for* as a marker of the RECIPIENT in GIVE constructions, giving rise to combinations such as *Have a doughnut for you* at 21 months.

3.2.6. More complex networks

In the preceding sections I have reviewed how RECIPIENT marking may be encoded in the same way as some other type of marking, such as benefactive, allative etc. Each of the languages reviewed illustrated a commonality between RECIPIENT marking and one other kind of function. It is possible, however, that a number of these senses may be present in the schematic network of a RECIPIENT marker, giving rise to more complex kinds of networks than we have hitherto seen. A question arises, then, as to which other meaning(s) the RECIPIENT marking sense of a morpheme should be most immediately related to.

Consider, from this point of view, the postposition *rò* in Kanuri (Saharan, Nigeria) as described by Hutchison (1981: 259–263), who refers to it as the "indirect postposition". Its uses include marking the RECIPIENT in a GIVE construction, as well as marking the benefactive and allative:

(41) a. *Shí-rò   yí-k-ìn.*
      3SG-to   give-1SG:SUBJ-TNS
      'I will give it to him/her.' (Kanuri, Hutchison 1981: 260)
   b. *Nyí-rò   yíwù-k-ìn.*
      you:SG-for buy-1SG:SUBJ-TNS
      'I will buy it for you.'   (Kanuri, Hutchison 1981: 260)
   c. *Kàsúwù-rò lèwó-n-ò.*
      market-to   go-3SG:SUBJ-TNS
      'He went to the market.'   (Kanuri, Hutchison 1981: 260)

What should one consider as the appropriate commonalities in these meanings: RECIPIENT-marking and benefactive, RECIPIENT-marking and allative, or all three as making up one commonality? We have seen in the previous sections that there is a good cross-linguistic basis for grouping together RECIPIENT-marking and the benefactive sense, as well as RECIPIENT-marking and allative. It is reasonable, therefore, to reflect the naturalness of both of these groupings in a schematic network. This means that the RECIPIENT-marking meaning will be grouped simultaneously with each of these other meanings, something which is provided for in Langacker's approach to schematic networks. Figure 19 reflects these observations about the relatedness of the meanings of Kanuri *rò*.[18]

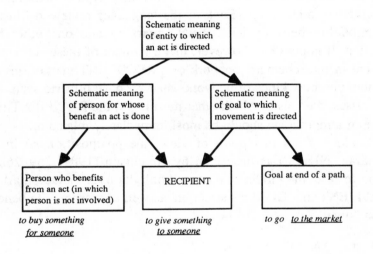

Figure 19. Kanuri *rò*

Iban is relevant here too. Some data from Iban was cited above as evidence of a GIVE construction with the RECIPIENT introduced by a form which is identical with a motion verb, namely *ŋagay*. There is an alternative GIVE construction, however, where the RECIPIENT is introduced by *ka,* instead of *ŋagay*. The preposition *ka* also appears with benefactive and allative meanings. The benefactive and allative meanings occur in complementary distribution: the benefactive occurs with human landmarks and the allative with non-human landmarks.

(42) a. *Iya   məriʔ surat ka aku.*
           he/she gave   letter to me
           'He/she gave the letter to me.'   (Iban, Scott 1956: 27)
     b. *Iya   məli   segerit   ka   aku.*
           he/she bought cigarettes BEN me
           'He/she bought cigarettes for me.'   (Iban, Scott 1956: 75)
     c. *Iya   rari   ka   laŋkaw ɲaʔ.*
           he/she ran   to   hut   the
           'He/she ran to the hut.' (Iban, Asmah Haji Omar 1983: 115)

This is a similar polysemy to that found in Kanuri, and, as in Kanuri, it would be arbitrary to insist on either RECIPIENT-benefactive or RECIPIENT-allative as being the only close relationship that the RECIPIENT use of *ka* has with other meanings. RECIPIENT has commonalities with each of these other meanings and these commonalities should be allowed for in any representation which purports to capture relatedness between the meanings of a morpheme.

Japanese *ni* is another example of a RECIPIENT marker which appears in a large number of other uses, including benefactive, locative, goal, human source, and agent in a passive construction, as illustrated in (43).

(43) a. *Ken   wa   watashi ni   hon   o   kureta.*
           Ken   TOPIC me   to   book ACC gave
           'Ken gave me the book.'
     b. *Ken   wa   Tokyo ni   itta.*
           Ken   TOPIC Tokyo to   went
           'Ken went to Tokyo.'
     c. *Ken wa   ototo   ni jidensha o   katte yatta.*
           Ken TOPIC younger brother for bicycle   ACC bought
           'Ken bought a bicycle for (his) younger brother.'

d.   *Ken*   *wa*   *Tokyo*   *ni*   *iru.*
     Ken   TOPIC   Tokyo   in   be
     'Ken is in Tokyo.'

e.   *Ken*   *wa*   *Taro*   *ni*   *hon*   *o*   *karita.*
     Ken   TOPIC   Taro   from   book   ACC   borrowed
     'Ken borrowed a book from Taro.'

f.   *Ken*   *wa*   *keikan*   *ni*   *korosareta.*
     Ken   TOPIC   policeman   by   was killed
     'Ken was killed by a policeman.'

g.   *Ken*   *wa*   *ureshisa*   *no*   *amari*   *ni*   *tobiagatta.*
     Ken   TOPIC   joy   POSS   greatness   because of   jumped
     'Ken jumped for joy.'

h.   *Ken*   *wa*   *shimbun*   *o*   *kai*   *ni*   *itta.*
     Ken   TOPIC   newspaper   ACC   buy   Connective   went
     'Ken went to buy a newspaper.'

i.   *Ken*   *ni*   *(wa)*   *hoshi*   *ga*   *mieru.*
     Ken   to   (TOPIC)   star   NOM   be visible
     'Ken can see the star.'

j.   *Ken*   *ni*   *(wa)*   *kodono*   *ga*   *hutari*   *iru.*
     Ken   to   (TOPIC)   child   NOM   two persons   exist
     'Ken has two children.'

Faced with such a range of functions, one might be inclined to simply label *ni* as an "oblique" marker and not attempt to give a semantically based characterization. I have no objection to calling a form like this an oblique marker as a way of indicating the very wide range of functions it can have. Furthermore, I agree that characterizing the morpheme in terms of a single, all-encompassing meaning would be difficult and, to the extent it succeeded, highly abstract. Such a characterization would be a highly schematic meaning at the top of a schematic network, rather more complicated than in the case of Kanuri *rò*. Following Langacker (1987: 381), I make no assumption that it is necessary to recognize a single, all-encompassing schematic meaning representing what is common to all uses of a morpheme and in the case of oblique markers like Japanese *ni*, it may not be illuminating to proceed in this way. Whether or not a single, highly schematic characterization of the meanings is appropriate, however, it is possible to identify commonalities on a smaller scale between certain groups of meanings, such as recipient-benefactive, recipient-allative etc. These intermediate level schemata are not invalidated just because the status of a single, highly schematic meaning is dubious. In the case of Japanese *ni*, some important observations about the commonalities which hold between the submeanings have been made by Kabata—Rice (1995). They argue for quite regular chains of meaning associations which give support to various groupings of the submeanings of *ni*.

3.2.7. THING as an instrument

What if one wishes to build on the basic structure in which the RECIPIENT functions as the object? In this case a goal image seems quite inappropriate as a way of construing the role of the THING. It is difficult to conceptualize the RECIPIENT as proceeding on to the THING, in the same way that one can think of the THING as proceeding on to the RECIPIENT. Instead, one must integrate a THING phrase in some way other than as a goal. Sometimes, the THING may be integrated by means of a very general morpheme, e.g. an oblique marker. Where the morpheme has a more specific function, it would appear to be the instrumental function which is most favoured as a way of integrating the THING. We find this in English with some donatory verbs, e.g. *I presented her with a book*, where *with* marks the THING transferred, as well as marking the instrument in clauses such as *I cut the tree with an axe*. West Greenlandic illustrates an instrumental morpheme marking the THING in a GIVE clause. In (44a), we have the instrumental suffix attached to the phrase functioning as the instrument with which the stabbing is done, while in (44b) the same suffix is attached to the THING in a GIVE clause.

(44) a. *Nanuq   savim-mi-nik   kapi-vaa.*
        polar bear knife-his-INST stab:3SGSUBJ:3SGOBJ-Indicative
        'He stabbed the polar bear with his knife.'
                        (West Greenlandic, Fortescue 1984: 214)

b. *Niisi   aningaasa-nik   tuni-vaa.*
Niisi   money-INST:PL   give:3SGSUBJ:3SGOBJ-Indicative
'He gave Niisi money.'

(West Greenlandic, Fortescue1984: 89)

In (44b), the suffix *-nik* is unambiguously the plural form of the instrumental (and contrasts with singular *-mik*). Since the verb agrees with a 3rd Singular object, the plural THING phrase *aningaasa-nik* cannot possibly be functioning as the object.

Babungo (Bantu, Cameroon) also integrates the THING into a GIVE construction through the use of an instrument marker:

(45) a. *ŋwé   sàŋ   zɔ̂   nə̀   mbàỳ.*
he   beat:PERF   snake   with   walking stick
'He has beaten a snake with a walking stick.'

(Babungo, Schaub 1985: 64)

b. *Mə̀   kɔ̀   Làmbí   nə̀   fá.*
I   give:PERF   Lambi   with   thing
'I gave something to Lambi.'

(Babungo, Schaub 1985: 60)

It may happen that the RECIPIENT-marking is handled in the same way as the marking of an instrument, though the morpheme may not be labelled as an instrumental. So, for example, Blansitt (1984: 141), citing Gildersleeve—Lodge (1898: 160), gives (46a) as an example of the THING appearing in an ablative case in Latin. But note that the ablative case in Latin is the case appropriate for typical instruments, as exemplified in (46b). In Latin, then, we still find an association between instrument marking and the marking of the THING in GIVE-type clauses in so far as both of these functions are realized by the same case marking.

(46) a. *Rubrium   corōnā   dōnāstī.*
Rubrius-ACC   crown-ABL   you-presented
'You presented Rubrius (with) a crown.'

(Latin, Gildersleeve—Lodge 1898: 160)

b.   *Litterās*   *stilō*   *scrīpsit.*
letter-ACC   pencil-ABL   wrote
'He/she wrote the letter with a pencil.'
                      (Latin, Gildersleeve—Lodge 1898: 160)

We may represent part of the schematic network of the instrumental morpheme in West Greenlandic as in Figure 20. This partial network would be appropriate for the other instrumental morphemes discussed above.

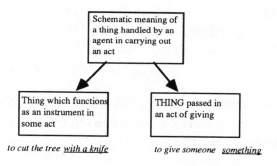

Figure 20.   West Greenlandic instrumental case

Often, a morpheme meaning instrumental also carries the meaning of accompaniment, i.e. the comitative. There is a close relationship between the comitative and instrumental senses. In both senses, there is typically a close physical proximity between the entities involved and this proximity is maintained while some event takes place. The closeness between the senses is evidenced by the frequency with which this pair of meanings occurs together, both associated with the same case or adposition (cf. Lakoff—Johnson 1980: 134–135). This is so in the case of English *with* and Babungo *nə̀*.[19] A morpheme carrying the senses of both instrumental and comitative may also mark the THING transferred in a GIVE clause. This is how English *with* is used with certain donatory verbs, e.g. *to present someone with something*, though not with *give* itself. The Babungo instrumental/comitative *nə̀*, on the other hand, is used with the basic GIVE verb, as mentioned above. The Babungo examples in (47) illustrate all the relevant meanings of this morpheme.

(47) a. *ŋwé   sàŋ   zɔ̂   nә̀   mbày.*
          he   beat:PERF   snake   with   walking stick
          'He has beaten a snake with a walking stick.'
                                          (Babungo, Schaub 1985: 64)

      b. *ŋwé   nyìŋ   nә̀   ŋwǐŋ   mī.*
          she   run:PERF   with   child   her
          'She ran away with her child.'
                                          (Babungo, Schaub 1985: 64)

      c. *Mә̀   kɔ̀   Làmbí   nә̀   fá.*
          I   give:PERF   Lambi   with   thing
          'I gave something to Lambi.'
                                          (Babungo, Schaub 1985: 60)

One might ask, then, whether the use of *nә̀* in Babungo to mark the THING transferred is more closely related to the instrumental sense, as in (47a), or to the comitative sense, as in (47b). As noted above, there is a close relationship between the meaning of THING transferred and instrumental and this argues in favour of subgrouping these two meanings. But nor is it difficult to see a commonality between a sense of accompaniment and THING transferred. Typically, the THING transferred in an act of giving is physically close to (and touching!) the GIVER and the RECIPIENT. This argues in favour of subgrouping the meanings of THING transferred and comitative. In the light of this, it is rather artificial to insist on subgrouping the function of marking the THING transferred with just one of these two other meanings (instrumental and comitative). It is more desirable that each of these subgroupings be reflected in the semantic representation. As with the complex networks described earlier, so in the case of Babungo, there will be more than one commonality which the THING enters into, as represented in Figure 21.

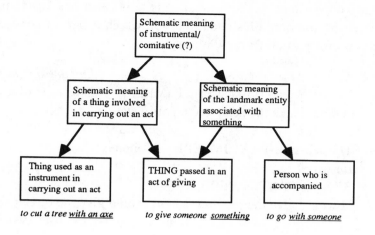

Figure 21. Babungo *nè*

3.2.8. Incorporated object

Nahuatl, as discussed in Tuggy (1989), integrates the THING into a GIVE clause by incorporating it into the verbal word. The construction is illustrated in (48).

(48)   *Ni-mitz-tlāl-maka.*
         I-you-(arable) land-give
         'I give you land.'   (Veracruz Nahuatl, Tuggy 1989: 129)

As part of the incorporation process, the noun *tlāl* appears in its bare stem form. Usually, nouns in Nahuatl have an absolutive suffix attached to them (unless they are possessed or pluralized). The normal form of "land", for example, is *tlāl-li.* As is common with object incorporation in other languages, this additional morphology is absent when the noun forms part of the verbal word. The RECIPIENT, on the other hand, appears as the (main) object in the form of the pronominal prefix *mitz.* (In Nahuatl, a verb stem together with prefixal subject and object may be a complete clause.)

Kunwinjku (Western Arnhem Land, Australia) also has an incorporated GIVE construction, illustrated in (49b), which is part of connected
discourse and follows on from (49a).

(49) a. *Kun-kurlah   a-ka-ni   djamun-djahdjam.*
        IV-pelt   1/3-take-PAST:IMPERF   dangerous-place
        'I would take the pelts to the police station.'
    b. *A-kurlah-wo-ni,   kun-warde*
        1/3-pelt-give-PAST:IMPERF   IV-money
        an-wo-ni.
        3/1-give-PAST:IMPERF
        'I would give them to him and he would give me money.'
                                          (Kunwinjku, Nick Evans 1994)

(49a) illustrates the use of the noun *kurlah* as an independent noun
phrase, functioning as the object of the verb "take". *kurlah* occurs with
its Class IV marker in this clause. In the continuation of the story in
(49b), the same noun appears as an incorporated object as part of the
GIVE word. In this function it does not appear with its class marker,
comparable to the absence of the absolutive suffix in the case of the incorporated object in Nahuatl. The discourse illustrated in (49) illustrates
also how object incorporation functions in Kunwinjku to track the noun
referent first introduced as an independent phrase. Note that in the second half of (49b), we have a new thing being given, namely *warde*
'money'. Again, this is introduced as an object noun phrase independently of the verb GIVE. Further reference to the giving of this money
could presumably rely on an incorporated construction.

3.2.9. *THING and RECIPIENT both obliques*

It may happen that both the THING and the RECIPIENT appear in a
GIVE construction as oblique phrases, i.e. marked in a way distinct
from the typical way in which subjects and objects are marked. As
elsewhere, so here it is important to appreciate the role of semantic extension in the schematic networks of morphemes, including adpositions

and cases. As an example of what appears to be oblique marking of both the THING and the RECIPIENT, consider the following sentences from the Amerindian language Kwak'wala (all Kwak'wala data from Neville Lincoln):

(50)   *Tom   c'ɔ* $\begin{Bmatrix} \check{x}a \\ sa \end{Bmatrix}$ *ɬuq'ʷi   la-q.*

         Tom   give $\begin{Bmatrix} \text{DO} \\ \text{INST} \end{Bmatrix}$ dish   to-him

         'Tom gives the dish to him.'   (Kwak'wala)

"Dish" appears as either a direct object phrase or an instrumental phrase and "him" appears as a directional phrase. The morpheme *la*, glossed as "to", is the verbal root "go". "Tom gives the dish to me" would require a directional phrase based on *gʷaǐ* 'come', similar to Cambodian, as discussed in Section 3.2.2. The use of the instrumental marker as an alternative to a direct object marker is by no means restricted just to the GIVE construction. We find, for example, *ǐa* alternating with *sa* in a number of cases, as in (51).

(51) a.   *nəpa* $\begin{Bmatrix} \check{x}a \\ sa \end{Bmatrix}$ *t'isṃ.*

          throw $\begin{Bmatrix} \text{DO} \\ \text{INST} \end{Bmatrix}$ stone

          'throw the stone'   (Kwak'wala)

      b.   *k'iʔs-ṇ   kəɬəla* $\begin{Bmatrix} \check{x}a \\ sa \end{Bmatrix}$ *siɬṃ.*

          not-I   fear $\begin{Bmatrix} \text{DO} \\ \text{INST} \end{Bmatrix}$ snake(s)

          'I do not fear snake(s).'   (Kwak'wala)

The use of the instrumental case in such constructions in Kwak'wala was commented upon by Boas:

The use of the objective and instrumental with different verbs shows great irregularities. On the whole, the objective is used only when the action directly affects the object; while in other cases, where a direction toward an object is expressed, periphrastic

forms are used. Whenever an action can be interpreted as per-
formed with an instrument, the instrumental is used, for which the
Kwā´g·uɬ has a great predilection. In many cases, however, both
instrumental and objective may be used, according to the point of
view taken. (Boas 1911: 544)

In the framework adopted here, the use of *sa* and *la* in the GIVE
construction illustrates extensions from what would appear to be the
more basic uses of these two morphemes marking instrument and "go"
respectively. We have already seen how an instrumental morpheme may
be extended to designate the THING given in languages such as West
Greenlandic and how the basic verbs "go" and "come" may be extended
to indicate directionality in GIVE clauses in Cambodian. Both these extensions are present in the schematic networks of instrumental *sa* and *la*
'go' in Kwak'wala.

Another example of a GIVE construction lacking any phrase marked
as a typical object is the following Kalkatungu sentence (Australian):

(52)   *Nyini   anyi-minha-n   nga-tyi   maa-tyi?*
        you   give-IMPERF-you   me-DAT   food-DAT
        'Are you giving me any food?'
                                    (Kalkatungu, Blake 1990: 57)

In this example, both the THING and the RECIPIENT appear in the dative case. A dative case is not unexpected as a way of encoding the
RECIPIENT in a GIVE scene, indeed it is a very common way of encoding the RECIPIENT, but it is unusual as a way of encoding the
THING. Before discussing (52), one should note that there are two
other, less problematical GIVE constructions in Kalkatungu, as shown
in (53).

(53) a. *Nyin-ti   anyi-mpa-n   maa   nga-tyinha?*
         you-ERG   give-PERF-you   food-ABS   me-ALL
         'Have you given food to me?'
                                    (Kalkatungu, Blake 1990: 57)

b. *Nyin-ti anya-ngi (ngai) maa?*
you-ERG gave-me (me-ABS) food-ABS
'Did you give me some food?'

(Kalkatungu, Blake 1990: 57)

The syntactic encodings of the THING and RECIPIENT roles evidenced in (53) are familiar from our overview of GIVE-construction types. As shown in (53a), and as discussed by Blake (1990: 43–44), the RECIPIENT with GIVE may appear in the allative. There is an alternative double object construction shown in (53b) with *ngai* and *maa* both in the absolutive case, i.e. a ditransitive construction with two objects. (It is possible for the "me" morpheme *ngi* to occur without case marking in this construction.) The parenthesis indicates that there can be a dual realization of the RECIPIENT in such clauses. Notice that there is no element labelled dative in either of these constructions.

Returning to (52), one should first clarify the basis for labelling the case of the objects as dative in this language. Barry Blake informs me of his criteria for labelling cases in languages which have hitherto not been described, in particular Kalkatungu:

> With a "new" language, I look for the large class of 2-place verbs that includes "smash", "bash", etc. and allot accusative to (the) patient. There is usually a minority class, as in Latin, of non-impingement/non-activity verbs. These take dative in Latin so on grounds of cross-language consistency, I allot the label dative to the corresponding case. (Barry Blake, p.c.)

This strategy is also described in Blake (1994: 144–145). Thus, the so-called dative in Kalkatungu is *not* a case which is to be thought of as prototypically involving a RECIPIENT. "Oblique" might just as well be chosen as a label for the case.

Regardless of what the most typical function of the Kalkatungu dative might be, one would need to recognize a polysemy in its range of functions. I would analyze the use of the Kalkatungu dative in (52) along the lines adopted for the analysis of allative, instrumental etc. in the earlier part of this chapter. Basic to the analysis is the recognition of the per-

vasive role of semantic extension in schematic networks of case morphemes. We have seen, for example, how the prototypical use of the instrumental case may be extended to include many types of PATIENTs in
Kwak'wala, as an alternative to object marking. Even Blake (1979:
343), in a discussion of the reconstruction of the history of Australian
languages, refers to the extension of the dative marker to the PATIENT
category in some languages. Proceeding in the same way with respect to
the Kalkatungu dative, one could say that the prototypical use of the dative (however that is defined) has been extended to mark each of the two
landmark phrases in (52). The use of the so-called dative case as an
alternative to the absolutive object ("2-3 retreat" in Blake's terms) is
widespread in Kalkatungu. It applies to the landmarks of some monotransitive verbs as well as ditransitives. So, for example, the verb "eat"
may occur with the thing eaten in the absolutive or the dative (Blake
1990: 43). The schematic network of the dative case in Kalkatungu thus
includes the functions of marking both THING and RECIPIENT.

The situation in Kalkatungu is a little more complicated, though. In
particular, the dative is extended to mark the THING, just when a dative
RECIPIENT is also present. Thus, we find (54c) but not (54a) or (54b):

(54) a.   *GIVE THING-dative RECIPIENT-allative
      b.   *GIVE THING-absolutive RECIPIENT-dative
      c.   GIVE THING-dative RECIPIENT-dative

I am not able to explain away this constraint on the use of the dative in
GIVE clauses in Kalkatungu. Nevertheless, (54c) is reminiscent of the
way in which the absolutive case may appear on both the THING and
RECIPIENT in a GIVE clause, as in (53b). One might therefore think
of the "double dative" construction as a variant of the "double
absolutive" construction, consistent with the variation between dative
and absolutive marking which is found elsewhere in the language.

3.3. Constructions with TAKE

In Chapter 2 we discussed aspects of the meaning of the TAKE predicate, which in some ways resembles GIVE and in other ways represents the converse of it. It is appropriate in the present context to discuss some of the similarities and differences which exist between TAKE and GIVE constructions.

In a number of Indo-European languages, the dative case marking typical of RECIPIENTs in GIVE constructions also appears as the marking on the person from whom something is taken. Compare the use of the dative case in the German and Czech sentences in (55).

(55) a. *Die Mutter gab dem Kind einen Apfel.*
the mother:NOM gave the child:DAT an apple:ACC
'The mother gave the child an apple.'   (German)

   b. *Die Mutter nahm dem Kind*
the mother:NOM took the child:DAT
den Ball weg.
the ball:ACC away
'The mother took the ball away from the child.' (German)

   c. *Hana dala Petrovi knihu.*
Hana:NOM gave Peter:DAT book:ACC
'Hana gave Peter a book.'   (Czech, Janda 1993a: 537)

   d. *Alena mi pořád bere čokolády!*
Alena:NOM me:DAT always takes chocolates:ACC
'Alena is always taking chocolates from me!'
(Czech, Janda 1993a: 537)

Identical marking of "human from whom something is taken" and RECIPIENT is also found in Sochiapan Chinantec (as described in Foris 1993: 352–353, 378). The preposition *ñí¹con²* marks an animate source (*the teacher* as in *The letter came from the teacher*), animate goal (*Kim* as in *Take this letter to Kim*), and the human RECIPIENT in an act of giving. Japanese *ni* also marks both the meanings of human RECIPIENT and human source, as illustrated in (43a) and (43e) above. In

Chamorro, the syntactic construction appropriate for a GIVE verb is also used with the TAKE verb, as shown in (56a) and (56b).

(56) a. *Ha   na'i   i   patgon   ni   leche.*
he/she gave the child the:OBL milk
'He/she gave the child milk.'

(Chamorro, Topping 1973: 251)

b. *Hu   amot   i   patgon   ni   bola.*
I took/snatched the child the:OBL ball
'I snatched the ball from the child.'

(Chamorro, Topping et al 1975: 13)

In both cases, there is a human direct object followed by an oblique phrase marking the thing transferred. This kind of construction is common in Chamorro, encoding a variety of semantic relationships, with the human direct object functioning as a RECIPIENT, source, benefactive, goal etc.

The apparent "reversal" of meaning found in such cases is not altogether uncommon within the dative category. So, for example, the dative case in Polish is closely associated with benefactive uses, as one might expect if RECIPIENT-marking is a central meaning within the category of the dative case. In addition, however, the Polish dative is used to denote a "malefactive" sense, referring to the person(s) disadvantaged or adversely affected by some action (cf. Rudzka-Ostyn to appear, a).

While one might propose that an extension to a semantic opposite be recognized as a legitimate category of semantic extension, I do not believe that the facts alluded to above support that approach. Instead, I believe that the opposite meanings, such as RECIPIENT and human source, should be viewed as being separate instantiations of a more schematic meaning associated with the relevant morpheme. Thus, in the case of the dative, as it is used in many Indo-European languages, a typical schematic meaning associated with that category is marking the experiencer, as discussed in Section 3.2.1. The sense of experiencer is easily compatible with the meaning of RECIPIENT in a GIVE clause, since the RECIPIENT comes to have control over the THING, repre-

senting something experienced by the RECIPIENT. A human or animate being from whom something is taken is also experiencing a change
in the state of affairs, just as much as the RECIPIENT in the act of
giving. Thus, each of the two meanings, RECIPIENT and human
source, are quite appropriate as more specific instantiations of the broad
category of experiencer. This way of construing the relatedness of
RECIPIENT and human source seems more plausible than appealing to
a dubious principle of antonymic extension. The benefactive and malefactive uses of the Polish dative, similarly, should be understood as instantiations of the experiencer category, rather than as evidence for a
meaning changing into its opposite. This is not to deny, however, that
antonyms can be a relevant factor influencing the course of diachronic
change. GIVE and TAKE, in fact, provide some support for this, in so
far as the form of one seems to sometimes influence the development of
the other, as discussed in Section 2.8.

In languages such as Czech and German, then, the TAKE construction rests on an extension of the schematic network underlying the dative case morpheme along the lines just discussed. This kind of extension
is diagrammed in Figure 22. The network shown in Figure 22 is to be
understood as a further possible addition to the network of a dative.

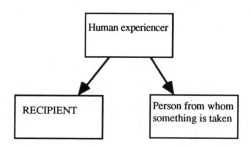

Figure 22. German and Czech dative

One would expect that the RECIPIENT sense to be the more central sense of such dative morphemes. The human source sense, as far as I am aware, never forms the core meaning of a case in case-marking languages. Again, this highlights the different status that a RECIPIENT has in a giving act, compared with the human source in a taking act. The RECIPIENT is crucial to the act of giving which is itself a basic interpersonal act. A human source, on the other hand, is not a crucial component of the act of taking (since there does not have to be any person from whom one takes things) and taking from someone does not seem quite as basic an interpersonal act as giving to someone is.

The schematic network depicted in Figure 22 contrasts with the situation where the two meanings, RECIPIENT and human source, are expressed differently, as in English *She gave the book to me* and *She took the book from me*. Compare also the uses of the allative and ablative cases in Finnish in (57) where these meanings are expressed quite differently.

(57) a. *Annan   kirja-n   tei-lle.*
         give:1SG   book-ACC   you-ALL
         'I give the book to you.'   (Finnish)

   b. *Mies   ottaa tavara-t   myyjä-ltä.*
         man:NOM   take   thing-PL:ACC   sales assistant-ABL
         'The man is taking the things from the sales assistant.'
                                                            (Finnish)

The English prepositions *to* and *from* have strong spatial senses as part of their central meaning, as do the Finnish allative and ablative cases. A pure allative sense (indicating a goal, either animate or inanimate) seems to be not easily compatible with an extension to the ablative sense, or vice versa. Where a case or adposition shows both allative and ablative meanings, one would expect that the two meanings are only relatable through some longer chain of associations or that both are specific instantiations of a more general schematic meaning, such as "direction".

3.4. The significance of schematic networks

Our discussion of schematic networks has revealed considerable diversity in the range of meanings evidenced by the morphemes which mark the THING and the RECIPIENT in languages.

Bearing in mind that it has not been possible to make very precise claims about central submeanings and the direction of extensions from one part of a network to another, I feel nevertheless that I can make some relevant suggestions (cf. also Heine 1990: 143–146). As far as prototypical meanings are concerned, I suspect that the RECIPIENT-marking and THING-marking functions of the morphemes we have looked at would be judged to be a relatively central meaning of the morphemes involved. The morphemes which have been considered are the ones which would commonly be used in GIVE constructions — they are not morphemes which have been extended in any novel and creative ways to "fit" into a GIVE construction. Recall, too, the basicness of the giving act in interpersonal relationships, as discussed in Chapter 1. As a general observation, I think we must recognize that we are dealing here with some commonly occurring and quite salient functions of morphemes. It leads me to suspect that the RECIPIENT-marking sense and the THING-marking sense are relatively central in the set of meanings of each of the morphemes considered.

The question of which submeanings of a morpheme might be considered as extensions from other submeanings is more difficult to address. In some of the examples of RECIPIENT-marking discussed above, I would tend to see the RECIPIENT-marking as basic and some other senses as extensions. This is how I would view the Russian and German dative. In these languages we see RECIPIENT-marking as a salient function of the dative and it is possible to construe some of the other uses of the dative as figurative extensions from that submeaning, as discussed earlier in this chapter. It is difficult to conceptualize the relationships in the opposite way, whereby there is some schematic meaning common to all the submeanings apart from RECIPIENT-marking which is figuratively extended to RECIPIENT-marking. In the case of morphemes which show a polysemy between RECIPIENT-marking and allative/locative uses, on the other hand, I would be inclined to see the RECIPIENT-marking as an extension of the allative/locative sense. Underlying this view is a cognitive bias towards viewing spatial relationships as even more basic than our understanding of giving acts. It strikes me as easier to construe the RECIPIENT as being like a goal to which something moves than to construe a spatial goal as being a figurative extension of a RECIPIENT. That is, it is easier to see movement to a GOAL in the prototypical act of giving than to see movement to a GOAL as an act of giving something to a RECIPIENT. Furthermore, I have not found any extensive diachronic evidence of a path of development from RECIPIENT marking to allative marking. Note that while Mandarin *gěi* 'give' has been extended to a variety of other meanings, including RECIPIENT-marking, benefactive, "allow", and agent marking in a passive construction, it has not been extended to mark the goal in a pure allative meaning (cf. Footnote 14 above). My view of the directionality here extends quite generally to other non-spatial submeanings of allative/locative markers. So, for example, I regard the spatial sense of *to* involving a path to some goal as the source for other senses of *to* as in *five minutes to six, being under an obligation to someone, the building faces to the north, I want to go* etc., rather than the other way around.

In the case of polysemy involving benefactive and possessive meanings the direction of extensions seems far less obvious to me. RECIPIENTs, benefactives, and possessors all make crucial reference to the role of a human in a relatively non-active role in a scene and moving from any one of these meanings to another seems plausible on general cognitive grounds. In a particular language, speakers may have clear intuitions about the directionality of the extension. It may be, for example, that a benefactive meaning is well entrenched for a morpheme while its use to mark RECIPIENTs is less well developed and felt as secondary. In such a case, speakers may sense an extension from a benefactive meaning to a dative meaning. Alternatively, a well entrenched dative morpheme may take on the role of benefactive marking. This may well be the case in Choctaw, based on the discussion in Davies (1986: 40–41). In Choctaw, there is an agreement marker on the verb which agrees with the RECIPIENT in GIVE clauses as well as the goal with (at least some) verbs of movement. This is called dative agreement by Davies. In addition, there is benefactive agreement whereby the verb is marked to agree with a benefactive. The dative agreement marking, however, also appears as an alternative to the benefactive agreement. Presumably, this represents an extension of the dative to benefactive.

Where the linguist does not have access to the intuitions of native speakers regarding the directions of extensions in cases of polysemy, one can only speculate, as I have done, on such matters. One may appeal to knowledge about attested historical developments to argue for the naturalness of a certain direction of extension, but one cannot equate diachronic facts with present-day intuitions of speakers. So, for example, there are words in English which are etymologically related but are not felt by ordinary speakers as being particularly close semantically, e.g. *flour* and *flower*. Thus, even when we can document the relevant period in the history of a semantic development in a language, speakers may or may not have an identical intuition. If the schematic networks are to represent aspects of the speakers' understanding of lexical items, then it is the intuitions which one must look to in constructing the network, not the historical facts. Similar comments may be made with regard to an appeal to general cognitive principles as a way of deciding on the supposed directionality of an extension of meaning. Such principles might be suggestive, but in the end it is the speaker who is the arbiter of the directionality. While I, as a linguist, am aware of certain historical tendencies and cognitive principles at work in language, I can only speculate on native speakers' judgements in any particular case. In representing the schematic subnetworks, I have preferred not to incorporate such speculations and have left the directionality of extension unspecified.

Regardless of what extensions one sees in the submeanings of the morphemes discussed above, it remains true that the RECIPIENT and THING may be treated as identical with other semantic roles from the point of view of clause organization. Underlying such polysemies are cognitive acts of categorization, or metaphorization. In saying this I am not suggesting that a native speaker carries out a creative metaphorical act. But creative acts of metaphorization on the part of speakers in the past are responsible for the range of meanings in the first place. Now, as part of the conventionalized images of a language, they have lost their novel, creative values. In exploring these conventionalized images, then,

I have been detailing some cognitive tendencies of (past) humans as reflected in (present) linguistic structures.

3.5. Integrating the morphemes

In previous sections we have reviewed the variety of cases and adpositions which may be employed in the construction of GIVE clauses across languages. This was done without paying close attention to details of the GIVE clause structure which now needs to be addressed. In this section I shall elaborate on the integration of the GIVE verb and its associated phrases (GIVER, THING, RECIPIENT) to form a complete clause. The framework will continue to be that of Cognitive Grammar. As a way of illustrating the Cognitive Grammar approach to combining the elements of a clause, I shall discuss each of the clause types shown in (58). These structures represent some of the most common types of GIVE clauses. The characterizations in (58) indicate the components of the structure abstracted away from particular word-order constraints which may be operative in a language.

(58) a. GIVE RECIPIENT THING
          e.g. *give me money*
      b. GIVE THING RECIPIENT$_{ALL}$
          e.g. *give money to me*
      c. GIVE THING$_{ACC}$ RECIPIENT$_{DAT}$
          e.g. *mir Geld geben* (German)

Figure 23 is a diagrammatic representation of the English construction exemplified by the tenseless and uninflected phrase in (58a), *give me money*. I have already introduced some of the relevant concepts, e.g. trajector (TR) and landmark (LM), in Chapter 2. These concepts appear in the representation of relational predicates. In particular, the version of *give* in *give me money*, which I will designate as *give$_1$*, includes in its profile a TR (the GIVER) and LMs (the THING and the RECIPIENT). This is essentially the same representation introduced as Figure 3 in Chapter 2. It features the spatio-temporal domain, which, although not the only domain relevant to GIVE, is a salient one and is convenient as a way of referring to the internal structure of GIVE. In the light of the difficulties inherent in identifying the THING or the RECIPIENT as the primary object in the English ditransitive construction, as discussed above, I have simply labelled both of these entities as LMs without further specifying one as primary. This seems the safest way to proceed with this construction. In this version of GIVE, all three participant entities are shown as elaboration sites (e-sites) which will need to be filled in order to construct a well-formed clause.

The *give me money* phrase is built up by integrating the components bit by bit. Although the order in which the components are combined is not crucial, it is convenient to show the integration happening in stages. The first stage I have indicated involves filling the RECIPIENT e-site with the morpheme referring to the speaker, which is realized variously as *I* or *me*. The meaning of this morpheme is shown as the highlighted SPEAKER entity in the speech situation. An arrow leading from the RECIPIENT e-site to the morpheme *I~me* represents the fact that this e-site is filled by the 1st Singular morpheme, realized as *I* when it functions as a TR and as *me* when it is a LM. A dotted line, or line of integration, further details the manner in which relevant parts of the 1st Singular morpheme are integrated into the relational predicate. In this case, the line of integration indicates merely that the SPEAKER is the part of the 1st Singular morpheme which will function as the RECIPIENT in the integrated structure. The result of this integration is shown as the new entity *give₁ me*, which is diagrammed as a rectangular shape to reflect its unit status as a well-entrenched combination within English. I follow Langacker (1987: 57–62) in recognizing familiarity and frequency of a structure as a basis for assigning unit status. Note that the result of the integration continues to be a relational predicate, preserving the basic nature of the *give₁* component, rather than being a nominal type of entity like the 1st Singular morpheme component. Dark outlining of the box surrounding *give₁* is the Cognitive Grammar convention for expressing this facet of the organization. *Give₁ me money* is then built up from *give₁ me* using the same devices to integrate *money* into the construction. The THING e-site is elaborated with a nominal

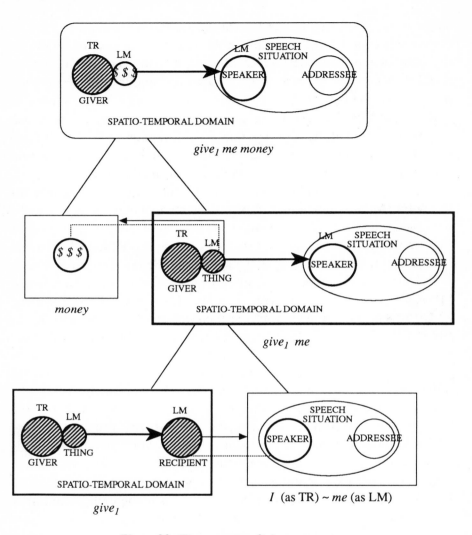

Figure 23. The structure of *give₁ me money*

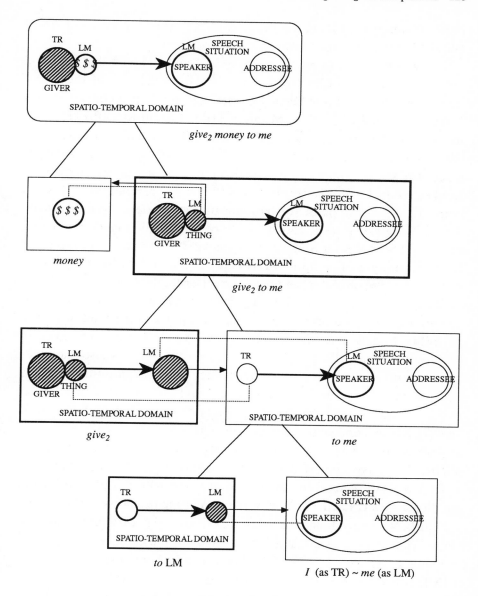

Figure 24. The structure of *give₂ money to me*

predicate *money*, yielding the structure at the top of Figure 23 in which both LMs have been specified.

The structure of *give me money* may be compared with that of (58b), *give money to me*, diagrammed in Figure 24. At the core of this structure is a slightly different version of the English GIVE predicate. In this version, labelled *give₂*, the LMs are a THING and a RECIPIENT, with the RECIPIENT imaged as a goal to which the THING moves. This is the version of GIVE which is relevant to all those constructions discussed above where the RECIPIENT is encoded as an allative. In English the path entity is constructed with the preposition *to* and this is a convenient starting point for building up the whole clausal structure. Thus, the *to* predicate is shown at the bottom of the diagram as being integrated with the 1st Singular morpheme. *To* defines a path traversed by a TR entity leading up to a LM entity and it is the LM entity which functions as the object of the preposition. Hence, the LM e-site is shown as being elaborated by the 1st Singular morpheme, yielding the phrase *to me*, here assigned unit status. The phrase *to me* is the kind of phrase permitted to elaborate *give₂*, and so these two entities are integrated to yield *give₂ to me*. The combination of *give₂* and *to me* is also shown as having unit status due to the frequency of this pattern. Lines of integration indicate the ways in which the understood TR and the LM of *to me* are integrated with the components of *give₂*. The elaboration of the THING is identical to what was done in Figure 23.

The use of a dative case in a GIVE clause, (53c), is diagrammed in Figure 25. I have suggested as a representation of the German dative, as used in a GIVE clause, the same kind of frame which is posited for the predicate GIVE itself. With the dative morpheme, however, only the RECIPIENT entity functions as an e-site. This way of representing the dative captures the idea that a core meaning of the German dative is the meaning of RECIPIENT in a GIVE type clause, as discussed above. The RECIPIENT e-site is filled by a LM version of the 1st Singular morpheme, *mir*. (I leave aside here the question of representing the different semantic structures associated with the different versions of the 1st Singular morpheme.) Thus, the dative *mir* contains within its representation all the basic components which go into GIVE itself, so that there is extensive sharing of the basic components: the GIVER subsumed in

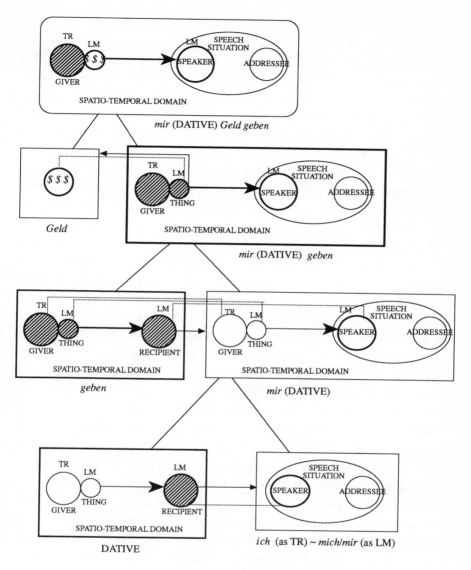

Figure 25. The structure of *mir Geld geben*

the dative morpheme is integrated with the GIVER subsumed in *geben*; the THING in the dative is integrated with the THING of *geben*; the RECIPIENT in the DATIVE entity is integrated with the RECIPIENT of *geben*. This is, in a way, the most perfect fit possible between a relational predicate and one of its arguments and it reflects the special association which exists between GIVE and dative (in its typical function). Once the combination *mir geben* is formed, then the rest proceeds as outlined for the other two constructions. I have simplified the representation of the German structure by omitting details about the nominative and accusative cases, each of which has its own associated structure (nominative associated with the AGENT TR and accusative with a PATIENT LM).

The representations in Figures 23-25 convey, successfully I hope, the similarities as well as the dissimilarities between the construction types. There is a basic similarity between all three constructions in so far as they all pertain to the transference of a THING to a RECIPIENT. Each of the representations reflects this much by showing a THING proceeding to a RECIPIENT. We see money proceeding to the SPEAKER in the topmost frame of each figure. This much is common to all three representations. At the same time, the Cognitive Grammar approach allows one to express the different images which underlie the three constructions. Compare, for example, the pair of diagrams in Figures 23 and 24, representing the structures of *give₁ me money* and *give₂ money to me*. In *give₂ money to me* we are invoking what is essentially a path image as the way of integrating the RECIPIENT into the GIVE clause. Figure 24 incorporates this notion of a path in the characterization of the preposition *to*. There is no comparable explicit "path" morpheme in the representation of the *give₁ me money* structure. In other words, while the two structures are similar in a "gross" kind of way, their semantic structures are different in the details of their composition.

The different building blocks which are utilized in Figures 23 and 24 correlate with differences in the semantics associated with the two structures. Earlier, in Section 3.1, we had occasion to remark on differences between the structures of *give me money* and *give money to me* involving properties such as "givenness" and "topicworthiness". Apart from these pragmatic differences, however, it is possible to characterize a difference in the semantics of each construction. Goldberg (1992b) reviews various attempts to deal with this difference before she proceeds to her own characterization in terms of the underlying event structures. The *give₁ me money* structure is characterized by her as meaning "agent successfully causes the transfer of a thing to a recipient", a sense which is centrally associated with this ditransitive structure. The *give₂ money to me* structure, on the other hand, may be paraphrased as "agent causes the movement of a thing along a path". A similar semantic distinction is suggested by the terms "donatory" (for the *give₁ me money* structure) and "destinatory" (for the *give₂ money to me* structure) in Davidse (to appear). These differences reside in the structures themselves and are relevant to understanding the preferences for one or the other of the syntactic frames with particular verb choices. Although both constructions are found with *give*, one or the other of the constructions may be required with certain combinations. For example, in causing someone to have a headache, it is difficult to understand the causation of the headache as an action which proceeds along a spatial path to the affected person. So, the destinatory structure is inappropriate. On the other hand, causation is quite generally understood as a kind of abstract transfer of an effect to some entity, as discussed in Goldberg (1992b: 60). Hence, the ditransitive construction, embodying the donatory viewpoint, is well suited to expressing such causation. In this way, one can motivate the extension of the ditransitive construction to *Kim gave Lee a headache* as well as explaining why one does not find **Kim gave a headache to Lee*. These semantic differences are reflected in Cognitive Grammar in the different substructures which appear as the components of the larger structures associated with the different meanings. These substructures directly incorporate the different images codified by the various morphemes.

3.6. Summary

One can see that there are several linguistic options available for imaging the GIVE scene, as described in this chapter. Although facts about our experience of acts of giving and our cognitive preferences for visualizing such acts are not by themselves able to unambiguously predict the linguistic facts, they nevertheless do serve as a useful context for better understanding the range of linguistic facts presented here.

The syntactic frames which occur with GIVE verbs are not arbitrary. Rather, they are motivated by facets of the base of GIVE as discussed in Chapters 1 and 2. The typical Indo-European dative case will include RECIPIENT-marking as one of its central senses, if not the most central, and the basicness and prominence of the giving act in human interaction is undoubtedly relevant to why a case should be so closely associated with the role of RECIPIENT. In the spatio-temporal domain of GIVE there is a movement of the THING to a RECIPIENT and this is what motivates the marking of a RECIPIENT as a goal or locative. In the control domain the RECIPIENT comes to be the new controller of the THING, motivating the encoding of the RECIPIENT in the same way as a possessor. In the domain of human interest the RECIPIENT benefits from the act of giving (in its prototypical manifestation) and this in turn motivates the marking of the RECIPIENT as a benefactive. In the force-dynamics domain one can observe a flow of energy from the GIVER through to the RECIPIENT, with the flow of energy proceeding through the manipulation of the THING. This facet of GIVE motivates the treatment of the THING as an instrument, enabling a successful interaction between the GIVER and the RECIPIENT.

Figure 26 summarizes the main options which are available cross-linguistically for encoding the GIVE scene, with the GIVER selected as the clausal trajector (grammatical subject). In this Figure, I have tried to suggest the ways in which particular syntactic frames (as suggested by their core semantic functions) are motivated by components of the GIVE predicate. The different domains which all form part of the meaning of GIVE provide the clues to understanding the various ways in which the THING and RECIPIENT are integrated into clausal structure. I have used arrows to show how different aspects of the

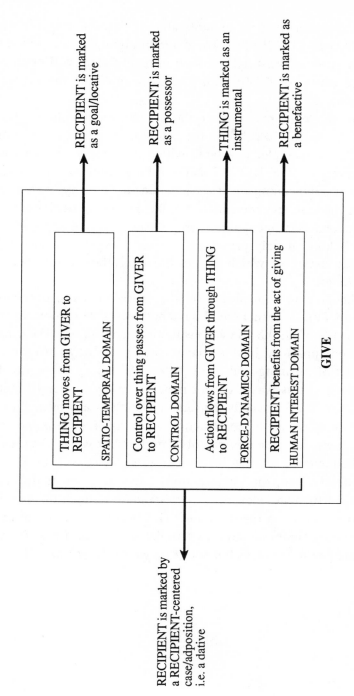

Figure 26. Literal GIVE and its associated clause structure

GIVE morpheme lead to, or motivate, a particular way of construing the THING or RECIPIENT. The diagram highlights the principal basis for each of these construals, though in reality there will often be more than one aspect of GIVE which helps to motivate the syntax which occurs with it.

Often, the case marking or the adposition which integrates the THING or the RECIPIENT in the clause structure is polysemous. The "dative", for example, is a label which may apply to many semantic roles, even if the RECIPIENT-marking function is typically a prominent submeaning of cases labelled in this way. Any attempt to describe the case and adposition morphemes which participate in GIVE constructions must recognize such polysemy. In the approach adopted here, this kind of polysemy finds a natural expression in the form of schematic networks which reflect the interrelationships between the submeanings.

In choosing to concentrate on the cross-linguistic diversity to be found in GIVE constructions, I have not been able explore in any great depth details of all the GIVE constructions considered. The glosses and translations provided in this chapter may not always bring out all the subtleties of meaning and use of the GIVE morphemes involved. In proceeding in this way I do not mean to imply that any literal GIVE construction carries exactly the same meaning as any other literal GIVE construction. A pair of constructions such as *give me money* and *give money to me*, for example, functions in different ways when it comes to their frequency and role in discourse, as discussed in Section 3.1. Semantically, too, the constructions carry with them different core meanings which are relevant to understanding some of the uses to which the two construction types are put. This becomes evident in the course of discussing figurative GIVE examples where one finds, for example, *Kim gave Lee a headache* but not **Kim gave a headache to Lee*.

Chapter 4. Constructions with figurative GIVE

4.1. Figurative GIVE

In Chapter 2 I characterized the prototypical meaning of GIVE with reference to a particular type of interaction between humans. In this chapter I will review the range of additional meanings which may be associated with the GIVE morpheme in languages. These will be meanings which involve something other than the transfer of some concrete object from one person to another. I will refer to all such meanings as "figurative", without any implication that such meanings are considered poetic or imaginative by native speakers. The term "figurative" is used in opposition to "literal" which I reserve for the "transfer of possession" sense. My interest lies in understanding the basis for the extension of meaning in each case, regardless of whether or not the figurative meaning is considered by native speakers or lexicographers to be one and the same morpheme as the GIVE morpheme in its literal meaning. The morphemes which I will be focusing on occur elsewhere with the meaning GIVE and I will gloss them as GIVE even when they have a figurative meaning, such as "cause" etc.

In what follows, I present an overview of the main directions in which GIVE is extended and offer some motivation for the extensions, without attempting to document each and every figurative extension which is possible. There is clearly a very large number of possible extensions, a number of which have been omitted from the present discussion. Nevertheless, I believe the examples included here are fairly representative of the general directions in which the extensions have occurred. I consider it more important to establish these general directions and to offer some explanation for them rather than to simply list every possible extension. The extensions are grouped into the following main categories and I will discuss each one in turn:

(1)   interpersonal communication
           emergence/manifestation
           causative/purpose
           permission/enablement
           schematic interaction
           recipient/benefactive marking
           movement
           completedness

Separating out the extensions into these eight areas is a necessary simplification I make in order to highlight the principal tendencies. Quite often, an extension relates to more than one of these areas, as will become apparent in the following discussion.

Within the framework developed by Lakoff (1987: 276), Lakoff—Turner (1989: 63), and Lakoff (1990: 48), literal GIVE would constitute the "source domain" and the figurative extensions would constitute "target domains". Expressed in these terms, this chapter is an attempt to document and motivate the various "mappings" which exist between the source domain and the target domains. Within that same framework, the Invariance Hypothesis, proposed in Lakoff (1990) and Turner (1990), has also been an important contribution to understanding such mappings, notwithstanding the trenchant critique of this hypothesis in Brugman (1990). This hypothesis holds that metaphorical mappings preserve all (in a "strong" version) or some (in a "weak" version) of the cognitive topology of the source domain. This hypothesis, at least in its strongest version, makes interesting claims about how the metaphorical mapping takes place. Support for this hypothesis can be found at many points in this chapter, where various syntactic and semantic facts about an extension in the meaning of a GIVE morpheme follow from one larger "equation" between the source domain and the target domain. While my own thinking about the GIVE extensions has benefited greatly from these works, as well as Lakoff—Johnson (1980), I have chosen not to couch the discussion wholly in terms of the metaphorical mappings (GOOD IS UP etc.) which are so central in these works. Presenting the discussion in such terms would require much more justification and explanation than is feasible here. Instead, I will discuss the similarities between literal GIVE and its figurative extensions in the terms already introduced in Chapter 2. Typically, this involves identifying one or more of the domains (in the Cognitive Grammar sense) which make up the complex matrix of literal GIVE: the spatio-temporal domain, the control domain, the force-dynamics domain, and the domain of human interest. By selectively focusing on one or more of these more specific domains which form part of literal GIVE, one is better able to articulate the facets of meaning which lead to a figurative extension.

For the most part, I will concentrate on GIVE morphemes without derivational affixes, verb particles etc. though, with some extensions, it is more natural to include such morphemes and where this is the case, they will be included. Derivational affixes, particles etc. may add various semantic effects to the GIVE morpheme. Lindner (1981) in an in-depth study of selected English verb particles and their associated semantics observed many properties of such particles which are relevant to GIVE constructions in English. So, for example, Lindner found that the *out* particle in English may be associated with a change from hiddenness to accessibility (Lindner 1981: 107–116) and this is relevant to its collocation with *give* in a phrase such as *to give out advice*. A full discussion of the semantics of GIVE morphemes in combination with derivational affixes, verb particles etc. will not be undertaken here.

Some extensions are what one might call grammaticalizations, with the erstwhile GIVE morpheme functioning more as a grammatical morpheme than a lexical item and, indeed, many of the extensions discussed in this chapter fall into this category. The semantic relationships which are explored in the following pages are therefore not just cases of polysemy, in the traditional sense, but also "heterosemy". I use this term as defined by Lichtenberk (1991: 476) for two or more meanings that are historically related but are associated with reflexes which belong to different morphosyntactic categories. Heterosemy is evident in various extensions of GIVE, including its extension to a causative suffix (as in Kunwinjku, discussed in Section 4.4.2), a purposive marker (as in Thai, discussed in Section 4.4.3), an agentive preposition (as in Mandarin, discussed in Section 4.5.6), and a verbal affix in a benefactive construction (as in Nez Perce, discussed in Section 4.7.2). Defined in this way, heterosemy contrasts, usefully, with polysemy which is usually understood to refer to the relatedness of meanings associated with one lexical or grammatical morpheme, belonging to one morphosyntactic category. An interest in the process of grammaticalization is characteristic of cognitive linguistics and it is therefore to be expected within this approach that reference will often be made to heterosemous relationships.

4.2.   Interpersonal communication

One of the most common ways in which GIVE is extended is to portray communicative acts between persons (or person-like entities). Some examples of this in English are shown in (2).

(2)   *give advice to someone, give my opinion to someone, give my best wishes to someone, give the verdict to the court, give orders to someone, give a report to someone, give information to someone, give our thanks to God for something, give my word to someone*

This extension is well represented in other languages. In (3) I have listed just a few of the many possible examples of this in other languages.[1]

(3)   a.   *Mi   diede   la   brutta   notizia.*
           me   gave   the bad   news
           'He gave me the bad news.'   (Italian)

      b.   *dare   il   buongiorno*
           give   the   good-morning
           'to say good-morning to someone'   (Italian)

      c.   *dare   la   benedizione*
           give   the   blessing
           'to give a blessing'   (Italian)

      d.   *Ti   darò   il   mio   giudizio.*
           you:OBJ give:1SG the   my   opinion
           'I'll give you my opinion.'   (Italian)

e. *dat'   telegrammu*
   give   telegram:ACC
   'send a telegram'   (Russian)

f. *davam   săvet* 2
   give   advice
   'give advice'   (Bulgarian)

g. *davam blagoslovija*
   give   blessing
   'give a blessing'   (Bulgarian)

h. *davam   mnenie*
   give   opinion
   'give an opinion'   (Bulgarian)

i. *davam   zapoved*
   give   order
   'give an order'   (Bulgarian)

j. *davam   informatcija*
   give   information
   'give information'   (Bulgarian)

k. *hálát   ad*
   thanks give
   'give thanks'   (Hungarian)

l. *pa   shauri*
   give   advice
   'give advice'   (Swahili)

m. *awèh slamet*
   give   greeting/blessing
   'to wish someone well'   (Javanese)

n. *hei   ta-ra*
   word   give-Purposive
   'to give orders'   (Rumu, Papuan)

o. *pahe   ta-ra*
   advice give-Purposive
   'to give advice'   (Rumu, Papuan)

The conceptual mapping underlying these examples is an easy one to make: the transmission of a message to someone is understood as the

giving of a thing to someone. The extension of GIVE to describe interpersonal communication is but one part of a larger "conduit metaphor"
which underlies and shapes much of our discourse (and thinking!) about
communication (Reddy 1979, Lakoff 1987: 450–451). In this particular
version of the conduit metaphor, the speaker is construed as a GIVER,
the message is construed as the THING which passes through the spatio-
temporal domain from the speaker to the addressee, and the addressee is
construed as the RECIPIENT. Telling something to someone thus
amounts to the verbal equivalent of giving. I have described the meanings involved here in terms of spoken communication, though this is a
simplification. Clearly, many of these communicative acts could also
take place in the written medium, or sign language. Russian *dat' telegrammu* 'give telegram', for example, must be construed as primarily
occurring in a written form. We have already discussed how GIVE
enjoys the status of a basic-level category in a hierarchy of human acts.
It is hardly surprising that it is utilized in conceptualizing other
interpersonal acts. Figure 27 is an attempt to capture this extension of
literal GIVE. It represents a portion of the schematic network
associated with a GIVE predicate in those languages where the predicate
is also used in the sense of TELL (with appropriate objects). The broken arrow indicates the direction of the extension from literal GIVE to
TELL. Here, and throughout this chapter, the GIVER in the GIVE
frame is designated as the trajector (in the sense of being the agent, instigating the act of giving) and the THING and RECIPIENT as landmarks. Corresponding to this, the speaker in the act of communication
is designated as the trajector and the message and the listener are designated as landmarks within the frame of verbal communication.

Despite the obvious parallels between the semantic structure of literal
GIVE and that of interpersonal communication, there are nevertheless
ways in which the structure of literal GIVE does not carry over to the
target domain. So, for example, in the case of literal GIVE, the GIVER
no longer has control over the THING passed to the RECIPIENT. In
the case of giving advice, an opinion, or information, on the other hand,
it is not the case that the speaker no longer has such advice or opinions
or information. The speaker "shares out" these kinds of information
with a RECIPIENT, rather than dispense with them altogether. This

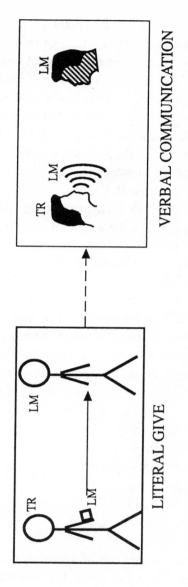

Figure 27. Extension of GIVE to verbal communication

would be an example of the Invariance Hypothesis applying in a "weak" form to this particular mapping: while much of the structure of literal GIVE is found also in the structure of interpersonal communication, not all of the structure carries over. In particular, inferences about the control over the THING are not identical in the source domain and the target domain. In this case, one might argue that properties of the target domain, in particular the way knowledge, ideas, opinions etc. are formed and retained, "override" the inferences which normally would apply as part of the metaphorical mapping.

Sometimes, the verbal communication takes effect through an intermediary, as in *Give my regards to Mary*, where a kind of greeting passes from me to Mary through the addressee. In English GIVE may carry this sense, though other languages may modify GIVE in some ways to bring out the difference between direct and indirect types of communication. In cases involving an intermediary in the transmission of a message, Bulgarian, for example, makes use of a prefix *pre-* derived from a preposition *prez* "through". In its basic spatial sense, the preposition traces the path or tunnel through which a trajector moves on the way to some goal. In its use as a prefix with verbs of communication, it functions in an analogous way to highlight a path of communication through an intermediate person.

(4) a. *pre-davam   săobštenie*
         through-give message
         'give (someone) a message'   (Bulgarian)
     b. *pre-davam   pozdravi*
         through-give regards
         'give (someone) regards'   (Bulgarian)

Although extensions to the domain of verbal communication are attested in many languages, it is not the case that the GIVE concept is naturally extended to take on all the meaning of verbal communication. Note, for example, that we do not use *give* in English as a substitute for *say/speak* in expressions like *I spoke (*gave) to her on the phone*, or *I said (*gave) something which upset her*. Likewise, one may not substitute *say* or *speak* for *give* in many of the phrases cited above: *give* (*say*, *speak*) *advice*, *give* (*say*, *speak*) *an opinion*, *give* (*say*, *speak*) *my best wishes to someone*, *give* (*say*, *speak*) *my word to someone*. With *give* it appears that one needs to construct it with an object referring to the communicated entity in order to have an interpretation in the communicative sense.[3]

It may also be observed that GIVE may function not just as a descriptive term but as a performative (*I give you my word*, *I give you my blessing*, *I give you my notice* etc.). It may be that the literal meaning of GIVE facilitates this extension. Just as literal GIVE involves a change in what the participants have control over, so figurative GIVE involves a change in the real-world state of one or both participants. Collocations with words meaning "word" are interesting in this respect. In many languages GIVE with singular "word" has the meaning of "promise", as in *give one's word*. Other examples are:

(5)   a.   *donner sa parole*
         give   one's   word
         'to give one's word'   (French)

     b.   *Sie gab ihr Wort.*
         she   gave   her   word
         'She gave her word.'   (German)

     c.   *Davam ti duma-ta si.*
         give:1SG   you   word-ART   REFL
         'I give you my word.'   (Bulgarian)

Note, however, that in Rumu the combination of GIVE with "word" *hei ta-ra* in (3n) above takes on the meaning of "to give orders". In English, French, and German it is the *speaker* who is put under an obligation by the words, while in Rumu it is the *addressee*. Possibly, the presence of a pronominal form referring back to the speaker in the English, French, and German examples and its absence in Rumu are relevant to this difference in interpretation.

The use of GIVE for the giving of a judgement, an opinion, a report, advice etc. is particularly common and properties of literal GIVE are relevant to this use. Literal GIVE includes in its profile a RECIPIENT who plays more than the role of being just a passive bystander. While not the instigator of the giving act, the RECIPIENT nevertheless is an essential component of the act and physically plays an active role in receiving the THING. (The RECIPIENT is not just a receptacle, in other words.) Giving is done with a particular RECIPIENT very much in mind and is not simply a matter of relieving oneself of something, followed by someone else coincidentally taking it. There is an implication with GIVE that a RECIPIENT is present and that the action is directed toward, and for the benefit of, the RECIPIENT. With judgements, opinions, advice etc., the communication occurs for the express purpose of providing something to an audience for the benefit of the audience. The audience is not incidental in these cases. Viewed in this way, one may find some motivation for relying on GIVE to conceptualize these particular communicative acts.

The basic dynamics of literal GIVE also appear well-preserved in the case of its extension to performances for an audience, even if the audience is not overtly expressed in the construction:

(6)   *give a concert, give a recital, give a performance, give a demonstration, give lessons, give a speech, give a lecture, give an address*

In other languages:

(7)   a.   *dare   una   commedia*
           give   a   play
           'put on a play'   (Italian)

      b.   *színdarabot   ad*
           play   give
           'to present a play'   (Hungarian)

      c.   *davam retch*
           give   speech
           'give a speech'   (Bulgarian)

      d.   *davam urotci*
           give   lessons
           'give lessons'   (Bulgarian)

e. *davam kontcert*
   give   concert
   'give a concert'   (Bulgarian)
f. *Kakvo davat   v   kino-to?*
   what   give:3PL at   cinema-the
   'What's on at the cinema?'   (Bulgarian)

Once again we recognize in these examples the crucial presence of the person(s) to whom the action is directed. It is the presence of the audience under particular conditions which is a prerequisite for the kind of performance illustrated above. GIVE, with its inherent involvement of a RECIPIENT, seems well suited to conceptualize this aspect of a performance. *Giving a party* and comparable expressions in other languages (Italian *dare una festa*) might be understood in similar terms but with the audience not just present to enjoy the entertainment but actively participating in it. A party, after all, is not a typical party unless and until the guests appear and make a contribution to the party atmosphere. There is in all these cases an implicit evolution of the spectacle over a period of hours. The "concert" or the "party" is not an entity which exists as a whole and is simply passed over to the audience. They are instead complex assemblies of people and things which require time in order to manifest themselves properly. They involve a kind of unfolding or evolution of an event which makes them appear similar in some ways to the use of GIVE in the emergent metaphors discussed in Section 4.3.1 (e.g. Italian *Questo terreno da ottimo grano* 'This land produces very good corn').

Sometimes, the role of the figurative RECIPIENT in interpersonal communication needs to be quite salient in order for GIVE to be extended to the situation. While this is less so in English, it is evident in other languages. Consider the restrictions on GIVE in the Polish data in (8), compared with counterparts of these sentences in English with *give*:

(8) a. *Marysia dała   mi   dobrą   radę.*
        Mary   gave   me   good   advice
        'Mary gave me good advice.'   (Polish)

b. *Marysia* $\left\{\begin{array}{c} \text{\textit{przekazała}} \\ \text{\textit{*dała}} \end{array}\right\}$ *mi* *wiadomość.*

Mary $\left\{\begin{array}{c} \text{transferred} \\ \text{*gave} \end{array}\right\}$ me message

'Mary gave me a message.' (Polish)

c. *Marysia* $\left\{\begin{array}{c} \text{\textit{wygłosiła}} \\ \text{\textit{*dała}} \end{array}\right\}$ *mowę.*

Mary $\left\{\begin{array}{c} \text{delivered} \\ \text{*gave} \end{array}\right\}$ speech

'Mary delivered/gave a speech.' (Polish)

Note that GIVE is extended to the giving of advice in Polish, as it is in English, but it is not similarly extended in the cases of giving messages or giving a speech. It appears that Polish GIVE requires the figurative RECIPIENT to be more integrated, as a participant, into the act than is required in the case of receiving messages or hearing a speech. Receiving messages or listening to a speech requires in a sense less involvement on the part of the figurative RECIPIENT than is the case with advising, where the person receiving advice is directly affected and is more clearly a beneficiary.

4.3. Emergence/manifestation of entities

Literal GIVE includes within its meaning the movement of a THING out of the GIVER's personal zone. The THING may be viewed, therefore, as emerging from out of some physical region, and it is this way of viewing the movement of the THING which motivates a large group of extensions involving emergence and manifestation of entities. Additionally, literal GIVE involves a further kind of emergence of the THING in the sense that there is an abstract motion of the THING out of a sphere of control of the GIVER and into the sphere of control of the RECIPIENT, as discussed in Section 2.3. In this more abstract sense, then, there is an emergence of the THING from the GIVER's sphere of control. Both these facets of the meaning of literal GIVE provide some motivation for the extensions of GIVE to emergence/manifestation. It might also be noted that in all the emergence/manifestation senses discussed below, there is some kind of motion involved, either concrete or abstract. Thus, one could also see these extensions as a subcategory of the extensions involving movement, discussed in Section 4.8.

4.3.1. Emergence

We begin with extensions relating to the emergence of one entity out of another. As used here, emergence will imply that there are two distinguishable entities involved in the process. Figure 28 is a highly schematic representation of this kind of extension. I have chosen to represent the control domain of the literal GIVE meaning in Figure 28, building upon the representation proposed for GIVE in Section 2.3. This representation includes a clear bounded region around the GIVER which is relevant to appreciating the extension to emergent senses. For the purposes of Figure 28, one could also think of the bounded region around the GIVER in Figure 28 more concretely as the physical space associated with the GIVER. In the emergent extensions of GIVE, there is a movement of some entity, the trajector, out of a bounded region which can be identified as some other entity, the landmark. A dotted circle is used in the representation of the schematic emergent sense to suggest some incipient form of the entity which eventually emerges. It is the movement out of a bounded region which is shared by literal GIVE and its emergent senses and this similarity is easily seen in Figure 28. In many of the emergent extensions, there is a causative component of meaning, in the sense that the trajector entity helps to make or cause the landmark entity to exist. This group of extensions, therefore, has much in common with the category of causative extensions dealt with in Section 4.4 (cf. also the discussion of causation and the making of new objects in Lakoff—Johnson 1980: 72–73).

Give milk, for example, may be used to refer to the production of milk by cows etc. In this case, the milk exists as such inside the animal and it passes from inside the body to outside the body. Other examples of emergence from animate beings are the expressions in (9).

(9)   a.   *tu   ta-ra*
           faeces   give-Purposive
           'defecate'   (Rumu, Papuan)

      b.   *dare una lacrima*
           give   a   tear
           'shed a tear'   (Italian)

      c.   *hōatu   rawa*
           give-away   anger
           'vent one's anger'   (Māori)

In the "give (away from speaker) anger" example in (9c), the words and actions which express the anger may be understood as the entity emerging from the person. This metaphor rests on the same kind of conceptualization of anger which underlies English expressions such as *an outburst of anger, she let out her anger, he exploded with anger, he couldn't contain his rage* etc. In all these expressions, the body is understood as a container for emotions, such as anger, and experiencing the emotion is understood as an entity coming out of the body. This idea has been explored in some depth in Kövecses (1986: 11–37, 1990: 50–68) and Lakoff (1987: 380–415). GIVE, which includes as part of its meaning the emergence of a THING from an abstract bounded region (the sphere of control of the GIVER), is highly appropriate as the source domain for conceptualizing the emission of emotions from the body. Although the schematic emergent sense, as diagrammed in Figure 28, does not require any human instigation, particular instantiations of the schema may involve humans as the trajectors, as in the examples in (9), and these humans may exert varying degress of control over the emergence of the landmark entities.

In Bulgarian, a prefix *iz-* appears with the GIVE stem in a set of expressions involving the emission of noise, as in (10).

(10) a.   *iz-davam   zvuk*
           out-give   noise
           'produce a noise'   (Bulgarian)

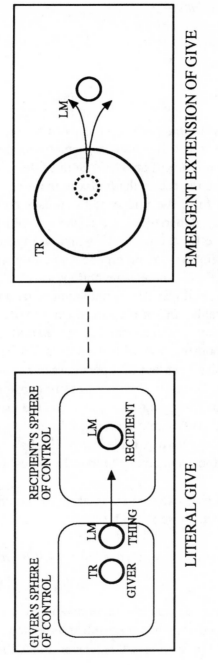

Figure 28. Extension of GIVE to (schematic) emergent sense

b. *iz-davam   ston*
    out-give   groan
    'to groan'   (Bulgarian)

c. *iz-davam   vik*
    out-give   cry
    'cry out'   (Bulgarian)

In its basic spatial sense the prefix *iz-* means "movement from the inside to the outside", but it also functions aspectually to express momentariness or a single occurrence of an event. Both of these senses appear relevant to appreciating the use of the prefix in these cases. The basic spatial sense helps to form the image of the noises emanating from the body, with the body understood as a container, while the momentary aspect is appropriate for these events, which are typically of short duration. While the notions of emergence and momentariness are attributable to the prefix *iz-*, these same notions are also closely associated with the semantics of GIVE. The combination of *iz-* and GIVE involves therefore a comfortable "fit" of meanings. Only verbal kinds of acts are expressed in this way in Bulgarian. So, for example, *davam* does not enter into similar construction with the words for "smile" or "shrug". The emission of noise from out of a person seems easily construed as a kind of emergence. Certainly it is more easily construed as emergence than, say, smiling or shrugging. Note, too, that the use of Bulgarian *iz-* in the examples in (10) is reminiscent of Lindner's (1981: 107–116) observations about the verb particle *out* in English, namely its use in constructions in which something hidden becomes accessible (in this case, perceptible).

English also has *give* expressions relating to the emission of noises from a person, such as those in (11).

(11)   *give a yell, give a scream, give a (little) laugh, give a call, give a shout*

Sometimes, these may be acts of communication and in such cases they may also be grouped together with the interpersonal communication extensions discussed in Section 4.2. However, I take the central meaning of most of these expressions to relate to the emission of a sound rather than actually communicating with someone. *Give a call*, of course, would always appear to involve some kind of communication.

Inanimate objects are also commonly understood as emitting certain properties. In English we tend to use *give off* in such expressions (*give off heat, give off a smell, give off light*), with the *off* emphasizing the separation of the property from its source. For the emission of smell, Bulgarian again reinforces the image of movement from out of a container by the use of the *iz-* prefix referred to above, as in (12a). It is possible, however, for the GIVE verb alone to carry this function in languages, as in the expressions in (12b)–(12d).

(12) a. *iz-davam mirizma*
          out-give   smell
          'to give (off) a smell'   (Bulgarian)

      b. *dare di luca*
          give the light
          'to give (off) light'   (Italian)

      c. *dare calore*
          give heat
          'to give (off) heat'   (Italian)

      d. *Słońce daje ciepło.*
          sun   gives warmth
          'The sun gives warmth.'   (Polish)

The emission of heat, sound etc. seems close to another type of extension, whereby GIVE is used to describe the appearance/impression which an object makes. In English, *give the appearance of* and *give an impression of* are examples of this, with an impression construed as something which comes from the object to a perceiver. In the Basque examples in (13), GIVE enters into a construction describing impressions.

(13) a. *Gazte ematen*   *du.*
          young give:IMPERF   AUX:3SGSUBJ:3SGOBJ
          'He seems young.'   (Basque)

b. *Arbola   horr-ek   urrutira   gizon-a   ematen*
   tree   that-ERG   afar   man-ABS   give:IMPERF
   du.
   AUX:3SGSUBJ:3SGOBJ
   'That tree looks like a man from a distance.' (Basque)

We have already had occasion to remark upon anger as an emotion which is construed as coming out of the body, in connection with the Māori expression *hōatu rawa* 'vent one's anger'. In (13), we are dealing not with emotions, but rather with characteristics of an animate or inanimate entity. As with emotion, however, properties of an entity may be visualized as residing in the entity and impressions on others are correspondingly understood as things which are emitted from the entity and proceed to the perceiver. Since this way of construing an impression involves an emergence of things (the properties of the entity making the impression), GIVE provides a suitable source domain for this image.

Brazilian Portuguese has an interesting GIVE construction conveying an impression, illustrated in (14).

(14)   *dar uma   de* $\begin{Bmatrix} boba \\ alegre \\ estudante \end{Bmatrix}$ *(em Z)*

       give a   of $\begin{Bmatrix} silly \\ merry \\ student \end{Bmatrix}$ (to Z)

       'to act $\begin{Bmatrix} silly \\ merry \\ like a student \end{Bmatrix}$ (to Z)'

                    (Brazilian Portuguese, Salomao 1990: 120)

The unusual feature of (14) is the use of a feminine article *uma* minus its head noun. Salomao (1990: 120) suggests that the noun *impressão* 'impression', or its slang counterpart *pintsa*, is missing from this construction, deleted, as it were, from its position after the article in the object phrase.

We might include here, too, the extension of GIVE to a marker of manner adverb. This is exemplified in (15).

(15) a.   *Khɲom rùət tÿu saːlaː-rìen   ʔaoy   rəhás.*
         I   run   go   school   give   quick
         'I run quickly to school.'   (Cambodian)
     b.   *Wîng   hây   réw.*
         run   give   quick
         'Run quickly!'   (Thai)

In these cases the quickness is a quality associated with the action carried out. I have no specific suggestion to make concerning the use of GIVE in (15), though I can see some parallels between the examples in (13) and (15). Recall that the impression a thing makes may be construed as something coming from the thing. Perhaps we should think of the manner of an action in a parallel way: a property, like quickness, associated with some action is understood as something produced, or generated, by the action? Understood in this way, GIVE is an appropriate source for carrying these senses because the literal meaning of GIVE is so strongly associated with the emergence of a THING from a bounded region, the sphere of control on the part of the GIVER. I do not offer these comments as a full explanation for the use of GIVE in (15), but I suggest they may be relevant.

A further subcategory of the emergence class of extensions relates to the creation of life. The notion of bearing fruit, for example, is something which may be expressed as the giving of fruit. This is possible in English, although a little marginal (*Our lemontree has been giving good fruit lately*). Italian and Basque examples are given in (16).

(16) a.   *Questo albero non   da   piu   frutti.*
         this   tree   NEG   gives   little   fruit
         'This tree no longer bears fruit.'   (Italian)

b.   *Zuhaitz hon-ek*   *ez*   *du*
     tree   this-ERG   NEG   AUX:3SGSUBJ:3SGOBJ
     fruiturik   *ematen.*
     fruit   give:IMPERF
     'This tree no longer bears fruit.'   (Basque)

In (16), the tree is understood as the GIVER and the fruit as the THING given. It is not only the specific living entity like "tree" which is construed as the source of a new living thing. "Land" is easily thought of in a similar way, being the repository of the nutrients and minerals which support crops growing in the ground. Hence, we find expressions such as those in (17).

(17) a.   *Questo terreno*   *da*   *ottimo*   *grano.*
     this   land   gives   very -good corn
     'This land produces very good corn.'   (Italian)

    b.   *Este*   *terreno da*   *un buen* *cultivo* *de* *maiz.*
     this   land   gives   a   good   crop   of   corn.
     'This land gives a good crop of corn.'   (Spanish)

    c.   *Zemja-ta tazi*   *godina*   *dade*   *dobra rekol-ta.*
     earth-the this   year   gave   good   crop-the
     'The land yielded a good crop this year.'   (Bulgarian)

Although the expressions in (16) and (17) do not involve any reference to a human participant, there nevertheless is a weak implication of such in the sense that the produce of the land is understood in these cases as being something for the benefit of the people of the country or the world. Possibly, this is relevant to why GIVE, which, in its prototypical manifestation, includes a human beneficiary in its base, is a preferred source for such metaphorical extensions.

    Human birth may also be conceptualized in terms of giving, as in (18).

(18) a.   *dare alla*   *luce*   *un bambino*
     give   to:the   light   a   child
     'to give birth to a child'   (Italian)

b. *Eman   nindu-zu-n   mundu-ra.*
    give   AUX-you:SUBJ-me:OBJ world-to
    'You brought me into the world.'   (Basque)

The examples in (18) differ from the preceding ones in that there is an overt figurative RECIPIENT: "light" in (18a), "world" in (18b). I take "light" to be metonymic for "world" here and both of these examples therefore incorporate an indirect reference to the world as a beneficiary of the act. In fact, one could think of both "light" and "world" here as metonymic for that part of the world which is the actual beneficiary, namely, the human race. Recall that, even in examples (16) and (17), it is arguably the case that there is some weakly implied beneficiary in the larger semantic frame. In other words, I believe there is a sense in which the world, more particularly the human race, is a kind of beneficiary in all of (16)-(18) and GIVE, with its implied beneficiary, lends itself easily to such extensions.

A closely related extension of GIVE describes biological growth, rather than reproduction. This sense is conveyed through a reflexive GIVE construction in Spanish, illustrated in (19).

(19)   *El   cultivo se   da   bien   este   año.*
          the   crop   REFL   gives   well   this   year
          'The crop is coming on well this year.'   (Spanish)

Growth may be thought of as emergence of a more mature living thing out of a more "primitive" version of itself — a seed or some less mature version of itself. Although different kinds of processes are at work in the change from seed to plant and younger plant to older plant, in both cases a new state of growth is arrived at through some kind of emergence. Since the crop in (19) may be thought of as growing more or less by itself, there is no obvious AGENT-PATIENT assymetry evident in the scene. A reflexive form of GIVE, in which there are no distinct AGENT and PATIENT entities, is therefore highly suitable for the expression of emergence involving a trajector producing some new form of itself.

The making of extra money out of already existing money in the form of profit, interest etc. has parallels to biological reproduction. So, for example, money may be deposited in a bank similar to the way in which seed may be sown in the ground; by leaving money in the bank, more money is earned through interest, just as a seed grows into a plant; eventually the money plus interest may be withdrawn in order to pay for some desirable object or experience, just as eventually a crop is harvested and eaten. These parallels support a mapping between the domains of agriculture and finance, which manifests itself in English expressions such as *investment growth, maturing of an investment* etc. Just as GIVE may be extended to some types of biological creation, so also it is extended to the earning of interest from an investment or the making of financial profit, as in (20).

(20) a. *Queste obbligazioni danno il 6%.*
          these   bonds   give   ART 6%
          'These bonds yield 6%.'   (Italian)

      b. *dare guadagni*
          give   profit
          'yield profit'   (Italian)

      c. *dać procent*
          give   interest
          'bear interest'   (Polish)

      d. *dać zysk*
          give   profit
          'yield profit'   (Polish)

Figure 29 represents a number of these specific emergent senses, as discussed above. Although by no means covering all the emergent senses which are attested cross-linguistically, it is helpful to see in one diagram some of the diversity which does exist. In this diagram, specific uses of GIVE verbs relating to the sense of emergence are shown as instantiations of a more schematic meaning of emergence. In the schematic meaning, there is an entity construed as the trajector (TR), corresponding to the clausal subject, and a distinct entity construed as the landmark (LM), corresponding to a clausal object. The trajector in these

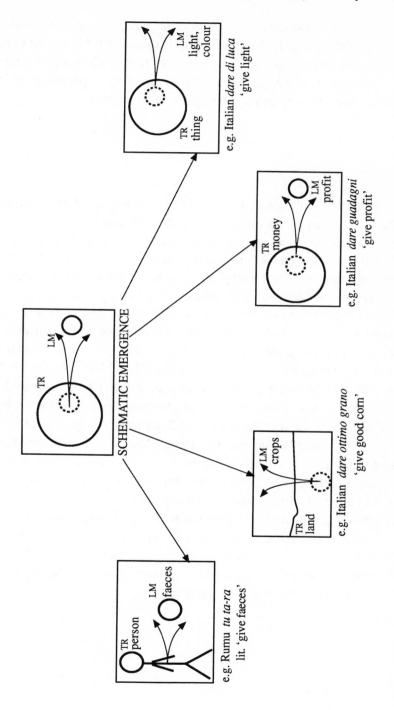

Figure 29. Examples of emergent senses based on GIVE

representations is the entity understood as being the cause of, and the entity responsible for, the landmark. The landmark entity in each case is understood as arising out of a container-like entity. The dashed circular outline is meant to suggest the real or imaginary presence of the landmark entity inside the trajector, prior to its emergence.

4.3.2. *Manifestation*

In the examples in the preceding section GIVE was used to conceptualize the emergence of an entity from some other conceptually distinct entity. This section focuses on a closely related concept, that of an entity manifesting itself or presenting itself. The manifestation of an entity is like the emergence of one entity from some source where the source is not evident or is backgrounded. Figure 30 represents this class of extensions. I have tried to convey the idea of manifestation of a thing by highlighting only a thing in the representation of the manifestation sense. An imaginary observer "sees" only the one thing, bearing in mind that the observer may only be "seeing" this thing in his/her imagination. The highlighted thing is shown as coming from some vague source, represented by the dashed lines forming some bounded region. Essentially, then, the manifestation of a thing involves the appearance of that one thing to an observer. The thing "comes" to an observer, but without coming from any clear source. As in the case of emergence, so also with manifestation, GIVE verbs are extended figuratively to express this concept. Since there is nothing corresponding to an agent in the notion of manifestation, GIVE verbs used to convey this sense tend to be used in constructions which lack the typical agent-patient contrast. The construction types favoured to convey the notion of manifestation of an entity are reflexive, impersonal, passive, and intransitive, and we shall look at examples of each of these in turn.

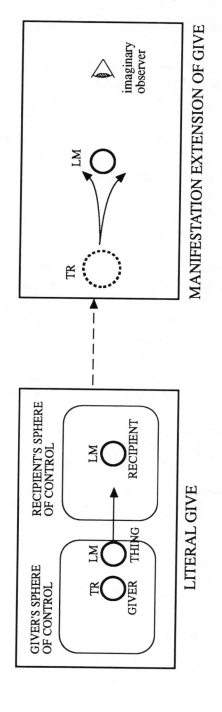

Figure 30. Extension of GIVE to (schematic) manifestation sense

4.3.2.1.   Reflexive GIVE

Literal GIVE provides the basic motivation for images of emergence of one entity from another. When emergent GIVE is constructed as a reflexive, then the sense of emergence out of a separate entity is transformed into some process involving just one entity in the real world. Example (19) above was an instance of this, where the resultant sense described the successful growth of crops. GIVE in a reflexive construction also provides a way of construing the manifestation of an entity as a kind of emergence of an entity out of itself. Manifestation is like a perceiver or cognizer seeing only an emerging entity appearing in a field of vision or cognizance, with the source of that entity indistinguishable from the entity itself.

A reflexive GIVE is found in "presentative" constructions, where it is typically a scene, situation, or event which presents itself. This construction is illustrated in (21). (21a)–(21e) describe manifestation of an event, either as reality or possibility. (English and French each have a similar construction based on a more marked donatory verb, namely *presents itself/se présentait*.) The Icelandic example (21f) combines reflexive GIVE with a dative of an experiencer giving rise to the meaning that something presents itself to the experiencer in the mind of the experiencer.

(21) a.   *Si   se   da   el   caso, ...*
           if   REFL   gives   the   event
           'If the circumstance should arise, ...'   (Spanish)

      b.   *Se   si   darà   l'occasione, ...*
           if   REFL   gives   the occasion
           'If the occasion presents itself, ...'   (Italian)

      c.   *Es   be-gab   sich,   dass ...*
           it   PRE-gave   REFL,   that
           'It happened that ...'   (German)

      d.   *Ako   ti   se   u-dade   văzmozhnost, ...*
           if   you   REFL   around-gave   opportunity
           'If an opportunity presented itself, ...'   (Bulgarian)

    e.   *Jeśli   się   da ...*
         if   REFL gives
         'If it is possible, ...'   (Polish)

    f.   *Gef-sk   mér   svá.*
         give-REFL me:DAT so
         'It seems so to me.'   (Icelandic)

Entities which have an inherent and verb-like complexity to them like "situation" lend themselves particularly well to this reflexive GIVE construction, as opposed to relatively simple thing-like entities such as "book" or "tree". "Situation" is low in terms of Givón's time-stability scale (cf. Givón 1984a: 51–52) and this may be a relevant factor. Temporally more permanent entities like "book" or "tree" may not be as easily construed as coming into existence as less stable entities like "situation". Or it may be that a certain threshold of internal complexity in the scene is required for such a construction. The idea of emergence of an entity out of another, which is assumed here to be the relevant aspect of GIVE underlying the uses of GIVE in (21), is a dynamic concept and this would be consistent with the reflexive construction also involving a relatively dynamic situation.

There are uses of reflexive GIVE in a number of Germanic languages which, in combination with an adverb "still", have to do with a situation presenting itself with an implication that the situation will evolve appropriately or improve, as in (22). The manifestation in these cases is seen as a positive, favourable occurrence.

(22) a.   *Det gir   seg   nok.*
          that gives REFL still
          'It will be all right.'   (Norwegian)

      b.   *Det ger   sig   nog   med tiden.*
          that gives REFL still with time
          'That will come round (all right) in the course of time.'
                                          (Swedish)

      c.   *Det giver sig   nok.*
          that gives REFL still
          'It will be all right.'   (Danish)

     d.   *Es   wird   sich   schon   geben.*
          it   will   REFL   already   give
          'It will follow/happen in due course.'   (German)

Another reflexive use of GIVE which seems relevant here is that illustrated in (23).

(23) a.   *Sie   gab   sich   ganz   natürlich.*
           she   gave   REFL quite   natural
           'She gave an impression of being quite natural.' (German)
      b.   *To such of those as spoke to me, I gave myself out as a Hindoo-Boodhist, from a distant province, bound on a pilgrimage.* (Wilkie Collins, The Moonstone, First published 1868. In 1966 edition p. 524.)

Here, the subject of the reflexive GIVE is a person who presents him/herself in a particular way. This use might also be called, appropriately, presentative, though here it is an individual presenting him/herself rather than an event or situation as discussed above. With a person functioning as the subject, it is more possible to view the person as agent-like than when the subject is an event or situation. This would certainly be the right interpretation for (23b), for example, which occurs in a context where the subject referent was quite consciously trying to create a particular impression.

4.3.2.2.   Impersonal GIVE

There exist impersonal constructions involving a two-place GIVE predicate. The impersonal GIVE constructions discussed in this section carry an existential meaning, with the thing referred to by the object phrase understood as the thing whose existence is described. A subject phrase may be represented by an "it" pronoun which does not refer to any specific entity in the scene or event being described, as in German, or it may be lacking altogether, as in Brazilian Portuguese and Jacaltec.

Either way, the impersonal construction with GIVE describes the presence or manifestation of some entity.

In German we find an impersonal *es gibt* construction, literally "it gives", which translates as "there is, there are ...":

(24) a.   *Es   gibt   viele   Kinder   in   den   Schulen.*
          it   gives   many   children:ACC   in   the   schools:DAT
          'There are many children in the schools.'   (German)
    b.   *Es   gibt   einen   Gott.*
          it   gives   one   God:ACC
          'There is one God.'   (German)

The "presented" phrase occurs in the accusative case, characteristic of direct objects in German. It contrasts with another construction in German with *es ist/sind*, which may also be translated as "there is, there are". Syntactically, the *es gibt* and *es ist/sind* constructions are quite different. For one thing, the *es* in *es ist/sind* only appears when there is no other constituent in clause initial position, unlike in the *es gibt* construction, where the *es* never deletes. Also, the verb "to be" in the *es ist/sind* construction agrees in number with the presented phrase which appears in the subject case of nominative, as in the examples in (25), taken from Hammer (1971: 221). This is quite different from the agreement pattern in the *es gibt* construction, where the verb is invariably in the 3rd Singular form, as is appropriate for an "it" subject. Thus, the noun phrase occurring in the *es ist/sind* construction has some subject-like properties while the noun phrase occurring in the *es gibt* construction is clearly a direct object.

(25) a.   *Auf   dem   Kaminsims   ist   eine Uhr.*
          on   the   mantelpiece   is   a   clock
          'On the mantelpiece there is a clock.'   (German)
    b.   *Es   ist   ein   Brief für Sie   da.*
          it   is   a   letter for you   there
          'There is a letter for you there.'   (German)

As far as the semantics of the two constructions are concerned, it is possible to make some distinctions between the two constructions. The distinction is not particularly easy to make and indeed there are occasions where either one is possible, as in the (26a)–(26b) and (27a)–(27b) pairs. These examples are taken from Hammer (1971: 220, 221).

(26) a. *Warum sollte ein Unterschied sein, zwischen einem weißen und einem schwarzen Mann?*

b. *Warum sollte es einen Unterschied geben, zwischen einem weißen und einem schwarzen Mann?*
'Why should there be a difference between a white man and a black man?'   (German)

(27) a. *Es war in diesem Winter wenig Schnee.*

b. *Es hat in diesem Winter wenig Schnee gegeben.*
'There was not much snow this winter.'   (German)

Despite some interchangeability between the two constructions, there are different nuances to the meanings involved. Hammer (1971: 219–222) succinctly summarizes these distinctions, the main ones being those in (28)–(29).

(28) *Es gibt* is used
    (a) to denote existence as such, without reference to a particular place;
    (b) to denote existence in a large area.

(29) *Es ist/sind* is used
    (a) to denote permanent or temporary presence in a definite and limited place;
    (b) to denote temporary presence in a large area.

Essentially, then, *es gibt* has to do with the existence of an entity, while *es ist/sind* has to do with the presence of some entity. The difference is nicely illustrated by the contrast between *Es gibt einen Gott* 'There is a/one God', where one is talking about the existence of God, and *Es ist jemand an der Tür* 'There is someone at the door', where one is talking about the presence of someone at a certain place. Also, when one is describing a picture, then one uses *es ist/sind*: *Im Hintergrund ist ein Wald* 'In the background there is a forest'. This is consistent with Hammer's characterization of *es ist/sind* as involving the description of something present somewhere, rather than the assertion of existence as such. There are ways in which the two concepts, existence and presence, imply each other: if something exists, one expects it to be present somewhere and if something is present somewhere, then it also exists. They are interrelated and it is not surprising that they are interchangeable in some situations.

There is no semantic component here of any physical emergence of an entity from out of another. It is possible, however, to approach an understanding of the construction as an abstract kind of emergence. Some grammar books of German in fact explain the construction as a figurative kind of giving:

> The origin and explanation of this phrase, "it gives" is: Nature (or Providence) gives (provides, produces). This is a clue to the uses of *es gibt*, e.g. *Es hat letztes Jahr eine gute Ernte gegeben* 'There was a good harvest last year'. (Hammer 1971: 221)

As shown by his choice of the "harvest" example, Hammer sees the occurrence of GIVE with such phrases as a conceptual link between the emergent GIVE sense and the presentative construction. With the harvest example, it may be possible to construe the subject *es* as "nature" or "providence" as suggested by Hammer. With the other example sentences cited above, however, this is not possible. Instead, one might think of the *es* in these cases as meaning the whole setting of the scene being described. English *it,* German *es* etc. may be thought of as having an "abstract setting" meaning, and this approach has been explored in the Cognitive Grammar framework (Smith 1985, Langacker 1991: 352–353, 365–367). In this view the presented thing may be thought of as being put into relief, or "thrown up" by the scene.

One may therefore think of *es gibt* as putting some entity on an imaginary stage for contemplation or comment. In so doing, attention is focused on that thing itself, rather than, say, its location somewhere. The effect is similar to what is achieved by the reflexive use of GIVE discussed in Section 4.3.2.1. The uses are similar in that neither of them postulates any other obvious entity as an energy source from which any emergence takes place. In the case of the reflexive, the entity itself is seen as its own energy source, while in the case of the impersonal it is the whole setting which may be thought of in these terms.

My explanation of the image underlying the *es gibt* construction may help in understanding why it should come to have the particular meanings it does have, as summarized above by Hammer. If *es* is to denote the whole setting of the scene, then it is natural for this type of *es* to be associated with the meanings spelled out for *es gibt* ("existence as such, without reference to a particular place" and "existence in a large area") rather than the more localized meanings of *es ist/sind* which include "presence in a definite and limited place".

Brazilian Portuguese uses an impersonal GIVE construction also in the sense of describing the manifestation of a thing, as illustrated in (30).

(30) a. *Deu   chuva   o   fim de semana   ineiro.*
          gave:3SG rain   the   weekend   entire
          'It rained throughout the weekend.'
                              (Brazilian Portuguese, Salomao 1990: 24)

      b. *Deu   meio-dia.*
          gave:3SG   midday
          'It's 12.00.'   (Brazilian Portuguese, Salomao 1990: 24)

      c. *Deu   um barulho na   televisão.*
          gave:3SG a   noise   in:the television set
          'There was a strange noise in the television set.'
                              (Brazilian Portuguese, Salomao 1990: 24)

      d. *Deu   praga   na   goiabeira.*
          gave:3SG   plague   in:the guava-tree
          'There is a plague in the guava-tree.'
                              (Brazilian Portuguese, Salomao 1990: 24)

Craig (1976: 109–110) mentions an impersonal, transitive use of Jacaltec *a'(a')* GIVE, illustrated in (31), which is used in construction

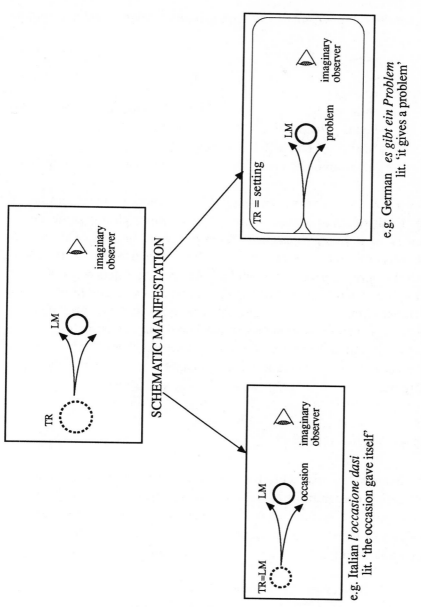

Figure 31. Examples of manifestation senses based on GIVE

with weather expressions to describe the existence of weather conditions.

(31)　a.　*Ch-a'*　　*cake.*
　　　　　ASP-give　wind
　　　　　'It is windy.'　　　　　　　　　　　(Jacaltec, Craig 1976: 109)

　　　b.　*Laŋan*　*Ø-y-a'-ni*　　　　　*ha'*　*nab.*
　　　　　ASP　　3ABS-3ERG-give-SUF　CL　rain
　　　　　'It is raining.'　　　　　　　　　　(Jacaltec, Craig 1976: 109)

The impersonal and reflexive GIVE constructions have similar effects. Each of them achieves the effect of highlighting some entity, which is, as it were, "presented" to an observer. In each of these constructions, the entity is presented without any obvious source from which the entity derives. In Figure 31, I have suggested ways of representing these two constructions which capture these facts. In the reflexive construction the entity highlighted is construed as simultaneously trajector and landmark, whereas in the impersonal construction the trajector is viewed as being the whole of the setting. They are both instantiations of the more schematic sense of manifestation shown at the top of the figure.

4.3.2.3.　Passive GIVE

A passive construction with the agent unspecified achieves the effect of highlighting one entity in a scene or event. A passive of GIVE may be used to express a manifestation sense. Scandinavian languages use a passive form of GIVE with an unspecified agent as a kind of presentative, comparable to the *es gibt* construction of German:

(32)　a.　*Det*　*gi-s*　　　　*løsning*　*på*　*problem-et.*
　　　　　it　　gives-PASS　solution　to　problem-the
　　　　　'There is a solution to the problem.'　　　　(Norwegian)

b. *Det gi-s karakterene "Bestått" og "Ikke bestått".*
   it gives-PASS the grades "Pass" and "Fail"
   'The grades are "Pass" and "Fail".'　　　　　(Norwegian)

c. *Det give-s lösning.*
   that gives-PASS solution
   'There is a solution.'　　　　　　　　　　　(Swedish)

d. *Der give-s börn som ...*
   there give-PASS children who
   'There are children who ...'　　　　　　　　(Danish)

The construction is reported as sounding sometimes formal or even archaic, but nevertheless is possible. Once again, there is no observable,
delineated energy source involved in this use of GIVE. An analysis
similar to what was done for *es gibt* suggests itself here, that is, the
whole setting presents a THING for viewing. The indiscernible nature
of the energy source means that the passive form is a particularly appropriate one as a way of presenting the THING.

In Polish, a passive GIVE with unspecified agent may be used in a
presentative kind of structure in which it is an event which presents itself to an experiencer, tantamount to the experiencer having the opportunity to carry out some act. Thus, in (33), the opportunity to meet the
Pope is construed as an event given to the experiencer.

(33)　　*Dane mi było spotkać Papieża.*
　　　　given me was meet Pope
　　　　'I had an opportunity to meet the Pope.'　　(Polish)

A passive past participle of GIVE occurs with a similar meaning in expressions such as *Given that the Government has withdrawn the funds,
...* or *dato che ...* (Italian) 'given that ...'. Here, *given* and *dato* serve to
present a fact or situation. Or, in Danish:

(34)　　*Det er givet at han kommer.*
　　　　that is given that he comes
　　　　'It is certain that he will come.'　　　　　(Danish)

4.3.2.4. Intransitive GIVE

We have seen how reflexive, impersonal, and passive constructions based on GIVE may be utilized to help achieve the semantic effect of the manifestation of a single entity. A final construction to consider here is intransitive GIVE, since an intransitive also highlights just one entity and, indeed, the intransitive use of *give* in the colloquial expression *What gives?* 'What's up/what's been happening?' would seem to fall into the category of manifestation. It asks about events which have happened or are about to happen. *Give* is intransitive in this construction and the interrogative *what*, referring to some event, is the subject. In thinking about the extension in the meaning of GIVE in this case, one might ask whether the subject *what* should be understood as a metaphorical GIVER or a metaphorical THING passed. Semantically, *what* seems to function more like a metaphorical THING, even though it functions grammatically as the subject. *Give* functions, in other words, like a "middle" voice: passive in meaning, active in form. The *what gives* construction should not be confused with the superficially similar German construction in (35).

(35)   *Was gibt's?*
          what gives:it
          'What's up/what's the matter?'   (German)

(35) is an inverted *es gibt* construction, with the object *was* fronted to initial position. In other words, (35) is a transitive clause in the active voice and the subject is "abstract setting" *es* in its contracted form, not the entity being presented.

4.3.3. GIVE as "become"

In some German dialects, a development of GIVE to mean "become" has occurred. In particular, in the Hessen, Trier, and Luxembourg ("westmitteldeutsch") dialects, GIVE has come to be used with a similar

range of meanings as we find with *werden* in standard German. Ex—
amples of GIVE meaning "become" are given in (36).

(36) a. *Wöttu   en   billhauer   gäwen?*
       want:you a   stone-mason   give
       'Do you want to become a stone-mason?'
       (19th century Hessen dialect, DWB, Vol.4 [1984]: 107)

    b. *Morje   gőste   braud.*
       tomorrow give:you bride
       'Tomorrow you will be/become a bride.'
       (19th century Trier dialect, DWB, Vol.4 [1984]: 107)

    c. *Ich   geb   'n Soldat.*
       I   give   a   soldier:ACC
       'I'm going to be a soldier.'   (Frankfurt dialect in 1900,
       Frankfurter Wörterbuch 1971: 809)

    d. *E   gët   pensionnéiert.*
       he   gives pensioned
       'He's going to be pensioned off.'
           (Luxembourg dialect, Schanen 1987: 38)

    e. *E   gët   bekannt.*
       he   gives well-known
       'He is becoming well-known.'
           (Luxembourg dialect, Schanen 1987: 38)

A way to understand this extension is to see it as a variation of the
emergence field of extensions. In particular, it seems close to the extensions discussed above associated with biological change, where GIVE is
used to conceptualize processes such as the reproduction and growth of
living things. In those cases we are dealing with an organic evolution of
one thing out of another. In the examples in (36), we are dealing with a
change in the state of a person which is not determined organically, but
rather by other factors. In other words, "becoming" may be construed
as a type of emergence of a new form of a thing, but not restricted to
organic growth.

There are other ways to understand the extension of GIVE to
"become", besides, or in addition to, relating it to the biological growth

metaphor. Both concrete and abstract types of motion are part of the meaning of GIVE (as described in Chapter 2) and these components of the meaning of literal GIVE relate in natural ways to the concept of "become". Most obviously, the movement of the THING in the spatio-temporal domain of GIVE might be seen as a source for the more abstract motion implied by the "become" sense. The abstract movement from one sphere of control to another sphere of control which is also present in the sense of literal GIVE provides another source for the abstract motion of going from one state to another. A reliance on concepts to do with motion as a way of conceptualizing change is widespread in languages. *Become* itself is an example of this, based as it is on the verb *come* (cf. also *it came to pass that...*). *Go* also has extensions to "become" in constructions such as *go crazy, the milk went bad* etc. Thus, the extension of GIVE to "become" may be understood as GIVE extended in its use to (abstract) motion from one state to another, comparable to other extensions of GIVE to movement expressions, as dealt with in Section 4.8. [4]

Brazilian Portuguese has a similar extension of GIVE to "become, change into" illustrated in (37).

(37) a. *Ele deu   em   linguista.*
       he gave:3SG in   linguist
       'He became a linguist, after all.'
                      (Brazilian Portuguese, Salomao 1990: 270)

   b. *Ele dá   prá   linguista.*
       he give:3SG for   linguist
       'He may become a linguist.'
                      (Brazilian Portuguese, Salomao 1990: 270)

   c. *Esse namoro   ainda vai   dar   em casamento.*
       this courtship still goes give:INF in marriage
       'This courtship will lead to marriage.'
                      (Brazilian Portuguese, Salomao 1990: 92)

As Salomao (1990: 98, 270) points out, there is an interesting difference in the extension of GIVE to mean actual change of state in construction with *em*, and an extension to possible change of state in construction with *prá* (cf. (37a) and (37b) above).

4.4. Causative/purposive

The meaning of literal GIVE has some connections, semantically, with two important notions in the study of language and logic: causation and enablement. These two notions have in common the idea that some entity/event A is a significant contributing factor towards some later event B (where "event" is understood in broad terms, referring to action, process, or state). Literal GIVE may also be understood in these terms, i.e. the GIVER (and the action associated with the GIVER) is a significant contributing factor to the RECIPIENT coming into control of the THING given. In very general terms, then, there is a schematic meaning which unites causation and enablement on the one hand, and both of these concepts and literal GIVE on the other hand.

Causation and enablement are clearly distinguishable: A causes B when A is identified as the sole or most salient factor contributing towards B; A enables B when A creates the possibility for B, with other factors also contributing to making B a reality. Put another way: A causes B when A makes B necessary; A enables B when A makes B possible. But they may also be construed as variations of each other. Causation could be construed as a stronger kind of enabling (enabling plus the realization of an event), or enabling could be construed as weak causation (causation without the actual realization of the event). While acknowledging some semantic overlap between these two notions, I nevertheless find it convenient to deal with the two notions in separate sections, i.e. Section 4.4 (the causation types of extensions) and Section 4.5 (the enablement types of extensions).

Causation has attracted considerable interest in the philosophical and linguistic literature. Of particular interest in the context of cognitive linguistics are works such as Shibatani (1976), Lakoff (1977), Eilfort et al (1985) (particularly the papers by Talmy in the preceding collections, namely Talmy 1976, 1985b) and Kemmer—Verhagen (1994). Clearly, causation is a complex notion which can be understood in many different ways. The examples in (38) illustrate some of these alternative notions of causation, though many more subtypes could be added:

(38)   a.   Event X causes event Y.
      b.   Person A causes event Y.
      c.   Person A causes some entity B (animate or inanimate) to change.
      d.   Person A causes person B to do Y.

Arguably, all three types are reducible to (38a), i.e. there is always some event A which is causally connected to another event, where "event" is understood broadly as action, process, or state. This is the position taken by Talmy (1976: 52): "The basic causative situation ... consists of a simple event ..., that which immediately causes the event, and the causal relation between the two".[5] While I agree that causation can be construed in this way, I do not believe it is the notion of causation which reflects ordinary human conceptualization of causation. Rather, I believe, following Lakoff (1977, 1987: 54–55), that causation is more appropriately characterized in terms of a human agent acting on a patient, along with the other properties detailed by Lakoff (cf. also Kemmer—Verhagen 1994: 118–119). This kind of characterization seems to accord better with the more basic linguistic structures which typify causative constructions in languages. It is not necessary that any particular notion of causation be singled out in considering extensions of GIVE to causative senses. Nevertheless, it should be noted that properties of literal GIVE are more consistent with certain types of causation. In particular, the fact that literal GIVE is an interpersonal act makes it more readily relatable to the interpersonal kind of causation, i.e. person A causes person B to do Y (38d above).

The idea of causation is often ascribed to the meaning of literal GIVE. Thus, the GIVER is said to be the entity which "causes" it that the RECIPIENT comes to have the THING. It should be noted that characterizing the GIVER as a causer is a way we may choose to conceptualize the GIVER, based on similarities between the GIVER and a prototypical causer. It is not something "given" in any objective reality. In the whole semantic frame of giving, there are various entities, events, and forces which contribute to a successful giving act. We may impose a causative structure on the scene by taking one of these entities, the GIVER, as a causer (and another entity, the RECIPIENT, as a causee). Indeed this conceptualization of GIVE is directly reflected in the morphological structure of GIVE in Ainu (Shibatani 1990: 48), where GIVE is formally a causative of a verb of possession (*kor-e* 'have-causative'). However "natural" it might be to construe the GIVER as a causer, it needs to be emphasized that this view of GIVE reflects our conceptualization of the act and should not be thought of as something present in the objective reality of the giving act.

4.4.1. GIVE as "have someone do something"

One extension found with GIVE involves the manipulation of another person in order to have that person do something, a sense which we may render in English as *have someone do something, get someone to do something, arrange for someone to do something*. This is what may be called the "manipulative" meaning. It is a meaning which is carried by GIVE in a number of languages:

(39) a. *antaa jonkun   korjata   jokin*
          give   person:GEN repair:INF   thing
          'to have a person repair something'   (Finnish)

      b. *Dajcie   to   stolarzowi   do naprawy.*
          give:2PL:IMP this   joiner:DAT   to repair:GEN
          'Have the joiner repair this.'   (Polish)

      c. *Mêe' hây lûuk pay phûut kàp fáráng.*
          mother give child go   speak with Westerner
          'Mother had her child go and speak with the Westerner.'
                                           (Thai)

      d. *Khɲom   ʔaoy ʔoːpùk tèɲ siəuphr̆u.*
          I   give father buy book
          'I had my father buy the book(s).'   (Cambodian)

In the examples in (39) there is not only a mapping from the GIVER onto the human causer, but also from the RECIPIENT onto a human causee. GIVER and human causer have in common that a person is involved and that person is a volitional human agent, instigating an action. RECIPIENT and human causee have in common that a person is experiencing some change in their behaviour due to the actions of another person. One might also see a parallel to the THING by construing the responsibility for the act as an entity passed over to the causee. Understood in this way, all three of the salient entities in the GIVE frame correspond to entities in the manipulation frame.

Note that some caution is required when classifying verbs as causatives. Sometimes, a causative-like morpheme may in fact be better classified as meaning "manipulation of a person", rather than a full-blown causative. Consider, for example, the Mandarin GIVE verb *gěi*. This verb has a well-established enablement sense as illustrated in (40a-c). The meaning extends also to some types of manipulation of persons, in the sense of having them do, act, or experience something against their will, as in (40d). But we do not find an extension to "pure" causatives, as shown in (40e-g).

(40) a. *Gěi   wǒ   bào-bao   háizi.*
          give me   hug   child.
          'Let me hug the child.'   (Mandarin)

      b. *Tā   zuó-tian   gěi   bu   gěi   nǐ   kàn diàn-yǐng?*
          he/she yesterday give not give you see movie
          'Did he/she let you see the movie yesterday?' (Mandarin)

      c. *Tā   gěi   hái-zi shuì-jiao.*
          he/she give child sleep
          'He/she let the child sleep.'   (Mandarin)

      d. *Tā   gěi   wǒ   shòu-zuì.*
          he/she give me   suffer
          'He/she made me suffer.'   (Mandarin)

      e. * *Tā   gěi   zhǐ   shāo   qi-lai.*
          he/she give paper burn   ASP
          'He/she made the paper burn.'   (Mandarin)

f. * *Tā   gěi   shū   diào   xià-qü.*
    he/she give   book   fall   down
    'He/she caused the book to fall.'   (Mandarin)

g. * *Tā   gěi   yǔ   xià.*
    he/she give   rain   down
    'He/she caused it to rain.'   (Mandarin)

As long as there is some kind of interpersonal manipulation (enticing, coercing, permitting, enabling etc.), *gěi* can be used, but it can not be used in the sense of causing an event to happen where there is no element of interpersonal manipulation. Thus, *gěi* is not appropriate to describe someone causing rain to fall down, or a book to drop.

4.4.2. GIVE as "cause"

Where the construction involves a causee (not restricted to humans or animates) which is made to exist or act in a new way, then the sense becomes more like a true causative, as opposed to a "manipulative". The Jacaltec GIVE verb *a'a'* (*a'a* or *a'* in certain contexts), as used in (41), might be considered an example of this.

(41) a. *Ch-ach   w-a'   xewoj.*
         ASP-2ABS   1ERG-give   to rest
         'I make you rest.'   (Jacaltec, Craig 1977: 362)

     b. *Tz'ayic x-'a'a-ni   tajoj   xil kape.*
         sun   ASP-give-SUF   to dry   clothes
         'The sun made the clothes dry.' (Jacaltec, Craig 1977: 376)

     c. *Cake   x-'a'a-ni-ayoj   ixim   awal.*
         wind   ASP-give-SUF-fall   CL   cornfield
         'The wind made the corn fall down.'

                                    (Jacaltec, Craig 1977: 377)

The causative construction in the first of these sentences has some different properties to the causative construction in the other two sentences and these differences are discussed in some detail by Craig. One major difference between (41a) and (41b–c) is the marking on the verb. In (41a), there is an ergative affix cross-referencing the causer, whereas this kind of affix is lacking in (41b–c). Semantically, there is a difference as to whether the causer is seen as a "direct agent" acting on the causee (41a), or as a kind of "indirect agent" where the causation involved may be less intentional, less immediate etc., as in (41b) and (41c).

The more general causative use relates to causing an event or thing, without any interpersonal manipulation entering into it. Many English *give* expressions relating to bodily acts may be thought of in this way: *give a yell, give a scream, give a call, give a shout, give a sigh, give a smile, give a shrug.* These expressions describe acts which people do involving parts of their bodies, even if the body parts themselves (tongue, shoulders etc.) are not named. The objects of *give* in these cases also exist as verbs in their own right and may be analyzed as deverbals (see also the discussion of such expressions in the section on schematic interaction, Section 4.6). In these expressions the base verb has been converted into a thing-like nominal. Note, however, that not all such deverbals are able to occur in this frame. *To give a sneeze* seems hardly possible as an alternative to the verb *sneeze* in its literal sense. Nor is it possible to say **give a little sneeze*, by analogy with *give a little cough* (in a literal sense or to indicate, say, a certain disapproval of a point being made by a speaker). Nor can one say **give a fall,* or **give a tremble*. This construction appears most felicitously with actions which can be controlled (yelling, screaming, shouting, shrugging etc.), as opposed to purely involuntary, reflex actions (trembling, falling down etc.). I take this to be a reflection of part of the core meaning of literal GIVE which involves a volitional, controlled act. Some of these phrases may nevertheless be used for relatively uncontrolled actions. The phrase *give a yell*, for example, could be used to describe a kind of reflex reaction to sudden pain inflicted. What seems important, however, is that these actions can also be instigated at will by a person. This would seem to be the necessary condition for the existence of the *give* phrase. There are other ways, too, in which these expressions display some of the literal sense of GIVE. For one thing, they refer to acts which are typically short in duration, i.e. perfective in nature, like the act of giving itself.

(Compare also the extension of GIVE predicates to perfective aspect markers in Section 4.9). Note that one might say *She gave a little cough* to describe one single cough, but one would not say **She was up all night giving coughs/a cough*. Furthermore, expressions like *give a cough/smile/laugh* contain within them the idea of an initiation or insti-gation of the act. Such expressions are not easily embedded within causative contexts where there is an explicit external cause of the action. Thus, it is not nearly as natural to say *Tickling her feet makes her give a smile* as it is to say *Tickling her feet makes her smile*. Most of these properties are relevant to the use of *give* in schematic interaction ex-tensions, discussed in Section 4.6.

One may include here also the Kunwinjku (Australian, Western Arnhem Land) examples in (42). Literal GIVE in Kunwinjku has the form *wo*, to which may be attached person and tense affixes. In addition, *wo* occurs as a verbalizing suffix with causative meaning. As a suffix, it may attach to an adjective, or a noun + adjective, to derive what Oates (1964: 60–61) calls a "compound verb root". In these examples, the adjective or noun in construction with *wo* is a thing or state which is created. (42a) illustrates literal GIVE in Kunwinjku, while (42b–e) illustrate the causative usage.

(42) a. *Galug bi-wo-ŋ   may?.*
      then   him-give-PAST   animals
      'Then he gave him animals.'[6]
                                  (Kunwinjku, Oates 1964: 91)

    b. *bele-wo*
       clear-give
       'make clean'   (Kunwinjku, Oates 1964: 61)

    c. *ware-wo*
       bad/mistake-give
       'make a mistake'   (Kunwinjku, Oates 1964: 61)

    d. *yag-wo*
       done-give
       'to finish'   (Kunwinjku, Oates 1964: 61)

e. *gug-buyiga-wo*
    body-another-give
    'to cause to change'   (Kunwinjku, Oates 1964: 61)

Further suggestive examples relating to a causative use of GIVE in other Australian languages may be found in Capell (1979: 255, 257, 272). Unfortunately, the number of examples given by Capell is too limited to draw firm conclusions about the full extent of this use of GIVE in the languages concerned.

One may note, too, the polysemy involving the GIVE and causative senses of the suffixal morpheme *-tia* in (Orizaba) Nahuatl, as described in Tuggy (to appear). The morpheme *-tia* may occur suffixed to intransitive verb stems and adjective stems, in which case it functions as a causative (a related form *-ltia* is used as a causative suffix with transitive verb stems). Thus, we have forms such as *kalak-tia*, literally 'enter-causative' = 'put/stick/pull/push in', *mik-tia* 'die-causative' = 'kill', *patio-tia* 'expensive-causative' = 'raise the price of'. Note that, as a causative, *-tia* is not restricted to any interpersonal kind of manipulation. The same suffix may also attach to noun stems to produce new verb stems with the approximate meaning of "give a [noun stem]". Examples of such derived verbs are *ama-tia* 'paper-give' = 'give documents to', *koton-tia* 'shirt-give' = 'dress in a shirt, give a shirt to', *misah-tia* 'mass-give' = 'celebrate a mass for', *tliokol-tia* = 'gift/charity/sadness-causative' = 'inspire pity in'. This way of expressing GIVE exists alongside the construction with the GIVE verb *maka* with an incorporated object (discussed in Section 3.2.8). Thus, we have the alternative expressions *tlakual-tia* and *tlakual-maka* both meaning 'food-give' = 'give food to, feed'.

Figure 32 sketches the extensions of literal GIVE to causative senses. In this diagram I have distinguished the "manipulative" sense, whereby one person causes another person to do something, as a bridge between literal GIVE and the more general sense of causation. The manipulative sense is closer to the original GIVE sense in so far as humans are typically involved in the interaction, whereas in the more general causative sense the causation may not involve human interaction.

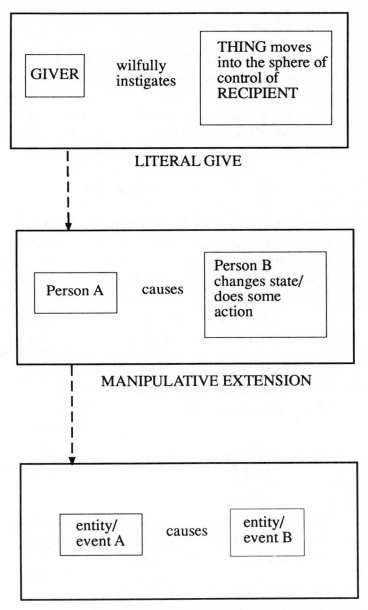

Figure 32. Extension of GIVE to causative sense

4.4.3. GIVE as a purposive marker

A further extension of the GIVE morpheme, closely related to the causative (and enablement) meanings, is the use of GIVE as a purposive marker/conjunction. In this use, it serves to connect two clausal structures with the meaning that the action of the first clause is done in order that the action/event of the second clause may take place. This use is illustrated in (43).

(43) a. *Tā   shuō gùshi gěi   wǒmen   tīng.*
          he/she tell story give   we   hear
          'He/she told a story for us to listen to.'   (Mandarin)

   b. *Bàba   xīnxinkǔku gōngzuò gěi   wǒ   shàng dàxuě.*
       father laboriously work   give me   go-to university
       'Father works hard so I can go to university.' (Mandarin)

   c. *Khɲom thʋɨ̀ː kaː ʔaoy   baːn cɔmnəɲ   craen.*
       I   work give get   profit   much
       'I work so as to have plenty of profit.'
                                    (Cambodian, Jacob 1968: 98)

   d. *Sùk   sâaŋ bâan hây   phɔ̂ɔ yùu.*
       Sook build house give father locate
       'Sook built a house for his father to live in.'
                                    (Thai, Filbeck 1975: 122)

A variant of this meaning in some languages translates as "until (some state is achieved)", as in (44).

(44) a. *Chit nía sa   sóe   hɔ̄   chin   chheng-khì!*
          this CL   clothing   wash   give   very   clean
          'Wash this garment until it is clean!'
                                    (Hokkien, Embree 1973: 89)

   b. *Kin   hây   ìm!*
       eat   give sated
       'Eat your fill!'   (Thai, Harrison—Sukcharoen ms)

In (44), the GIVE morpheme introduces a subordinate clause/phrase which describes the desired endpoint of the activity expressed by the main clause. It could be seen as a subcategory of the purposive sense. The constructions in (44) relate an earlier activity to a later *state*, whereas the constructions in (43) relate an earlier activity to some later *activity*.

Intentionality and purposefulness are strongly associated with the transfer of control over the THING in the GIVE frame. The GIVER intends that the RECIPIENT has control over the THING. This component of the meaning of literal GIVE helps to motivate the extension of GIVE to a purposive marker. Note, too, that the act of giving commonly leads to a further event in which the RECIPIENT makes some use of the THING passed, as discussed in Section 2.6. This aspect of literal GIVE could also be seen as motivating an extension of GIVE to a purposive marker. The heterosemy of one form being used as a verb GIVE and as a purposive marker may well be facilitated by an impoverished verbal morphology in the language. This might enable a form to more easily function in quite different ways syntactically, without appearing to be "degenerate" in its structure. Certainly in the case of Chinese and the Southeast Asian languages cited in (43) and (44), there is relatively little, or no, verbal morphology, lending some support to this hypothesis.

4.5. Permission/enablement

We now turn to the permission/enablement group of extensions of literal GIVE. As mentioned at the beginning of Section 4.4, enablement and causation share some semantic properties. Enablement (and the closely related concept of permission) is like the causation of a potential for some event rather than the causation of the necessity of some event. Our discussion of permission/enablement is thus a natural sequel to the discussion of causation in the preceding section.

Notions of permission/enablement have been explored in many linguistic and philosophical studies. Of particular relevance here are the discussions of permission and enablement in works such as Johnson

(1987: 41–64), Talmy (1988), and Sweetser (1990: 49–75). These three discussions all deal with different types of permission and enablement. A major distinction relevant to the enablement meaning is that between a negated restriction and positive enablement. A negated restriction removes an already existing or potentially present barrier thereby allowing some event to happen. A positive enablement imparts some capability or force to an entity and in that way allows an event to happen. Sweetser (1990: 53) suggests two appropriate images to convey the difference between these two types of enablement: a negated restriction is like an open garage door which allows a driver to start on a journey; positive enablement is like a full gas tank in a car which also, though in a different way, allows the driver to start on a journey. If we think about literal GIVE in terms of negated restriction versus positive enablement, then it seems to fall well and truly into the category of positive enablement. The act of giving transfers a THING to the RECIPIENT and this in turn allows the RECIPIENT to do something he/she otherwise would not have been able to do. Giving is the imparting of something rather than the removal of a barrier. It is the notion of positive enablement which is the larger schematic meaning shared by literal GIVE and most of the enablement senses. As with causation, it is the interpersonal type of enablement ("person A enables person B to do something") which seems closest to literal GIVE in its cognitive topology.

In the remainder of Section 4.5 I will elaborate on the details of some of the connections between literal GIVE and the permission/enablement extensions. I will also include, in Sections 4.5.6 and 4.5.7, discussion of some unusual extensions of Mandarin GIVE which are relatable to the enablement sense.

4.5.1. *"Give permission" type*

A very direct way in which GIVE is utilized in constructions relating to permission and enablement is by explicitly combining it with object nouns with the meaning "permission", "opportunity" etc., as in (45). In these cases, the notion of enablement/permission is contributed most obviously by the noun rather than the verb GIVE, and one should not categorize these uses as instances of GIVE being extended to mean permission. Nevertheless, it is relevant to include such cases here to illustrate the ease with which GIVE enters into constructions with such nouns. The collocation of GIVE with such nouns is itself indicative of a close semantic association between GIVE and permission/enablement.

(45) a. *give someone the right(s) to something, give someone the possibility of doing something, give permission to someone*

   b. *davat' pravo*
      give   right:ACC
      'give the right to'   (Russian)

   c. *davat' vozmozhnost'*
      give   possibility:ACC
      'enable'   (Russian)

   d. *dare il permesso*
      give the permission
      'give permission'   (Italian)

   e. *Ciò gli diede l'occasione di rivedere l'amico.*
      that him gave the opportunity to see again the friend
      'That gave the opportunity of seeing his friend again.'
                                        (Italian)

   f. *pa ruhusa*
      give permission
      'give permission'   (Swahili)

   g. *mem-beri izin*
      TRANS-give permission
      'give permission'   (Malay)

The use of words such as "right(s)" and "permission" in these GIVE constructions is an indication of a pervasive metaphorical equation of rights and possessions. Rights to act in certain ways may be conceptualized as abstract things which are possessed, taken, and given in the same way as concrete possessions. In English, one may *have permission, give permission to someone,* and *take permission away from someone,* parallel to *have a book, give a book to someone,* and *take a book from some-*

one. Literal giving thus maps neatly onto the granting of permission: the permitter corresponds to the GIVER, the rights to the THING passed, and the permittee to the RECIPIENT. The correspondence in conceptual structures is reminiscent of the way in which giving maps so comfortably onto interpersonal communication, as discussed earlier.

Languages may also employ GIVE with noun phrases which are metonymically associated with rights to act, proceed, control something etc. Examples of this sort are given in (46).

(46) a. *give way to someone, give the wheel (of a car) to someone, give someone the floor, give ground to someone*

  b. *davat' dorogu*
    give   way:ACC
    'give way to'   (Russian)

  c. *davat' mesto*
    give   place:ACC
    'make room for'   (Russian)

  d. *mem-beri-kan   jalan   untuk...*
    TRANS-give-BEN   way/road for
    'give way to...'   (Malay)

While all these expressions are extensions from literal GIVE, they themselves have both literal and figurative interpretations. In their literal interpretations, the nouns which appear as syntactic objects in these cases do indeed refer to spatial entities which may play some role in the overall meaning. So, in *giving way* to someone, the person may have before them an actual way along which he/she proceeds. This is the use in a sentence like *When you come to a stop sign you must give way to all traffic*. It is also possible to use the expression more figuratively, without *way* referring to any clearly laid out physical path, as in *The older members of the Cabinet should give way to the younger members* or *I'm not going to give way to him on this issue*. In these more figurative interpretations of *give way* there is the sense of "pass over control" but no clear physical path is opened up. Similarly, in *giving the wheel to X*, X may take hold of an actual steering wheel in a car, but it is possible to use the expression without any physical wheel being involved: *It is time for the older members of Cabinet to give the wheel to the younger members of parliament.* Here, the idea of a change in control over the Cabinet is understood in terms of a change in control over a vehicle, so the vehicle imagery (which includes the wheel) is the source domain for the more complex target domain of political government. But there are aspects of driving a vehicle which are, in turn, partly understood with the help of more basic concepts, such as construing the passing of responsibility of driving in terms of GIVE. The extension of GIVE in such cases goes hand in hand with a choice of nouns as syntactic object which have strong associations with rights, precedence, dominance etc. *Way*, for example, refers in its literal sense to a path one proceeds along and so lends itself to standing for the rights to proceed.

With literal GIVE, the more salient part of the overall meaning is probably that a thing changes hands, with the concomitant change in possession an intangible and less striking component of meaning (though nevertheless real). With *give way* and the other expressions in (46), on the other hand, it is the change in control over something which is the more salient aspect of the overall meaning, with the literal meaning of *way* backgrounded.

4.5.2. *"Give someone a book to read"* type

There is another way in which the idea of a positive enablement can manifest itself with GIVE, as illustrated by *She gave me a book to read.* Here the literal GIVE of *She gave me a book* forms part of the whole sentence both in form and meaning. Added to this is an explicit expression of the projected use which the RECIPIENT will make of the THING passed. In doing so, one is really only giving overt recognition to an aspect of the complex matrix of GIVE which is typically present but not always expressed, as discussed in Chapter 2. Typically, one gives a thing to a person so that the person may make some use of that thing. The addition of *to read* in *She gave me a book to read* makes this aspect explicit rather than just leaving it implicit. One may observe the same phenomenon in other languages, as in (47).

(47) a. *Ich   gab   ihm   eine   Tasse   ·Tee.*
         I   gave him:DAT   a   cup:ACC   tea
         'I gave him a cup of tea.'   (German)

   b. *Ich   gab   ihm   eine   Tasse   Tee   zu   trinken.*
         I   gave him:DAT   a   cup:ACC tea   to   drink:INF
         'I gave him a cup of tea to drink.'   (German)

   c. *Tā   gěi   wǒ   dōngxi.*
         he/she gave me   thing
         'He/she gave me something.'   (Mandarin)

   d. *Tā   gěi   wǒ   dōngxi chī.*
         he/she gave me   thing eat
         'He/she gave me something to eat.'   (Mandarin)

Although these examples involve the use of literal GIVE, rather than figurative extensions, it is useful to consider them in the present context. They show how *even* in the literal use of GIVE, the idea of enablement of a RECIPIENT to act in some way is not far beneath the surface. The addition of the verbal word in these examples, in a sense, "completes" the GIVE sentences by bringing more of the meaning of GIVE into profile. Conceptually, the *Give someone a book to read* type of structure is a bridge to the "pure" enablement senses.

4.5.3. "Give someone to think" type

A construction which is quite common is the use of GIVE with a verb of mental activity, with the whole construction having the sense of imparting information. This exists in English in expressions such as *give someone to understand* and its passive counterpart *to be given to understand*. These expressions might also be categorized as interpersonal communication, or as causatives. I have included them here since they share with the class of permission expressions the sense of enabling, in this case enabling another person to have access to some knowledge or information. (48) illustrates this use in other languages.

(48) a. *dat'*   *komuto*   *znat'*
     give:INF   someone:DAT   know:INF
     'let someone know, inform someone'   (Russian)

     b. *dać komuś*   *do*   *zrozumienia*
     give someone:DAT to   understanding:GEN
     'to give someone to understand'   (Polish)

     c. *Mi dava ad intendere*   *che*   *il*   *conto era pegato.*
     me gave to understand   that   the   bill   was paid
     'He gave me to understand that the bill was paid.' (Italian)

     d. *Ich gab ihm*   *zu verstehen,*   *dass ...*
     I   gave him:DAT   to   understand, that
     'I gave him to understand that ...'   (German)

     e. *antaa jonkun*   *ymmärtää,*   *että ...*
     give person:GEN   understand:INF, that
     'give a person to understand that ...'   (Finnish)

     f. *mem-beri-tahu*
     TRANS-give-know
     'to inform'   (Malay)

There can be subtle nuances which attach to some of these expressions. In English a sentence like *I was given to understand that I would have a computer in my office* seems most appropriate in the situation where there is some disagreement or some question about my right to a computer. It suggests a relatively subjective understanding of the situation, along the lines of *The way I understand it is...* It would be consistent with having obtained the information indirectly, without the information being made absolutely clear. As such it contrasts with a sentence like *I was informed that I would have a computer* which has a more matter-of-fact tone to it, consistent with an explicit communicative act passing on this information. These facts may be seen as another instance of the widespread iconicity discussed by Haiman (1985: 102–159), whereby the lengthier structure (*give to understand*) corresponds to greater conceptual complexity. A *give to understand* construction in another language may not have exactly the same additional connotations as the English sentence, but one can expect some additional nuances, beyond what one finds with a simple verb "inform".

The sense of GIVE in this construction has strong connections with literal GIVE and there are multiple mappings which hold between literal GIVE and the *give to understand* type of extension. There is a source of information, corresponding to the GIVER; there is information which is communicated, corresponding to the THING passed; there is a person who receives information, corresponding to the RECIPIENT. There is, furthermore, a resulting new mental state of the RECIPIENT (his/her understanding of the situation). This might be put into a correspondence with the new control over the THING which a RECIPIENT has or with the acts which a RECIPIENT may carry out as a result of having being given the THING. This kind of extension is also classifiable as interpersonal communication, as discussed in Section 4.3.

4.5.4. GIVE as "enable"

In the preceding section we saw how a construction like *He gave me to understand that I would be promoted* involves a reference to some information being passed, with *give* taking on more the meaning of "enable, lead to". In such a sentence, there is still something definite which passes between people (words, information, a document etc.). One may also find GIVE with a meaning approximating "permit, enable, let, help, bring about" without any implication at all that any physical object has passed between the persons involved. I take all these particular meanings to be instances of a larger schematic meaning which we may simply characterize as "enable". "Permit", for example, is that specific kind of enabling by which a person exercises some authority in the social domain, enabling the permittee to act in some way. In order not to clutter up the discussion with the plethora of verbs which refer to enabling of different kinds, I will discuss these various meanings by referring to the more schematic "enable" sense. This extension can be found in a number of languages:

(49) a. *Emu   ne   dali   govorit'.*
      him:DAT   NEG   gave:PL   speak:INF
      'They didn't let him speak.'   (Russian)

b.   *Dajte   mne   podumat'.*
     give:IMP   me:DAT   think:INF
     'Let me think.'   (Russian)

c.   *Nie   dali   mi   wejść.*
     NEG   gave:PL   me:DAT   enter:INF
     'They wouldn't let me in.'   (Polish)

d.   *Te   ne   mu   dadoxa   dori   da   opita.*
     they   not   him   gave   even to   try
     'They didn't even let him try.'   (Bulgarian)

e.   *antaa   jonkun   mennä*
     give   person:GEN   go:INF
     'allow a person to go'   (Finnish)

f.   *Wǒ   yàu   kàn,   tā   jiǔ   gěi   wǒ   kàn.*
     I   want   look,   he/she   then   give   me   look
     'If I want to look, he/she will let me.'   (Mandarin)

g.   *Mêe'   hây   lǔuk   pay   duu   nǎng.*
     mother   give   child   go   watch   movie
     'Mother let her child go and see a movie.'   (Thai)

h.   *Khɲom   ʔaoy   nèək daə-lèɳ.*
     I   give   you   walk-play
     'I'll let you go for a walk.'   (Cambodian)

i.   *Ia   mem-beri   dia   lari.*
     he   TRANS-give   he   run
     'He let him escape.'

                         (Indonesian, Echols—Shadily 1963: 53)

English examples of this use can be found from earlier periods, including the examples in (50), taken from the collection of poems *Leaves of Grass*, by Walt Whitman (1819–1892).

(50) a.   *Give me to warble spontaneous songs recluse by myself ...*
           (line 10 of the poem *Give me the Splendid Silent Sun*)

      b.   *Give me to hold all sounds ...* (line 138 of the poem *Proud Music of the Storm*)

      c.   *Give me to bathe the memories of all dead soldiers ...* (line 34 of the poem *Ashes of Soldiers*)

The examples in (49) and (50) all involve enabling a person to do something, rather than just enabling a situation to come about. Enabling someone to do something is closer semantically to the sense of literal GIVE involving, as it does, a human RECIPIENT (in its prototypical use). It seems natural, therefore, to deal with this kind of enabling before turning to the more generalized enabling of events which may not involve the enabling of a human.

I have already indicated above, in broad terms, how I see a general kind of motivation for enablement extensions from literal GIVE. Both literal GIVE and enablement involve an entity being a key factor in making some event possible. (This is true also of causation.) If one just focuses on the core of the meaning of GIVE ("the GIVER passes control of a THING to the RECIPIENT"), then the relationship of the GIVER to the final state of the RECIPIENT is closer to causation than enablement. In giving, the GIVER does not just act in order that the RECIPIENT has the potential to control the THING, which would be enablement. Rather, the GIVER acts to bring something about and the result is indeed realized, and so is more like causation. Thus, although the semantics of literal GIVE, narrowly defined as above, do provide some motivation for the enablement extension, the connection between GIVE and the enablement sense seems less straightforward than that between GIVE and the causation sense.

As a way of better understanding how the enablement extensions might be related to literal GIVE, some additional aspects of GIVE need to be brought into the discussion. Consider the set of sentences in (51).

(51) a. *She gave me an apple.*
      b. *She gave me an apple to eat.*
      c. *She gave me to eat.* = 'she enabled me to eat' (as in Whitman's use of *give*)

As discussed in Chapter 2, one must recognize that there is, typically, as part of the giving act, an intention (and a consequence) that the RECIPIENT will do something with the THING transferred. Thus, a sentence such as (51a) would usually refer to a situation where there is an intention on the part of the GIVER that I would eat the apple. In a framework which tries to reflect experiential reality in characterizing the semantics of morphemes, a full semantic description of GIVE will include some reference to this aspect of giving. In Cognitive Grammar terms, we say that GIVE as used in (51a) profiles the transfer of an apple, with the projected subsequent action on the THING by the RECIPIENT relegated to the unprofiled part of the larger complex matrix of the morpheme. In (51b), that subsequent act of eating is given overt expression, so that the larger sense of the whole clause profiles the idea of enabling me to eat an apple. The notion of enabling is encoded in this sentence by the concatenation of the relevant substructures (a clause followed by an infinitive). In (51c), the notion of enablement is included in the profile of the verb *give*. Any idea that a concrete object has been passed to someone is only present as one of the typical scenarios which might instantiate an enabling act. The extension to "enable" is fully complete when the passing of an object is not normally even one of the possible scenarios consistent with the enabling. Whitman's use of *give* in (50a), for example, involves enabling without the transference of any particular object.

Understood in this way, the extension from literal GIVE to enablement involves a change in the relative salience of components of the overall meaning of literal GIVE. What is only weakly implied in (51a), the enabling of me to eat, becomes the focus of meaning in (51c); what is directly asserted in (51a), the transfer of a concrete object, is only weakly implied in (51c) as a typical way in which the enabling happens. This is comparable to the kind of profile shift seen in the use of *wash* in *I washed the clothes* and *The clothes washed clean*. Washing will typically lead to a clean state of the thing being washed and one should recognize that the thing in a clean state is typically part of the larger frame of transitive *wash*, even though it is not designated as such by the predicate. The copula-like use of *wash* in *The clothes washed clean* differs from transitive *wash* by including in its profile the final state of the thing being washed and backgrounding the interaction between the washer and the thing.

I suggest (51a–c) as no more than an aid to understanding the conceptual links between the "enable" sense and literal GIVE. In particular, I do not mean to suggest that (51a–c) must be the historical path along which such a development must occur. There are semantic similarities between literal GIVE, even in its narrow meaning of passing something from one person to another, and "enable" which would motivate the extension. Both involve what is typically a person-to-person act; the act starts with one person and ends with another; and there is a clear directionality in the flow of the action. These parallels facilitate, even if they do not fully motivate, an extension of GIVE to "enable" without the need to rely on the weakly implied component of enabling in literal GIVE.

Figure 33 summarizes the enablement group of extensions. As with the causation group, here too the enablement extensions involving an interpersonal act ("person A enables person B to do something") are conceptually closest to the sense of literal GIVE. Hence, the interpersonal enablement is shown as a bridge to the more general enablement senses.

There is a useful parallel one may draw between the enablement extension of GIVE as observed, say, in Mandarin *gěi* 'give; let' and English *tell*. Compare (52) and (53).

(52) a. *Wǒ gěi nǐ yí běn shū.*
       I give you one CL book
       'I'll give you a book.'   (Mandarin)

    b. *Wǒ gěi nǐ kàn.*
       I give you look
       'I'll let you look.'   (Mandarin)

(53) a. *I told her the truth.*

    b. *I told her to leave.*

In the case of both *gěi* and *tell*, we see a verb being extended to the domain of interpersonal control or manipulation. GIVE and "tell" have some common characteristics which lend themselves to this kind of extension: both are relatively "basic" verbs; they are typically person-to-person acts; there is a clear directionality in the flow of the action; there is some thing which proceeds from one person to the other. It is not surprising, then, that *tell* in English is extended in a way comparable to GIVE in Mandarin. There is a difference, of course, in so far as *gěi* is

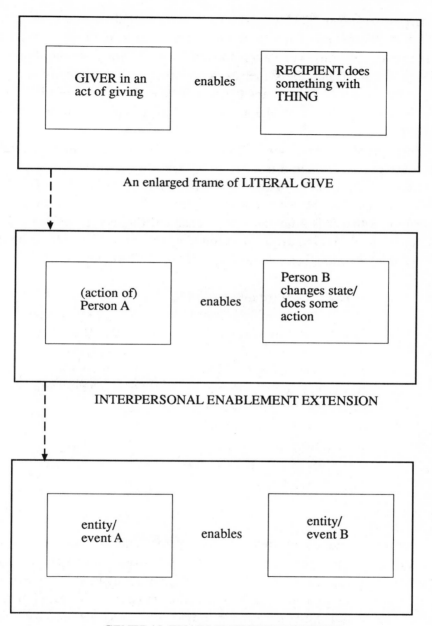

An enlarged frame of LITERAL GIVE

INTERPERSONAL ENABLEMENT EXTENSION

GENERAL ENABLEMENT EXTENSION

Figure 33. Extension of GIVE to enablement sense

extended to mean "enable", while *tell* is extended to mean "order". Possibly, the nature of the basic meanings plays a role here, though I have no convincing explanation for the facts. So, for example, telling things to people may be somehow more "forceful" than giving something to someone? Or perhaps the benefactive component of GIVE is not very compatible with the sense of ordering someone to do something?

In proceeding from literal GIVE to "enable", it seems most natural to consider cases where it is a person who enables another person to do something, consistent with the basic dynamics of literal GIVE. Nevertheless, a more general sense of "enable" exists which does not presuppose that it is a human who is enabled. English *let*, as in *He let the car roll down the hill,* is an example of this more generalized kind of "enable". So, too, is the Finnish use of GIVE illustrated in (54).

(54) a.   *Anna   koiran   juosta!*
           give-2IMP   dog:GEN   run:INF
           'Let the dog run!'   (Finnish)

      b.   *antaa   veden   jäähtyä*
           give   water:GEN   cool:INF
           'to let the water cool down'   (Finnish)

      c.   *antaa   sen   tapahtua*
           give   it:GEN   happen:INF
           'to let it happen'   (Finnish)

4.5.5.   GIVE as a hortative

A morpheme with the meaning of "enable" may sometimes be used as a hortative in languages, carrying the sense of urging and encouraging some action. English *let* may be used in this way, as in *let's go.* Since GIVE can occur with an "enable" sense in languages, as discussed in the preceding sections, it is not surprising that GIVE may also take on this hortative use. This is illustrated in (55).

(55) a. *Dài!*
          give
          'Come on!'   (Italian)
      b. *Davaj   igrat'!*
          give:IMP play:INF
          'Let's play!'   (Russian)
      c. *Davaj   sygraem!*
          give.:IMP play:1PL
          'Let's play!'   (Russian)
      d. *Dai   da   napravim   tova!*
          give:IMP PARTICLE do:1PL   this
          'Let's do this!'   (Bulgarian)
      e. *Adjunk   a   menés-nek!*
          give:1PL the going-DAT
          'Let's go!'   (Hungarian)

The Russian examples illustrate alternative syntactic structures possible
with this sense of GIVE. The Imperative *davaj* may be followed either
by the infinitive (e.g. *igrat'*) or by the 1st Plural Perfective finite verb
(e.g. *sygraem*). There is even a third structure in Russian with *davaj*
followed by a finite clause structure with *ja* 'I' as the subject, as illustrated in (56).

(56)   *Davaj   ja   pomogu   tebje!*
          give:IMP I:NOM   help:1SG   you:DAT
          'Come, I'll help you!'   (Russian)

Since we know that the hortative sense can be related to an "enable"
sense, as with English *let*, it is reasonable to see the evolution of a hortative sense from literal GIVE as relating to the enablement idea
associated with GIVE. The imperative GIVE in (55) and (56) is used by
a speaker to advocate some action. In so far as it is meant to help bring
about some action, it functions like a positive enablement. The hortative
use of GIVE is also closely related to the inceptive extensions discussed
in Section 4.8.2.

4.5.6.   Agentive preposition in Mandarin

We turn now to an intriguing puzzle in Mandarin, where the GIVE morpheme *gěi* is also used as a marker of the agent in a passive construction. In the following example, *māo* 'cat' is understood as the entity which did the eating:

(57)　　*Jīnyú　　gěi　　māo　　chī-le.*
　　　　 goldfish　give　cat　　was eaten-ASP
　　　　 'The goldfish was eaten by the cat.'　　　　　　　(Mandarin)

In (57) "cat" functions like an object or landmark for the GIVE morpheme, and yet semantically it seems quite unlike landmarks of GIVE. The animate landmark of literal GIVE, the RECIPIENT, is closely associated with the endpoint of action, as the entity to which the action "flows". In (57), on the other hand, the action of eating originates with the landmark ("cat"). We seem to have, then, an unexpected and dramatic reversal of what one would expect in an extension of GIVE.

I believe that a number of considerations motivate this use of *gěi* in Mandarin, without any one of these considerations being seen as the sole basis for the extension. One of the relevant factors to consider is the fact that *gěi* is used in contexts like those discussed earlier, involving an enablement sense, as in (58a) and (58b).

(58)　a.　*Tā　　gěi　　wǒ　dōngxi　　chī.*
　　　　　he/she　give　me　something　eat
　　　　　'He/she gave me something to eat.'　　　　　　　(Mandarin)
　　　b.　*Tā　　gěi　　hái-zi　shuì-jiao.*
　　　　　he/she　give　child　sleep
　　　　　'He/she let the child sleep.'　　　　　　　(Mandarin)

In (58), *gěi* is still the literal GIVE, but a subsequent action involving the THING given has been included in the overall profile of the sentence. In elaborating the basic GIVE structure in this way, we are overlaying an additional kind of role onto the RECIPIENT who now is also understood as the trajector with respect to the additional predicate "eat". In (58b) the enablement sense attaches to *gĕi* itself and there is no suggestion that any THING has to be handed to a RECIPIENT. Quite clearly, it is "child" in (58b) which is the trajector with respect to the verb "sleep". In both sentences in (58), then, the noun phrase to the right of *gĕi*, a position associated with the landmark of *gĕi,* functions as a trajector with respect to the following predicate. Relating the agentive marking function of *gĕi* in (57) to the uses of *gĕi* in (58) helps to motivate the agentive marking function. In both (57) and (58), *gĕi* is followed by a noun phrase which functions as the trajector of some other verbal predicate.

Secondly, one must bear in mind an historical fact about Mandarin, namely that there has been a general trend in the history of Mandarin involving a word order shift from SVO to SOV (cf. Li—Thompson 1975: 185). Where there is a sequence of verbal predicates in a clause, the trend has been for the second predicate to be construed as the main verb and the first predicate as part of the complement of the main verb. One manifestation of this trend has been the depletion of semantic content of the first verbal predicate in a series and the simultaneous enhancement of semantic content of the second predicate (cf. Givón 1975: 93). This larger fact about the history of Mandarin syntax is surely relevant to an account of the *gĕi* passive, though I do not mean to suggest that the passive construction must have emerged out of GIVE uses simply by a gradual semantic shift. I stress that more than one factor needs to be considered in accounting for the passive construction. Nevertheless, this historical fact about Mandarin takes us further towards our goal by providing some motivation for the weakened semantic bonds between *gĕi* and the noun phrases which flank it in the passive construction.

Thirdly, there is a certain slipperiness to the semantic role played by a noun phrase at the beginning of a sentence in Mandarin, related no doubt to a pervasive topic-comment structure in the language. In particular, it is possible for initial noun phrases to be interpreted as either the trajector or the landmark of the following verbal predicate. Contextual and pragmatic factors usually result in only one possible interpretation and the frequency of actual ambiguities like this in the real world is therefore relatively low. Nevertheless, ambiguity is possible with the right choices of lexical items, as illustrated in example (59), taken from Chao (1968: 72).

(59)   *Zhèi yú bù néng chī le.*
       this fish NEG can eat PARTICLE
       'This fish cannot be eaten any more.'
       or 'This fish cannot eat any more (it is sick).' (Mandarin)

This variability in the semantic function of the initial noun phrase in Mandarin would obviously help to smooth the way for the development of a *gěi* structure in which the initial noun phrase functions like a patient rather than an agent.

Finally, one can point to the existence of cognitive similarities between an agent role in a passive construction and a benefactive sense. There is a benefactive prepositional use of *gěi* 'for the benefit of' whereby *gěi* occurs in the same position in the clause as the agent of a passive, i.e. immediately before the main verbal predicate. Note that a benefactive phrase is typically also the motivation for an act, i.e. the NP in the benefactive *gěi* + NP phrase refers to a person who not only benefits from some act but who is also, in a weak sense, the cause of the act. It is this aspect of the benefactive sense which makes it comparable to the agentive sense. The agent of an act and the person for whose benefit an act is carried out both play a part in setting the act in motion.

I offer these considerations, then, as an attempt to relate the use of *gěi* in the passive construction to other facts about *gěi* and the structure of Mandarin. No one of these seems to completely explain away the *gěi* passive construction, but when taken together, I believe these considerations do help to make the existence of this construction understandable.

4.5.7. *Mandarin emphatic*

There is yet another unusual use of the GIVE morpheme in Mandarin which deserves attention. Mandarin *gěi* appears in imperative clauses lending a kind of emphasis to the command. So, the sentences (60a) and (60b) are semantically similar, but (60b) gives an extra emphasis to the command.

(60) a. *(Nǐ) chī-fàn!*
          you eat
          '(You) eat!'   (Mandarin)

      b. *(Nǐ) gěi wǒ chī-fàn!*
          (you) give me eat
          '(You) eat!'   (Mandarin)

Gěi must be used with a following 1st person pronoun (*wǒ*) in this use. (60b) could also have the "enable" meaning ("You let me eat"), which is semantically quite distinct from the emphatic meaning. I am not concerned with the "you let me eat" reading here. Given the semantic distance between the enablement sense and the emphatic use of *gěi*, it does not seem very promising to attempt to directly relate them.

One way to approach the use of *gěi* in (60b) is to think of it as a kind of benefactive. *Gěi* has a well established use in Mandarin as a benefactive marker. One could argue that the sense of a 1st person benefactive encourages a more emphatic interpretation of the imperative. This would make it comparable, though not identical, to the dative *mir* in a German sentence such as *Fahr mir nicht zu schnell!* 'Don't drive too fast!', where the *mir* accentuates the speaker's involvement and concern. Another possible approach to motivating the emphatic use of *gěi* may be to relate it to the agentive marking use discussed in the previous section. This is, in fact, the approach taken in Liang (1971: 166–73), a dissertation written within the framework of generative grammar. In particular, Liang derives (60b) from an underlying structure in which there is an explicit performative verb *jiào* 'order'. The *gěi wǒ* phrase originates, then, as the agentive phrase accompanying the passive of the underlying performative verb *jiào*. This derivation is sketched below in (61).

(61)   *Wǒ   jiào   nǐ   [nǐ   qù   chī-fàn].*
             I   order you you go eat
             'I command you to eat!'

-->   *Wǒ   jiào   nǐ   [Ø   Ø   chī-fàn].*
          I   order you   eat

-->   *Nǐ   gěi   wǒ   jiào   [Ø   Ø   chī-fàn].*
          you give-Agent me   order-Passive   eat

-->   *Nǐ   gěi   wǒ Ø [Ø   Ø   chī-fàn].*
          you give-Agent me   eat
          'You eat!'

Liang's derivation is a way to understand the semantics but I believe this use of *gěi* can be motivated without resorting to deletion transformations of the sort proposed by Liang.

To approach an understanding of this use of *gěi*, it is convenient to start with some observations about English *by*. As is well known, *by* functions as the agentive preposition in the passive construction, as in (62a). In addition, it serves as a preposition with a meaning like "in recognition of the authority of ...", especially with verbs relating to the taking of an oath, as in (62b–c). Notice also that this latter use is further extended to various exclamative uses, where there may not be any literal sense of taking an oath, as in (62d–e).

(62) a. *The hunter was killed by a vicious tiger.*
      b. *I swear by God/the Bible that I will avenge her death.*
      c. *The Immigration people went by the book in processing his application.*
      d. *By Heavens/Jove, that's an unusual sight!*
      e. *I'll get you for this, by God!*

In comparing the uses of *by* in (62a–c), we see both the sense of "by the agency of ..." and "by the authority of ...". Uniting both senses is the

more schematic idea of an entity controlling some action which can be
further specified as either an agent (in the context of actually
performing actions) or a figure of authority (in the context of a power
structure involving humans and symbols of authority). As may happen
with expressions relating to symbols of authority, they may be weakened in their semantic content to exclamatives with various nuances, as in
(62d–e).

One may think of the agentive marking and the emphatic uses of *gěi*,
repeated below as (63), as being related in a similar way.

(63) a. *Jīnyú   gěi   māo   chī-le.*
      goldfish give   cat   was eaten-ASP
      'The goldfish was eaten by the cat.'   (Mandarin)

   b. *(Nǐ)   gěi   wǒ   chī-fàn!*
     (you)   give   me   eat
     '(You) eat!'   (Mandarin)

In (63a), *gěi* has the sense of "by the agency of ...", as described in the
preceding section. In (63b), on the other hand, *gěi* has the meaning of
"by the authority of...". This is the same pairing of meanings which is
found in the case of English *by* phrases, as explained above. In (63b),
wǒ 'I, me' is no longer the trajector of the verb "eat" but refers to the
authority by which the eating is done.

4.6. Schematic interaction

GIVE sometimes occurs in constructions where it appears to contribute
little more than the idea of an interaction between entities, as in *give the
car a wash*. The nature of the interaction is spelled out by some other
phrase in the construction, often based on a verb or action-like word
(*wash* in the example quoted). There are many expressions in English
which fall into this category. In this type of construction, illustrated
further in (64), the nature of the action is conveyed largely by the second NP following *give*.

(64) a. *give the car a push*   (= *push the car*)
      b. *give someone a shove*   (= *shove someone*)
      c. *give the house a clean*   (= *clean the house*)
      d. *give the floor a sweep*   (= *sweep the floor*)
      e. *give the floor a scrub*   (= *scrub the floor*)
      f. *give the rope a pull*   (= *pull the rope*)
      g. *give it a try*   (= *try it*)
      h. *give someone a scare*   (= *scare someone*)
      i. *give someone a hug/kiss*   (= *hug/kiss someone*)
      j. *give the ball a kick*   (= *kick the ball*)

In the examples in (64) we find a ditransitive *give* construction functioning as a paraphrase of transitive verbs as shown in parentheses. I take the second noun of the ditransitive construction (*push, shove, clean* etc.) to be a deverbal. The paraphrase, or near-paraphrase, relationship illustrated in (64) has attracted some attention in the recent literature (see in particular the interesting discussion and references in Dixon 1991: 336–362). Grimshaw—Mester (1988: 229–230) suggest an analysis of the *give* paraphrase in terms of a process called "Argument Transfer". *Give* is viewed as having an incomplete argument structure, like some other "light verbs" in English, e.g. *make, put, take*. The deverbal noun, on the other hand, is analyzed as having a complete argument structure which is "transferred" to *give*. One could proceed in a roughly comparable way in Cognitive Grammar, along the lines suggested by Langacker's analysis of periphrastic *do* (cf. Langacker 1991: 205–206) and I sketch an analysis along these lines below. The idea underlying both these approaches is that *give* is associated with a relatively schematic meaning ("someone interacts with something/someone") which combines with the more richly elaborated deverbal predicate to form a new semantic whole.

Apart from contributing a highly schematic verbal component to the whole meaning of the expression, *give* appears to contribute other elements of meaning as well. It is possible to isolate elements of intentionality, energy flow, and punctual or perfective aspect in its use. Before providing the data which bring out these various components of the meaning of *give* as used in examples like (64), one should note that there appears to be a kind of formal constraint on the use of a deverbal in the *give* construction, to the effect that it exists as a deverbal independently of its use in the *give* construction, as discussed by Stein (1991: 7–8). So, for example, with the deverbal *push* one can say not only *I gave it a push*, but also *Do you want a push?*, *I got a big push* etc. If we try to construct a sentence such as **I gave the song a sing*, its unacceptability might then be explained away as simply a result of the non-existence of a deverbal *sing*. If we want to tease out the semantic factors influencing the use of the *give* construction, then, we must use deverbals which have independent existence.

Consider, then, *spill* which is used both as a verb and as a noun (presumably based on the verb, hence deverbal) independently of the *give* construction, as in *There has been an oil spill off the coast*. Notice that we do not find pairs such as those in (65).

(65) a. *I spilled the milk.*
       b. **I gave the milk a spill.*

A clear difference semantically between *spill* and the deverbals in (64) is the involuntary nature of *spill*. It is understood that spilling is strongly associated with something one does accidentally and this seems relevant to the impossibility of (65b). That is, the *give* construction is associated with an intentional component of meaning. Compare also (66a) and (66b).

(66) a. *Lin missed the show.*
       b. *Lin gave the show a miss.*

Both *miss* and *give (something) a miss* have the sense of "not experience (something)", but the *give* construction must be interpreted as an intentional act of avoidance, whereas the plain verb could be intentional or non-intentional.

Another component of meaning present in the *give* construction is a momentary, punctual, or perfective sense, consistent with the extensions of GIVE noted in Section 4.9 below. Notice that in (67a), *was kicking* can easily be used to describe an ongoing activity carried out over a prolonged period, while *was giving a kick* is not possible.

(67)   a.   *Tom was kicking the ball the whole afternoon.*
      b.   **Tom was giving the ball a kick the whole afternoon.*

If one tries to ascribe some meaning to (67b), it would be that Tom's kick took the whole afternoon. The use of the indefinite article in the *give a kick* construction may also be relevant here, emphasizing the singularity of the kicking. If one pluralizes *kick*, one can have a sentence such as *Tom gave the ball lots of kicks during the afternoon.* But it still seems awkward to use the progressive aspect *?Tom was giving the ball lots of kicks during the afternoon.* The conclusion is that the *give a [deverbal]* construction strongly suggests a momentary, singular action. Consider also the impossibility of **give the ball a hold* (in spite of the independent existence of a nominal use of *hold* as in *He had a good hold on the ball*). In at least one of its main uses, the verb *hold* refers to an on-going stative relationship and this is presumably a factor contributing to the unacceptability of **give a hold*.

Furthermore, where there is a transference of energy from one entity to another, the transference of energy has to be from the subject referent to the object referent. Compare (68a) and (68b).

(68)   a.   *I gave the ball a good throw.*
      b.   **I gave the ball a good catch.*

In the case of throwing an object, the thrower initiates the energy flow and the object thrown is an energy sink, so the energy flow is outwards from the subject referent. In (68b), on the other hand, the subject referent functions most obviously as an energy sink. The ball comes to rest in the hands of the catcher and energy flows from the ball to the catcher. This is not the entire story, of course. Catching a ball is not the same as a ball landing in someone's hands. To catch a ball, one must also initiate some activity affecting the ball. However, the role of the catcher as a kind of endpoint in the energy flow seems to make a stronger impression than the role of the catcher as the initiator of the catch. This orientation in the energy flow of catching seems relevant to understanding why (68b) is unacceptable.

These nuances of the *give* construction, compared with the corresponding plain verb construction, are familiar as features associated with higher transitivity as discussed in Hopper—Thompson (1980) and Rice (1987). The relatively high transitivity inherent in the *give* construction does not reduce to any simple presence or absence of a feature, as can be seen in the variety in the *give* constructions reviewed here. It is helpful to consider the features of the *give* constructions with respect to the different domains which are relevant, as proposed by Rice (1987: 78–88). So, for example, when physical entities are acting upon each other, as in *give the ball a kick*, the flow of energy involved results in a change in the location of the affected entity *(the ball)*. In the case of *give the show a miss*, on the other hand, we are dealing more with a state of mind of a person with respect to some event and there is no obvious effect on the object referent *(the show)*. Instead, the flow of energy manifests itself as a mental activity directed towards some entity. These different properties should be understood as related to the different effects associated with transitivity in different domains.

The properties of this *give* construction are consistent with and motivated by properties of literal GIVE. Intentionality is very much present in the mental world of the giver in the characterization of literal GIVE, as well as in many of its extensions. It is present in the interpersonal communication extensions and the extensions relating to permitting, enabling etc. Extensions of GIVE to benefactive marking, as discussed in Section 4.7.2, also typically involve an intention that someone be the beneficiary. The momentary, perfective element inherent in the *give* construction is a further example of the "completedness" group of extensions discussed in Section 4.9, motivated by an inherent perfectivity in literal GIVE. The flow of energy which is present (though understood differently in the different domains) has its source in the clear flow of energy (outwards) from GIVER (through the thing) to the RECIPIENT.

It is significant that this particular *give* construction makes use of the ditransitive alternative in English, rather than the monotransitive + *to* phrase alternative (**give a wash to the car, *give a push to the car,* *give a shove to the man* etc.). There is evidence elsewhere in English that the double object construction is the preferred construction type where the activity has a stronger effect on the RECIPIENT. Compare the examples *I teach English to high school students* and *I taught Sue English*. The former sentence construes the high school students as a more peripheral part of the activity, without any strong assumption that they actually learn anything. The latter sentence, on the other hand, suggests more strongly that Sue in fact successfully learnt English through my teaching. Recall also from the discussion in Section 3.5 that the construction of *give* sentences with a *to* phrase tends to impose a path-like image on the scene, creating subtle differences between the ditransitive and monotransitive + *to* phrase constructions. The figurative extension of *give* in the schematic interaction extension is basically an interaction between two entities and does not involve any literal or figurative path along which an entity moves, and so it seems appropriate that the ditransitive construction is employed rather than the construction utilizing the path image of *to*.

In Figures 34 and 35 I suggest Cognitive Grammar representations of the two phrases *wash the car* and *give the car a wash*, minus the articles. In the representation of *wash the car* in Figure 34, the lexical item *car* elaborates the landmark of the two place predicate *wash* (represented in highly schematic form). The diagram at the top represents the result of filling the elaboration site with a lexical item. In Figure 35, I have sketched out the *give the car (a) wash* counterpart. This construction builds upon a version of *give*, labelled *give3* (so numbered in order to distinguish it from the versions of *give* discussed in Chapter 3). This version of *give* profiles an interaction between an AGENT and a PATIENT, with the interaction imaged as a transfer of the action from the AGENT to the PATIENT. A lexical item *car* elaborates the PATIENT site, giving rise to an intermediate phrasal construction *give car*, though nothing important hinges on whether it is *car* or *wash* which is first combined with *give*. The ACTION argument of this predicate functions as an elaboration site which can be filled by the deverbal *wash*. Deverbal *wash* is a THING and hence the outer circle is in profile, just like a nominal. But the semantic structure of the nominal consists of a relational predicate (again in highly schematic form).

Correspondence lines associate the trajectors and landmarks of the combining predicates as shown. The result is the diagram shown at the very top for *give car wash*, consisting of the same type of interaction between entities as for *wash car*. The expressions differ in the way these final semantic structures are built up.

Brazilian Portuguese has a similar use of GIVE, illustrated in (69). In this construction, the preposition *na* 'in' is used to integrate the entity affected by the action into the clause structure. The use of *na* in this construction is in contrast to the use of *prá* 'for' to introduce the RECIPIENT in the literal GIVE construction. This difference in the choice of prepositions is considered significant by Salomao (1990: 131), who sees the use of *na* in (69) as reflecting the neutrality of the RECIPIENT entity with respect to the action. *Prá*, on the other hand, is associated with a RECIPIENT who typically benefits from an action and so is an unsuitable choice for a preposition in these figurative extensions.

(69) a. *O   jogador deu   um   chute na   bola.*
          the   player   gave   a   kick   in:the ball
          'The player kicked the ball.'
                          (Brazilian Portuguese, Salomao 1990: 131)

      b. *Ela deu   um   tapa   nele.*
          she gave a   slap   in:him
          'She slapped him.'
                          (Brazilian Portuguese, Salomao 1990: 131)

      c. *Maria   deu   um   beijo   na   sua   filha.*
          Maria   gave a   kiss   in   her   daughter
          'Maria kissed her daughter.'
                          (Brazilian Portuguese, Salomao 1990: 131)

      d. *A professora deu   um   castigo   nas   criancas.*
          the teacher   gave   a   punishment in:the children
          'The teacher punished the children.'
                          (Brazilian Portuguese, Salomao 1990: 131)

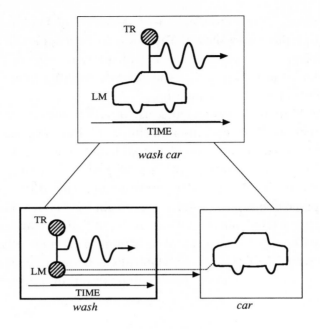

Figure 34. Representation of *wash car*

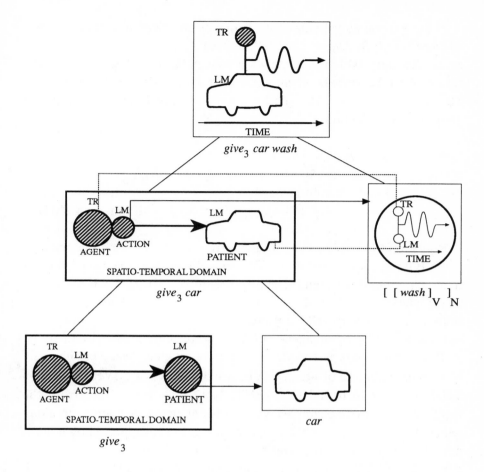

Figure 35. Representation of *give car (a) wash*

In the Australian language Ungarinjin, as described in Rumsey (1982: 74) and briefly in Capell (1979: 236–239), the GIVE morpheme serves as an auxiliary which contributes a schematic action structure to the clause, with the verbal content elaborated with an uninflected verb root. This is illustrated in (70). The auxiliary in such cases carries all the grammatical inflections.

(70)   *Njidbidj a-ŋu-ŋuḷu-n.*
         to hook MASC:OBJ-1SG:SUBJ-give-PRES
         'I hook them together.'
                                    (Ungarinjin, Coate—Elkin 1974: 403)

Rumsey (1982: 118) lists 14 auxiliaries, each of which occurs with some limited set of verb roots. To some extent, the selectional restrictions which hold between the auxiliary and the verb root can be semantically characterized. In the case of the auxiliary *ŋuḷu*, which also functions as a main verb GIVE, Rumsey characterizes its semantics as involving an action by an agent causing a non-agent to move to a patient. In these cases, *ŋuḷu* is functioning in a way which preserves the basic conceptual structure of literal GIVE, which involves a GIVER causing a THING to move to a RECIPIENT. Note that this differs from the English *give a wash* examples where it is not easy to see any path along which a thing moves. Rumsey's characterization is supported by a number of examples of verbs which can take a *ŋuḷu* auxiliary in Coate—Elkin (1974). Thus, *ŋuḷu* is an appropriate auxiliary for use with verb forms such as: *dodani* 'collide, bump into', *dor* 'bump, hit', *dudug* 'powder, sprinkle, shower (with spears)', *gura* 'collide, bump'. As Rumsey (1982: 119) points out, however, a semantically based approach to characterizing the class of verbs occurring with *ŋuḷu* is only partly successful. There are verbs in the class which do not fit the semantic characterization above, such as: *laj* 'like, desire, want', *djomali* 'get big, mature', *daŋgan* 'take the strain'. While the class of verbs can not be fully characterized semantically in any obvious way, it would be quite misguided to declare the class completely arbitrary since that would ignore the clear semantic basis for the core of the class.

4.7. Recipient/benefactive

Properties associated with the RECIPIENT in a giving act motivate extensions of literal GIVE to marking RECIPIENT phrases with verbs of transfer and to marking benefactive phrases. Recipients and beneficiaries have much in common and often both the sense of "someone who receives something transferred" and "someone who benefits from some action" are present as part of the meaning of phrases described in grammars as benefactive or recipient. It is appropriate, therefore, to group these extensions together.

A useful contribution to our understanding of this group of extensions from GIVE is Lord (1993: 31–45), who provides some comparative data on such extensions in African and Asian languages, as well as Caribbean creoles. Throughout her discussion, Lord emphasizes the relevance of a serial verb configuration in each of the languages she considers. Sometimes a sequence of [V NP] [GIVE NP] is analyzable as a sequence of two VPs, each with its own full verb and accompanying object. At other times the same sequence of forms is better analyzed as a sequence of VP and prepositional phrase. The two analyses are not always easy to keep apart. This is especially so in languages where verbs and prepositions are not easily distinguished in their morphology and syntax. A formal similarity between verbs and prepositions in a language is undoubtedly a factor in promoting a transition from a full verbal meaning like GIVE to a prepositional meaning like RECIPIENT or benefactive marker.

As detailed below, GIVE may extend to either RECIPIENT marking or benefactive marking. Another verb which may extend in the same direction is "show", though there are differences. GIVE and "show" in Twi (Benue-Kwa, Ghana), as discussed in Lord (1993: 31–33), provide an interesting contrast in this respect. The GIVE verb *ma* may also be used as a benefactive marker meaning "for the benefit of, on behalf of, with respect to". The verb *kyerẹ* "to show", on the other hand, is used to mark a general RECIPIENT, e.g. marking the person to whom something is said. This difference in the extensions can be related to properties of the basic verbs. "Show" involves an audience which "receives" a visual image without any implication that the audience is in any way affected as a result. Showing is directionalized to an audience, but does not necessarily mobilize the audience. Giving, on the other hand, involves not only a flow of action to a RECIPIENT, but, as discussed in more detail below, the RECIPIENT comes to be in control of a THING which would normally be used in some way by the RECIPIENT. Note also that GIVE often occurs with the nuance of "give as a present" (hence something explicitly meant for the benefit of the RECIPIENT), whereas one does not normally just "show" something as a present. Hence, while an extension to RECIPIENT marking can be motivated for both GIVE and "show", an extension to benefactive marking is more strongly motivated by the semantics of GIVE than "show".

4.7.1.   GIVE as a RECIPIENT marker

A morpheme GIVE appears in some languages with the function of marking the RECIPIENT with verbs of transfer. As mentioned above, this development in the use of GIVE is not uncommon in serial verb languages, in which verbal morphemes more readily take on more purely relational or prepositional characteristics. In such cases, the GIVE morpheme functions as a relational predicate helping to integrate a RECIPIENT into the clause structure. Like GIVE, a RECIPIENT marker invokes a scene in which some transfer takes place. Unlike the basic meaning of literal GIVE, however, a RECIPIENT marker will not normally be restricted to just the GIVE frame. Rather, it would normally occur with some larger class of verbal predicates, for example all donatory verbs. Also, a RECIPIENT marker will often be distinguished from a full verbal predicate by failing at least some of the diagnostic tests for verbs in the language concerned. However, as discussed below, some morphemes which seem to contribute little more than RECIPIENT marking to the meaning of a clause might still be classifiable as a verb (as in Yoruba and Akan).

Compare the uses of the GIVE morpheme as a main verb in (71a, c, e) with the RECIPIENT marking use in (71b, d, f).

(71) a. *Wǒ   gěi   tā   yì   fen   lìwù.*
        I   give   him/her   one   CL   present
        'I gave him/her a present.'   (Mandarin)

   b. *Wǒ   sòng-le   yì   fen   lìwu   gěi   tā.*
        I   present-ASP   one   CL   present   give   him/her
        'I gave a present to him/her.'   (Mandarin)

   c. *Chán   hâi   nǎnsǐ: kè: dèk.*
        I   gave   book   to   child
        'I gave a book to a child.'   (Thai)

   d. *Chán   sòng   nǎnsǐ: hâi   dèk.*
        I   sent   book   give   child
        'I sent a book to a child.' / 'I sent a book for the child.'
                                                       (Thai)

   e. *Ó   fún   mi   nî   owó.*
        he/she   gave   me   PREP   money
        'He/she gave me some money.'
                              (Yoruba, Pulleyblank 1987: 989)

   f. *Ó   tà   á   fún   mi.*
        he/she   sold   it   give   me
        'He/she sold it to me.' [7]   (Yoruba, Pulleyblank 1987: 989)

Sometimes, the verb of transfer may actually involve a handing over of something, but it may be extended to more abstract types of transfer. In Mandarin[8], for example, *gěi* functions as a marker of the RECIPIENT with predicates such as: *jì* 'mail, send', *huán* 'return (something)', *chuán* 'pass on', *jiāo* 'hand over', *mài* 'sell', *shǎng* 'bestow', *tuō* 'trust', *shū* 'donate', *fù* 'pay'. Even so, there are restrictions on the use of RECIPIENT *gěi*, referred to in Li—Thompson (1981: 384), some of which may be understood by reference to the basic literal meaning of GIVE. One might note, in particular, that it does not function in the broad sense of an indirect object as that category is understood in some languages. RECIPIENT *gěi* may not be used, for example, to mark the person from whom something is taken with the verbs *tōu* 'steal', *yíng* 'win', *qiǎng* 'rob', *duó* 'snatch'. This contrasts with German, where the person deprived of the object in such cases may be expressed with the same (dative) case otherwise used for the

RECIPIENT with GIVE-type verbs: *Er raubte mir das Geld* 'He robbed me of my money', with *mir* 'me' in the dative case. The directionality inherent in the literal meaning of GIVE is clearly preserved in its function as a marker of RECIPIENT. To label RECIPIENT *gěi* simply as indirect object or "3" (as in Relational Grammar) does not do justice to the close relationship which RECIPIENT *gěi* still bears to the literal GIVE sense of *gěi*. RECIPIENT *gěi* may not be used with another set of verbs too, namely those having to do with communication, including: *gàosu* 'tell', *dāyìng* 'promise', *huídá* 'answer', *wèn* 'ask'. This restriction is all the more remarkable in the light of the fact that GIVE is easily extended to construe acts of communication in some languages, as discussed in Section 4.2. The directionality implied by the acts of communication is consistent with literal GIVE in the sense that there is another person to whom the action is directed. But in Mandarin the RECIPIENT *gěi* still requires, apparently, an actual physical transaction, and communication appears to be too intangible to qualify.

Li—Thompson (1981: 384) mention another constraint on the use of RECIPIENT *gěi*, namely the impossibility of RECIPIENT *gěi* occurring with GIVE *gěi,* as in:

(72) ?/* *Tā   gěi   qián   gěi   wǒ.*
      he/she give money give me.
      'He/she gave money to me.'   (Mandarin)

The unacceptability here is ascribed to the same form *gěi* being repeated in such close proximity. I acknowledge that the double *gěi* construction is rejected by some speakers, but I have also encountered Mandarin speakers who will accept it in colloquial language. It might also be noted that Chao (1968: 318) refers to the double *gěi* construction (using the same example, but with RECIPIENT *gei* shown as toneless, *gěi qián gei tā* 'give money to him') as not only possible but "quite common". Though the constraint may not be felt strongly by all Mandarin speakers, the constraint certainly does operate for some speakers of Mandarin and Chinese dialects. The Southern Min dialect of Chinese Teochew provides another interesting example of this kind of constraint. In this dialect, there are two synonymous verbs GIVE : [k'ɯk] in a low falling tone and [puŋ] in a mid level tone. My informant allowed the two forms to occur with each other (*He* [k'ɯk] *a book* [puŋ] *me* and *He* [puŋ] *a book* [k'ɯk] *me*), but did not allow the same GIVE form to be used twice within the one clause (**He* [k'ɯk] *a book* [k'ɯk] *me* and **He* [puŋ] *a book* [puŋ] *me*). A similar phenomenon seems to occur in the Northern Min dialect Fuzhou, where there are also two verbs GIVE: [k'øyʔ] in a low to mid rising tone and [puɔŋ] in a high level tone. My informant rejected a double occurrence of the same form for GIVE in that dialect, comparable to the Teochew judgements.

The syntactic status of the RECIPIENT-marking morpheme can vary from more verb-like units to more adposition-like units. Pulleyblank (1987: 989) explicitly rejects an analysis of the GIVE morpheme *fún* in the Yoruba data above as a preposition, in favour of an analysis of it as a verbal predicate (it can take object clitics and can be nominalized, just like verbs). The Mandarin use of RECIPIENT-marking *gěi*, on the other hand, is argued to be a preposition and not a verb in Liang (1971: 157), on the basis that it cannot be negated, put into an interrogative Verb-*bu*-Verb construction, or suffixed with aspect markers — all tests used by Liang for verbhood in Mandarin.[9] Zhang (1990: 313–315) adds some further arguments for an analysis of RECIPIENT-marking *gěi* as a preposition rather than a verb.

In Figure 36, I have shown diagrammatically the extension of literal GIVE to its function as a non-verbal RECIPIENT marker, as in Mandarin. As a RECIPIENT marker, the predicate is defined with respect to a general "donatory" frame which is intended as a cover term for three-place predicates such as "transfer", "give", "contribute", "send" etc. In the representation of literal GIVE in this diagram, I have included the profiled time axis, which has usually been omitted in previous diagrams, in order to simplify representations. In this case, however, the profiling or non-profiling of the time dimension is relevant, since this is a feature which helps to distinguish literal GIVE (where the time dimension is profiled) and the RECIPIENT marker (where the time dimension is excluded from the profiled portion of the predicate).

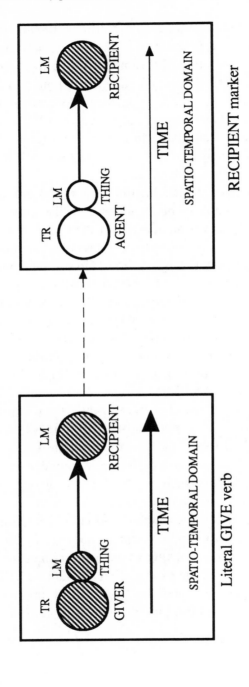

Figure 36. Extension of GIVE to RECIPIENT marker

4.7.2. *GIVE as a benefactive*

In some languages, the RECIPIENT with donatory verbs is marked in the same way as a benefactive, meaning "for the sake of" or "on behalf of". These senses, RECIPIENT marking and benefactive, are closely related, both focusing on the person who experiences some change in state as a consequence of an act. Also, each sense weakly implies the other. The senses co-occur in a relationship of polysemy in many languages. In Chamorro, for example, the same form *pära* marks RECIPIENT as well as benefactive, as illustrated in (73).

(73) a.   *Hu na'i i lebblu pära i taotao.*
         I   gave   the   book   to   the   man
         'I gave the book to the man.'   (Chamorro)

     b.   *Man-ma'cho'chu i famagu'un pära i atungu'-niha.*
         PL-work   the   children   for   the   friends-their
         'The children worked for their friends.'   (Chamorro)

As noted in the preceding section, a GIVE morpheme may be extended to function as a RECIPIENT marker. Hence, it is not surprising that one also finds literal GIVE extended to a benefactive meaning alongside its use as a RECIPIENT marker:

(74) a.   *Tā gěi wǒ zào-le yì dōng fángzi.*
         he/she   give   me   build-ASP   one   CL   house
         'He/she built a house for me.'   (Mandarin)

     b.   *Ông ấy bán sách cho tôi.*
         he   sold   books   give   me
         'He sold books for me.' / 'He sold books to me.'
                           (Vietnamese, Liem 1979: 57)

     c.   *ʔɔːpùk tɛɲ siəʋphʉu ʔaoy khɲom.*
         father   buy   books   give   me
         'Father buys books for me.' (Cambodian, Jacob 1968: 141)

d. *Chán   sòng   nǎnsɨ̀:   hâi   dèk.*
   I   sent   book   give   child
   'I sent a book for a child.' / 'I sent a book to the child.'
                                              (Thai)

e. *átsá   kìbɔ̀è   kúki   Kòfi   kúki   mɛ́.*
   he-paid   money   give   Kofi   give   me
   'He paid the money to Kofi for me.'
                                    (Siya, Ghana, Ford 1988: 144)

Examples of GIVE extended to mark benefactive may also be found in the Senufo (Africa) languages (see Carlson 1991: 214), where the GIVE morpheme appears as a postposition. Matisoff (1991: 427–431) provides examples from a number of Southeast Asian languages.

As with the extension of GIVE to RECIPIENT marking function, there is some variability as to the syntactic nature of the GIVE morpheme in its benefactive marking function. In Mandarin, benefactive *gěi* is preposition-like and fails tests for verbhood such as occurring with aspect markers. In Akan (Nigeria), on the other hand, the benefactive use of GIVE appears more verb-like on account of its ability to take the same kind of morphology as does a canonical verb, as in the following examples (tones not shown) from Schachter (1974), cited by Baker (1989: 523–524):

(75) a. *Me-yɛɛ   adwuma   me-maa   Amma.*
        1SG-do   work   1SG-give   Amma
        'I work for Amma.'   (Akan, Baker 1989: 523)

     b. *Ma-yɛ   adwuma   ma-ma   Amma.*
        1SG:PERF-do work   1SG:PERF-give   Amma
        'I have worked for Amma.'   (Akan, Baker 1989: 524)

As discussed in Chapter 2, there is an element of benefit to the RECIPIENT in the frame of prototypical GIVE. Even when GIVE is used in a relatively literal way, a benefactive nuance may be present and may be felt as a salient part of the meaning. With "true" benefactive phrases, there does not need to be anything actually given to the beneficiary (*I peeled the potatoes for her, I walked the dog for our neighbour* etc.). In most cases, however, there is at least a weak implication that the beneficiary is also a RECIPIENT. Consider sentences like *I sang a song for her, I wrote a poem for her*, where *her* can be construed as a kind of RECIPIENT of the song/poem, as well as a beneficiary. In other words, the two concepts of RECIPIENT and beneficiary weakly imply each other, even though they may be distinguished conceptually. The purely benefactive use and the purely RECIPIENT use of GIVE represent limiting cases along a continuum, understandable through the common experiential association between RECIPIENT and beneficiary in the frame of giving.

Sometimes, the benefactive function of the GIVE morpheme may be restricted in ways which reveal a close connection still with the literal GIVE sense. An example of a relatively limited extension of GIVE to benefactive is seen in Cantonese (following the transcription system in Huang 1970):

(76) a.   *Chit pìng-gwó béi ngóh.*
        cut apple   give me
        'Cut an apple for me.'   (Cantonese)

    b.   *Bàh-bā jaahn chín   béi   ngóh.*
        dad   earns money give me
        'Dad earns money for me.'   (Cantonese)

    c.   ?/* *Cheung gō   béi   ngóh.*
        OK *Cheung gō   béi   ngóh tèng.*
            sing   song give me   hear
        'Sing a song for me.'   (Cantonese)

    d. * *Jà   go pìng-gwó béi   ngóh.*
        hold CL apple   give me
        'Hold the apple for me.'   (Cantonese)

    e. * *John heui Wellington   béi   ngóh.*
        John go Wellington   give me
        'John went to Wellington for me.'   (Cantonese)

In the "cut apple" and "earn money" sentences, the GIVE morpheme has as its landmark a person who is transparently a RECIPIENT of the THING named earlier in the sentence. The receiving of the THING is, however, not completed but only implied as a potential consequence. Consequently, it is natural to translate the GIVE morpheme in these sentences as a benefactive "for" in English. In the case of the "hold the apple" and "go to Wellington" sentences, on the other hand, there is no connection, or at best only the most indirect connection, with the handing over of something. In (76d–e), it seems significant that the person landmark of the GIVE morpheme is not functioning as a RECIPIENT of any named action. That is, Cantonese GIVE only allows a benefactive meaning in contexts where the beneficiary has the potential of receiving something. The "sing a song" case appears somewhat intermediate. To the extent it is acceptable (not all speakers accepted it), one must presumably think of the song as "going out" to a hearer, so that the hearer functions like a RECIPIENT. It is useful to compare these facts with another Chinese dialect, Hokkien, as in (77), where we find the GIVE morpheme extended to a "true" benefactive, where the beneficiary does not need to be a RECIPIENT of anything passed. The Hokkien sentences are transcribed following the system in Embree (1973) with some symbols modified to conform more to common linguistic practice.

(77) a. *Chiat pîn-kó hō̄   goá.*
          cut   apple give me
          'Cut an apple for me.'   (Hokkien)

      b. *Pa-pa thàn lúi   hō̄ goá.*
          dad   earns money give me
          'Dad earns money for me.'   (Hokkien)

      c. *Chhiũ koa hō̄   goá.*
          sing   song give me
          'Sing a song for me.'   (Hokkien)

      d. *Gīm pîn-ko hō̄ goá.*
          hold apple give me
          'Hold the apple for me.'   (Hokkien)

      e. *John khì Wellington hō̄   goá.*
          John go   Wellington give   me
          'John went to Wellington for me.'   (Hokkien)

In the case of Hokkien, the position of the GIVE morpheme in the clause is the same regardless of whether it is used in the sense of RECIPIENT or benefactive. This might be seen as facilitating a subtle transition to a benefactive sense. One could not reason in the same way in the case of Mandarin, however. Mandarin *gěi* in a "true" benefactive sense occurs before the main verb (which I will refer to as the preverbal position), whereas *gěi* marking RECIPIENT occurs after the main verb (the postverbal position).

In Figure 37, I have sketched a benefactive extension from literal GIVE. In this diagram I have focused on the relevant aspect of literal GIVE, which is the domain of "human interest", as described in Section 2.5. The benefactive preserves this benefactive bias of literal GIVE and makes it the central component of the meaning. As shown in the diagram, the benefactive (as exemplified by Hokkien *hɔ̃*) is not restricted to donatory acts and does not necessarily involve any RECIPIENT.

With the benefactive extension of GIVE one finds constructions where the morpheme functions as a verbal affix rather than as an adposition. Examples of this sort from Amerindian languages (Nez Perce, Sahaptian, and Klamath) in the northwest of the United States are discussed by Rude (1991: 186–187). Consider, for example, the pair of examples in (78).

(78) a. *Tom hi-'ní-ye*　　　*wálc 'áayato-na.*
　　　Tom 3SUBJ-give-PAST knife woman-OBJ
　　　'Tom gave the woman the knife.' (Nez Perce, Rude p.c.)
　　b. *Wálc páa-ny-a'n-ya*　　　　　*'áayato-na.*
　　　knife 3SUBJ:3OBJ-make-BEN-PAST woman-OBJ
　　　'He made the woman a knife.' (Nez Perce, Rude 1991: 186)

The benefactive marker in the second example, appearing as *-a'n,* is the same root as the Nez Perce verb GIVE in the first example, appearing as *'ní*. Both these forms are phonologically conditioned variants of a basic form *-'eni*. Similar facts hold in the other languages discussed by Rude.

In Japanese, there is an interesting relationship which holds between the GIVE verb *ageru* and a benefactive sense.[10] The GIVE morpheme

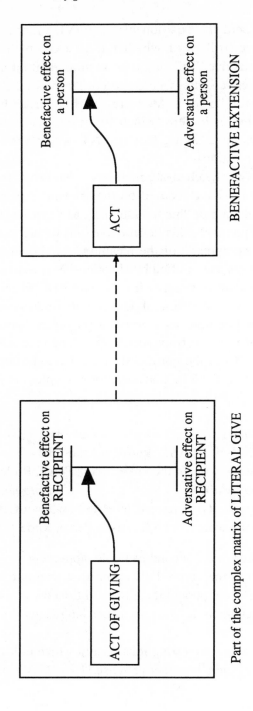

Figure 37. Extension of GIVE to benefactive sense

ageru appears preferentially as part of a larger verbal complex when a beneficiary, followed by *no tame ni* 'possessive sake indirect object' occurs. Compare (79a), without any benefactive phrase, and (79b) with one.

(79) a.   *Watashi wa*   *piano o*   *hiita.*
      I   TOPIC   piano OBJ   played.
      'I played the piano.'   (Japanese)

     b.   *Watashi wa*   *kanojo no*   *tame ni*   *piano o*
       I   TOPIC   her   POSS   sake   IO   piano OBJ
       hiite   *ageta.*
       play   gave
       'I played the piano for her.'   (Japanese)

This is similar to what is found in Marathi, as described by Hook (1991: 66), where we also find a close relationship between GIVE and the presence of a benefactive phrase. In Marathi, GIVE functions as a kind of verbal predicate, forming what is traditionally called a "vector" in a "compound verb" construction. In Marathi, the function of GIVE as a vector is limited to two situations: either a situation involving outward movement, consistent with "movement away" extensions discussed in Section 4.8.1, or a situation in which an action is done for another's benefit. In the latter case, it occurs with benefactive phrases, as illustrated below:

(80)   *Maajhaa saaThi he kaam kar-un de-Sil*   *kaa?*
       my:OBL sake   this job   do-CP   give-FUT   Question
       'Will you do this job for me?'   (Marathi, Hook 1991: 66)
       (CP stands for "conjunctive participate", capitalized letters
       stand for retroflex sounds.)

4.8.   Movement

Central to the GIVE frame is the transfer of the THING from the GIVER to the RECIPIENT. As such, the GIVE frame presents us with a clear image of movement from one physical location to another. In the complex matrix that constitutes the full meaning of literal GIVE, there are additional features which qualify as "abstract motion". For example, there is a transfer of control which forms part of giving, which accompanies the physical movement of the THING. The transfer of control is obviously closely related to, but still distinguishable from, the physical movement of the THING. Also, the force dynamics of GIVE, as observed in Section 2.4, has the structure of a flow of action from the GIVER to the RECIPIENT. Taken together, these features combine to make literal GIVE a natural source for images of movement. Indeed, almost all the extensions of GIVE considered thus far can be construed as involving abstract motion of some sort: interpersonal communication, emergence, manifestation, permission, enablement, causation, schematic interaction, even benefactive marking.

Examples of an extension of GIVE to concrete motion are shown in (81). The use of *sich begeben* in (81a) is somewhat formal.

(81) a. *Sie   be-gab   sich   von   Mannheim   nach Berlin.*
          she   PRE-gave REFL from Mannheim   to   Berlin
          'She went from Mannheim to Berlin.'   (German)

      b. *Di   con-migo   en   Paris.*
          1SUBJ:gave   with-myself to   Paris
          'I went to Paris.'   (Spanish)

A "goal" phrase (*nach Berlin, en Paris*) is required, at least in German, in order for these constructions to be complete. I have no specific suggestion as to why this is so, except to note that various extensions of GIVE do seem to require supporting morphemes (derivational affixes, adpositions etc.) which are closely integrated with the meaning of the verbal predicate. Recall, for example, that the extension of Bulgarian GIVE to uses such as *iz-davam ston* 'to groan' requires the prefix *iz-* 'movement from inside to outside' (also involving movement!), as discussed in Section 4.3.1. In the case of motion verbs, there is always a departure point and a destination point implicit in the frame of the verb and their inclusion as elaboration sites in the profile of a motion verb is not surprising.

The use of *sich (nach ...) begeben* in German may be compared with *betake oneself, take oneself off to a place* in English. It is as though one part of the self functions as an agent and another part as the patient. In the case of *sich begeben*, the agent part of the self "pushes" the patient part into movement, whereas in the case of *take oneself*, the agent part is "pulling" the patient part along with it. Another archaic variant of *sich begeben* occurred in a construction *sich einer Sache begeben* 'to renounce a thing', with *eine Sache* 'a thing' in the genitive case. The underlying image here is of abstract motion of a person away from the thing which is being renounced. The use of the genitive in a kind of ablative sense is consistent with some other uses of the genitive in German and other languages.[11]

A more abstract kind of motion based on GIVE appears in the examples in (82), where the motion concerned is a presentation of some entity in the mind, or to the mind. This use is also classifiable as examples of the manifestation group of extensions discussed in Section 4.3.2.

(82) a. *Anglijskij jazyk   dajot-sja   jemu   legko.*
         English   language   gives-REFL   him:DAT easily
         'English comes easily to him.'   (Russian)

     b. *U-davat   li   ti   se   čuzhdi ezitci?*
         PRE-give Interrogative you REFL foreign languages
         'Do foreign languages come easily to you?'   (Bulgarian)

4.8.1. GIVE as "movement away"

If one adopts the perspective of the GIVER, then the THING is viewed as not just moving but going away from the GIVER. This is reminiscent of the facts about Ik, discussed in Section 1.2.1, where the Ik verb GIVE behaves as though it had an inherent orientation "away from GIVER" with respect to directional affixes. In this respect, the Ik verb GIVE is similar to the verb "go". The sense of movement away or disappearance can be found with the extensions of GIVE in (83).

(83)   a.   *Das   Fieber   gibt   sich.*
      the   fever   gives   REFL
      'The fever is going down/away.'   (German)

    b.   *Hōatu,   me   waiho   maua.*
      give (away)   PARTICLE   leave   us
      'Go ahead, leave us.'   (Māori)

In the German example, the fever is viewed as an entity which disappears by removing itself away from a field of vision or cognizance. In the Māori example, the form of GIVE used is the "give away" form, contrasting with the "give here" form *hōmai*. The "give away" form is appropriate here where the sense is that of proceeding out of view. A related "movement away" sense seems also to be relevant to the use of GIVE as a "vector" in Marathi. According to Hook (1991: 66), the GIVE vector is favoured in a compound verb construction where there is an outward movement which the object referent undergoes:

(84)   *Tyaana   katsraa   Taak-un   dilaa.*
       he:ERG   trash   throw-CP   gave
       'He threw out the trash can.'   (Marathi, Hook 1991: 66)
       (CP stands for "conjunctive participate", capitalized letters stand for retroflex sounds.)

Another type of abstract motion based on GIVE involves the sense of "facing in a certain direction", as in English *give on to* (for some speakers). (85) illustrates this in other languages.

(85)   a.   *Ikkunat   antavat   pohjoiseen.*
      windows   give   north:ILLATIVE
      'The windows face to the north.'   (Finnish)

    b.   *La   ventana   da   al   norte.*
      the   window   gives   to:the north
      'The window faces the north.'   (Spanish)

c. *A   janela   dá   no   jardim.*
the window gives in:the garden
'The window opens to the garden.'
(Brazilian Portuguese, Salomao 1990: 90)

Unlike German *sich (nach ...) begeben* 'to go (somewhere)', there is no actual motion in such examples. But there is an abstract motion involving a path along which the view from some point "leads out". Nothing physical, of course, is emitted, but the orientation of the thing is construed as though one's vision proceeds out in some direction or to some other type of landmark. Our own way of describing orientation in English using expressions like *lead out to, look out on* also contain within them a similar metaphor.

4.8.2.   GIVE as "movement into"

If one focuses on the movement of the THING into the sphere of the RECIPIENT in the act of giving, then one has a source for extensions of GIVE relating to (concrete or abstract) movement into a region. The movement could be quite literal and the examples in (81) above include as part of their meanings a literal movement to a new locality. A more specific "movement into" sense is found in the extension of Brazilian Portuguese *dar* constructed with *no* 'in', illustrated in (86).

(86)   *O   navio   deu   no   rochedo.*
the ship gave in:the rock
'The ship hit the rock.'
(Brazilian Portuguese, Salomao 1990: 85)

In addition, there are extensions of GIVE which involve an abstract motion whereby an entity moves into a new state or commences a new activity. The extension of GIVE in some German dialects to a sense of "become, change into", discussed in Section 4.3.3, could be considered an example of moving into a new state, as well as being construed as a kind of emergence. Some additional examples where GIVE takes on the sense of "begin" are given in (87).

(87) a.   *Si*   *diede*   *a gridare* *come* *un pazzo.*
        REFL 3SG:SUBJ:gave to shout   like   a   mad
        'She/he began to shout like a madman.'   (Italian)

    b.   *giva* *sig*   *ill* *att* *springa.*
        give REFL to   run
        'to start running'   (Swedish)

    c.   *Hän*   *anta-utu-i*   *puheisiin*
        she/he give-REFL-PAST   conversation:ILLATIVE
        rehtorin   *kanssa.*
        headmaster:GEN   with
        'She/he entered into conversation with the headmaster.'
                                  (Finnish)

4.9.   Completedness

Giving is typically an event of brief duration resulting in a final state, obviously distinct from the initial state. Thus, in the final state of affairs, the THING is located in the sphere of control of the RECIPIENT, whereas initially it is located in the GIVER's sphere of control. These characteristics of literal GIVE would appear to be the basis for the extension of GIVE to senses which I have grouped together under the label of "completedness". The same characteristics also have some relevance to the peculiarities of the schematic interaction extensions of GIVE, as discussed in Section 4.6.

The abruptness and completedness which form part of the meaning of literal GIVE make GIVE a strongly perfective verb. One can appreciate this by reflection on the meaning of the predicate itself, but there are in addition facts about literal GIVE in languages which point to an inherent perfectivity in GIVE. One piece of evidence for the perfectivity of literal GIVE may be found in the use of the verbal prefix *ge-* in earlier periods of German. In modern German, the prefix *ge-* is part of the marking which appears on the past participle of a verb (cf. infinitive *singen* 'sing' and past participle *gesungen* 'sung'). Already in the period of Old High German, this prefix was well established in this function. With some verbs, however, it was not used or was used only rarely. Even at the time of Middle High German, for example, the prefix still did not appear with the verbs *finden* 'find', *komen* 'come', *treffen* 'meet', and *werden* 'become'. Occasionally, according to Paul (1969: 188), the prefix is also missing in the case of *geben* 'give' and *nemen* 'take'. The explanation offered by Paul (1969: 188) is that most of these verbs are of a perfective nature to begin with (and this would certainly apply to GIVE), making the addition of the perfectivizing prefix redundant. Another piece of evidence comes from Russian. In Russian, most verbs exist in both an imperfective and perfective form. In the overwhelming majority of cases, a simple stem will be imperfective and the perfective will be formed from that stem through the addition of a prefix, e.g. *čitat'* 'write (Imperfective)' and *pročitat'* 'write (Perfective)'. There is, however, a small number of verbs where the simple stem itself functions as a perfective, including: *past'* 'fall', *leč'* 'to lie down', *sest'* 'sit down', *det'* 'put', and *dat'* 'give' (Vilgelminina 1963: 21). Once again, the morphology associated with GIVE shows this verb to be one of a set of inherently perfective verbs.

Although I have no examples where it is the morpheme GIVE which appears as the perfective marker, transforming the aspectual nature of the accompanying verb, there are examples where a grammaticized GIVE occurs with perfective type verbs. One example of this is found in Hindi-Urdu where GIVE functions as a so-called "vector", i.e. an auxiliary-like component, in the compound verb construction with a meaning sometimes described as perfective. The discussion by Hook (1991: 66–74) suggests, however, that the usual function of GIVE in this construction in Hindi-Urdu is not really to perfectivize the main verb, as the main verb is typically one which already contains the idea of completedness. It would appear more correct to speak of GIVE in this construction as indicating the presence of a perfective element of meaning in the verb phrase, rather than creating it. This would be comparable to the use of GIVE with the main verb in Japanese together with an explicitly marked benefactive phrase, as discussed in Section 4.7.2.

Some examples of the use of GIVE with perfective-like main verbs are given in (88).

(88) a. *Is   mE   us   ne   teraa naam le   diyaa.*
          this in   he   ERG   your name take gave
          'He implicated you in this.' (Hindi-Urdu, Hook 1991: 67)

      b. *Aaxirkaar us   ne   mujh   ko paise   de   diye.*
          finally   he   ERG   me   to money   give   gave
          'At last he gave me the money.'
                                      (Hindi-Urdu, Hook 1991: 67)

      c. *MAI ne   uske hoThO ko   TaTol-naa Suruu kar diyaa.*
          I   ERG her   lips   DAT feel-INF   start   do gave
          'I began to feel her lips.'
          (Hindi-Urdu, Hook 1991: 6, cited from Vaid 1970: 13)

Chatterjee (1988: 75) notes a similar phenomenon in Bengali, where the GIVE morpheme *de-* functions as the vector in compound verb formations. In Bengali, too, it would appear that GIVE as a vector occurs preferentially with perfective-like verbs. It is used, for example, with the verbs "touch", "bite", "cut", but not with "hear" or "smell".

   The Turkish use of GIVE as a kind of auxiliary, illustrated in (89), is relevant here as another illustration of the inherent perfectivity of GIVE.

(89)   *Geli-ver!*
          come-give
          'Come quickly/just come!'   (Turkish)

As an auxiliary, Turkish GIVE implies ease and quickness in the completion of an act, although the meaning can not simply be reduced to these properties. Tarring (1886: 107) characterizes the semantics of the auxiliary GIVE in terms of "promptitude, readiness, facility, offhandedness" and "cheapening ... or making light of an action." Properties of literal GIVE, including its inherent perfectivity, are relevant to these nuances of auxiliary GIVE. The idea of "offhandedness" and "making light of an action" may reflect a further metaphorical mapping from quickness of an act to unimportance of an act.

While the notion of perfectivity refers to the internal structure of a verbal predicate and is distinct from the time at which an event happens, there is nevertheless a conceptual connection between perfectivity and the location of an event in the past. It is the concept of completedness which is common to both of them. In the case of perfectivity, the completedness is observable within the time span in which the event takes place, whereas locating an event in past time means one sees the whole event as completed with respect to the present (or some other point of temporal reference). This link between perfectivity and past time is relevant to the extension of a GIVE morpheme to past tense contexts in addition to the perfective contexts mentioned above. Based on the discussion in Hook (1991: 62–63), it appears that the GIVE vector in a compound verb construction in Hindi-Urdu occurs comfortably in contexts referring to past, completed events. This is illustrated in (90), though note that here it occurs with a GIVE main verb (in the main clause) which also strongly favours a GIVE vector.

(90)   *Jab   tak   aap   yahAA   aae   us ne   mujhe   ciTThii*
        when   by   you   here   came   he ERG   me   letter
        de   dii   thii.
        give   given   had
        'By the time you came here, he had given me the letter.'
                          (Hindi-Urdu, Hook 1991: 62)

4.10. Overview of the main categories of extension

Having now dealt with the main categories of figurative extensions of literal GIVE, it is appropriate to reflect on the full set of meanings represented in these extensions. While it is necessary to look at each one of these main categories in turn, it is also useful to take a "bird's-eye view" of the whole semantic terrain which we have been exploring. This means collecting our main observations about the extensions of literal

GIVE into one larger map showing the directions in which extensions proceed, cross-linguistically.

4.10.1. *The network of GIVE meanings*

The main directions in which literal GIVE extends, cross-linguistically, are summarized in Figure 38. In this diagram I have shown only the broad categories, as used in the preceding sections, without attempting to include every submeaning which is found. The broad categories alone are quite sufficient to demonstrate the diversity of meanings found amongst the extensions. The meaning of literal GIVE, which functions as the source for all these extensions, is shown in the centre of this network of meanings, reflecting its central role in the discussion of these extensions. I have grouped together meanings which share some obvious commonalities, as discussed in the preceding sections. So, for example, enablement and causation both involve one entity having some role in determining some later event and these two large areas of extensions are therefore grouped together.

I have not attempted to incorporate into Figure 38 many claims concerning the order in which extensions must happen. I have done this only for extensions in the area of enablement and causation. As discussed in Sections 4.4 and 4.5, it is the interpersonal kind of enablement/causation ("person A enables/causes person B to do something") which is conceptually closest to the semantics of literal GIVE. Consequently, it seems reasonable to posit this kind of enablement/causation before the extension to the more general sense ("event A enables/causes event B") or to the purpose sense ("person A does something so that event B can happen"). Determining an actual order in which figurative extensions of GIVE must happen, chronologically, would be an enormous task and one which falls outside the scope of this study. Nor have I attempted to represent in Figure 38 all the commonalities which one might perceive amongst the various extensions. Abstract motion of some sort is not only evidenced in the "change of location" group of senses, but is arguably a component of other meanings too, such as interpersonal communication, enablement, causation, sche-

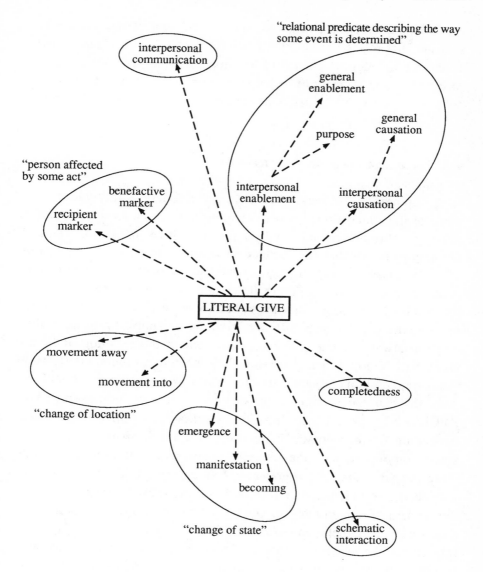

Figure 38. Overview of the figurative extensions of GIVE

matic interaction, and change of state. An element of causation is present not just in the causation extension, it is also part of enablement, schematic interaction, change of location, and interpersonal communication. There is a danger of losing sight of the main trends if all this detail is included and such detail is consequently omitted from Figure 38.

4.10.2. Motivating semantic extensions

It is important to observe that there are alternative motivations for some of the connections between meanings. This is a familiar situation in any synchronic account of polysemy which relies on the intuitions of the linguist to establish the connections between meanings. In the course of the discussion in this chapter, I have had occasion to point out some of the alternative ways to motivate certain extensions. Even when one focuses on just a single link between two senses, there are alternative motivations which can be offered. It would be simplistic to think that one can always isolate just one component of the meaning of literal GIVE which motivates an extension. The meaning of literal GIVE itself is so complex in its semantic structure that it is normally not possible to draw the boundaries around just one component of its meaning. The RECIPIENT, for example, functions simultaneously in various ways, depending on the domain: it represents a kind of spatial goal in the spatiotemporal domain, the centre of a new sphere of control over the thing passed in the control domain, an energy sink in the force-dynamics domain, and the person typically benefiting from the act of giving in the domain of human interest. Distinguishing the various domains, as I did in Chapter 2, helps in our description of meanings, but at the same time it must be recognized that the domains are closely interrelated and one can not entirely ignore any domain in the description of part of the meaning of GIVE. If I appear to have done this in my discussion of the figurative extensions, it is because I am directing attention to what I consider to be the *most* relevant component of the meaning of literal GIVE at that point in the discussion, rather than the *only* component of meaning which is relevant.

Consider from this point of view the extension of a GIVE verb to a "permit" sense, as found in Russian, Mandarin, Finnish and many other languages. Common to these senses of "give" and "permit" is the idea of enabling a person to do something. This seems to me to be one of the more obvious commonalities between the two senses and this was the basis of the discussion of this type of extension in the overview in Section 4.5. But further reflection will reveal other parallels between the senses, involving all the domains of meaning which we have recognized. This is illustrated in Figure 39. Each of the domains which make up the meaning of literal GIVE provides some motivation for the extension. In Figure 39 this is shown by arrows leading from each domain in literal GIVE to a corresponding domain of the "permit" sense. In addition, I have tried to characterize what the source and target domains have in common. It is the sum of all these commonalities which sanctions the extension.

A full account of the extensions of literal GIVE would require a comparable degree of detail for each extension. More generally, one must always be prepared for multiple motivations in the extension of meaning. The more conceptual complexity in the meaning of the source morpheme, the more motivations one is likely to find, whether one is thinking about synchronic relatedness of meanings, i.e. schematic networks, or diachronic paths of evolution of these meanings.

Note, finally, that there is a kind of motivation for extensions in the use of GIVE morphemes which relates to the forms of constructional types in a language. I have been focusing on semantic motivations for figurative extensions, but one must also consider aspects of the form of the figurative extensions. In many cases, the form of an extended sense of GIVE is a form which has independent existence in the language and this in turn provides some additional motivation for the new use of the GIVE morpheme. For example, German has extensions of literal GIVE which involve impersonal, reflexive, and impersonal reflexive constructions as illustrated in (91).

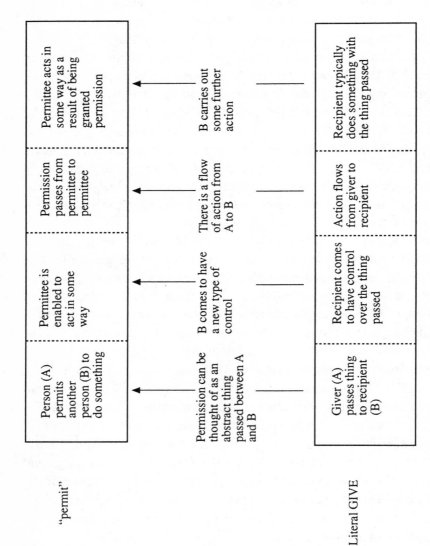

Figure 39. The multiple motivations for the extension of GIVE to "permit"

(91) a. Impersonal:

     Es gibt sieben Universitäten in Neuseeland.
     it gives seven universities in New Zealand
     'There are seven universities in New Zealand.' (German)

   b. Reflexive:

     Das Fieber gibt sich.
     the fever gives REFL
     'The fever is going away.'   (German)

   c. Impersonal reflexive:

     Es be-gab sich, dass...
     it PRE-gave REFL that
     'It happened that...'   (German)

Each of these construction types (impersonal, reflexive, impersonal reflexive) exists in German quite independently of the figurative GIVE uses. That is, one must recognize for German these three constructional types, each with its own characteristic form and schematic meaning. In accounting for these figurative uses, then, one can appeal to already existing morphological/syntactic devices as part of the explanation of why the new uses are possible. The extension of literal GIVE in (91) elaborates the polysemy of existing construction types rather than creating brand new construction types. Thus, it is no coincidence that languages such as German, Italian, Spanish are rich in figurative extensions of GIVE involving grammaticized reflexive and impersonal constructions but lack extensions of GIVE to preposition-like uses meaning benefactive. These languages have well-established reflexive and impersonal construction types but do not have well-established serial verb type constructions in which morphemes are ambiguous between verbs and prepositions. Certain African languages and Chinese dialects, on the other hand, behave in exactly the opposite way: they have well-developed preposition-like uses of GIVE morphemes, but lack reflexive and impersonal types of extensions. This reflects the availability of different conventional devices in the languages.

4.11.   Miscellaneous extensions

The discussion in the preceding sections has attempted to identify the main directions in which GIVE verbs have been extended cross-linguistically. However, GIVE is such a productive source for metaphorical extensions, including grammaticalizations, that it would be wrong to assume that my classification exhausts all the possibilities for such extensions. In this section I shall briefly comment on various additional extensions.

4.11.1.   Metonymies

Metonymy is as evident in the use of GIVE verbs as it is elsewhere in language. An expression such as *give someone the boot* 'to fire someone, to sack someone', for example, makes reference to a *boot* metonymically. *Boot* is associated with kicking something away from oneself, and kicking something is a way of imaging the sacking of a person from a job. *Boot* in this expression is thus used metonymically for an act (kicking) which is metaphorically extended to conceptualize another act (sacking someone). Salomao (1990: 79) describes an interesting use of metonymy with GIVE verbs in Brazilian Portuguese to describe the weather. So, for example, in response to a question about the state of the weather, one could reply as in (92). Here, the reference to the beach or swimming pool is understood as indicating that the weather is sunny, a good volley ball game as indicating that the weather is sunny and not windy etc.

(92) *Está dando* $\left\{\begin{array}{l}praia\\piscina\\um\ vôlei\ bom\\uma\ blusinhe\ leve\end{array}\right\}$.

is give:GERUND $\left\{\begin{array}{l}\text{beach}\\\text{swimming pool}\\\text{a good volleyball game}\\\text{a light sweater}\end{array}\right\}$

'It is the kind of weather for $\left\{\begin{array}{l}\text{the beach}\\\text{the swimming pool}\\\text{a good volleyball game}\\\text{a light sweater}\end{array}\right\}$ ',

(Brazilian Portuguese, Salomao 1990: 79)

Body parts are particularly productive in metonymical uses with GIVE verbs. The meanings of such expressions vary considerably from language to language, depending on the cultural associations connected with the particular body part. In contemporary English, we find expressions such as: *give a hand, give one's hand in marriage, give a leg up, give lip, give cheek, give fingers* 'make an obscene sign with the fingers', *give teeth* (*to legislation* etc.), *give someone the elbow, give someone the cold shoulder*. The OED offers the following examples from earlier English:

(93) a. *The mothers use to beare their children at their backs...they give them the brest over their shoulders.* With meaning 'to present or expose to the action of a person or thing'.

   b. *to give back* (obsolete.) 'to retreat, turn tail, run away' (1591, Shakespeare, Two Gentlemen v, iv, 126): *Thurio giue backe, or else embrace thy death.*

   c. *to give one the back* (obsolete) 'to turn away from, disregard him'.

   d. *to give a back* (obsolete)(at leap-frog, etc.) 'to bend the body so as to present a surface which may be jumped over'.

Other languages offer many other metonymies which I will not try to document here. Suffice to say that a full understanding of such metonymies often requires an understanding of larger cultural facts pertaining to the culture. In Jacaltec, for example, an expression which is literally "give big stomach for me!" functions as an idiom with the meaning "be patient with me!" (Craig 1977: 396). To understand how a word with the meaning of "stomach" comes to be used in this idiom, one needs to appreciate the existence of a number of metaphors in Jacaltec based on "stomach", which is associated with various emotions and mental states (Craig 1977: 274). So, for example, "I would like to sing/play" is expressed as "My stomach would like to sing/play etc" (Craig 1977: 315); "I am sad that he is going" is expressed as "My stomach is burning that he should go" (Craig 1977: 256). The "give big stomach" construction is thus part of a larger, coherent system of metaphor which needs to be considered in a full account of the semantics of the construction.

4.11.2. People giving people

Not only inanimate things, but people, too, can be "given", as in *give one's daughter in marriage*. The phrase presumably has its origins in a social context where daughters were "owned" in quite a literal sense and, to the extent that is true, it builds directly on the idea underlying literal GIVE, namely that there is a transfer of ownership. Other related uses of GIVE involve not so much the transfer of ownership of a person as putting someone under the care or protection of some person or institution, such as a convent or school. In Polish, for example, it is the GIVE verb *dać* which is used in the expression "to send someone to school". Another instance of giving of people is in Tikopia (Polynesian), where the GIVE verb *sori* is used with human PATIENTs to mean "consign person to spirits, with harmful intent" (Firth 1985: 449–450). In Hawaiian, GIVE figures in a construction meaning "to commend to one's care" (Lorrin Andrews 1985: 131). Craig (1977: 385) comments on the "frequent lending and borrowing of children among neighbours and relatives to help with daily tasks" in the Jacaltec

community she studied in connection with the use of the GIVE verb
a'(a') in sentences such as (94).

(94)   *Xc-ach   y-a'   ix   munlahoj tet ya'.*
          ASP-2ABS 3ERG-give she to work   to   CL
          'She gave you to her (older woman) to work.'

                                        (Jacaltec, Craig 1977: 385)

Ya' is the classifier for a respected non-deity, here referring to an older
woman.

A reflexive construction with GIVE is possible where one assigns
oneself to the care or authority of another as in *give oneself to God* and
comparable uses in other languages. A particularly common meaning of
reflexive GIVE with human subjects has to do with surrendering to an
enemy, police, etc., as in (95).

(95) a. *dar-si   al   nemico*
           give-REFL to:the enemy
           'give oneself up to the enemy'   (Italian)
      b. *Nie dajmy   się.*
           not   give:1PL:IMP REFL:ACC
           'We mustn't give in.'   (Polish)
      c. *Die Festung hat   sich   dem   Feind   er-geben.*
           the fortress has   REFL the   enemy:DAT PRE-given
           'The fortress has surrendered to the enemy.' (German)

The sense of surrendering to an enemy is close also to the sense of sex-
ual subjugation, as in *She gave herself to him.* In other languages:

(96) a. *Sie   gab   sich   einem Mann   hin.*
           she   gave REFL a   man:DAT Directional
           'She had sexual intercourse with a man.'   (German)
      b. *Tja   mu   se   ot-dade.*
           she   him   REFL PRE-gave
           'She had sexual intercourse with him.'   (Bulgarian)

There is another common usage of GIVE in a reflexive construction where it is used to conceptualize the idea of a person's addiction, devotion, or dedication. The target of the giving may be a person, an influence, life style, cause etc. This is seen in the expressions in (97).

(97) a. *Er hat sich dem Teufel er-geben.*
 he has REFL the devil:DAT PRE-given
 'He has given himself to the devil.' (German)

b. *se donner au jeu*
 REFL give to gambling
 'to be addicted to gambling' (French)

c. *dar-si agli studi*
 give-REFL to:the study
 'devote oneself to study' (Italian)

d. *dar-si al bere*
 give-REFL to:the drink
 'to take to drink' (Italian)

e. *Hän anta-utu-i opiskelemaan*
 she/he give-REFL-PAST study:ILLATIVE
 historiaa.
 history:PARTITIVE
 'She/he devoted her/himself to studying history.' (Finnish)

f. *Hän anta-utu-i juopottelemaan.*
 she/he give-REFL-PAST boozing:ILLATIVE
 'She/he gave her/himself up to drink.' (Finnish)

Common to many of these extensions of the THING to a human is the notion of putting the person into a position of being under the influence, authority, or control of some entity. This can be seen as reflecting one of the properties of literal GIVE which involves putting a THING into the sphere of control of the RECIPIENT.

An interesting expression in English which might appear to fall in the category of giving people is *I give you the Queen!* However, there is certainly no transfer of ownership or custodianship of the Queen. Rather than connecting it with the other extensions dealt with in this section, I believe it is better understood as being like the presentative uses of GIVE described earlier. *I give you the Queen!* is best understood as equivalent to something like "I put before you (on an imaginary stage) the person called the Queen (for you, the audience, to react to)". *I give you the host* would be analyzed in the same way.

4.12. Overview of figurative extensions of GIVE and TAKE

While not attempting here to give a full account of figurative extensions of TAKE, it is interesting nevertheless to make some comparisons between GIVE and TAKE with regard to the kinds of figurative extensions they exhibit. As pointed out in Chapter 2, there are similarities and differences between literal GIVE and TAKE and these prove relevant to understanding the similarities and differences between figurative GIVE and TAKE.

If we begin with the spatio-temporal domain, we may note that literal GIVE and TAKE both involve, in a very conspicuous way, the movement of some object through space. We have already seen how reflexive GIVE may give rise to verbs of motion, as in German *sich begeben* 'to go'. TAKE, even in a non-reflexive usage, can extend to senses relating to motion. So, for example, *Kim took off* means that Kim left (suddenly). In *Kim took Lee to the pictures, take* combines the sense of motion and accompaniment. We also find a reflexive use of *take* in archaic English *betake oneself*. We see, then, that both German *sich begeben* and *betake oneself* construe (typically human) locomotion as a reflexive action, in the one case as "giving oneself to somewhere" and in the other case as "taking/bringing oneself to somewhere". The same sense of locomotion is achieved here despite the semantic oppositeness of the source predicates GIVE and TAKE. It must be stressed that GIVE and TAKE appear as "opposites" only with respect to certain semantic dimensions (involving, among other things, the direction of the movement of the thing relative to the subject). They are not opposites in the sense that one implies movement and the other doesn't. It would be misleading to say that predicates which are opposite in meaning have given rise to an identical figurative extension in this case. The predicates we begin with, GIVE and TAKE, are semantically complex and to the extent their meanings have some elements in common, they have been extended in an identical way.

As mentioned already, the movement of the thing is in opposite directions with respect to the subject referents of GIVE and TAKE, i.e. *away* from the GIVER and *to* the TAKER. Consistent with this, it seems natural to understand a person communicating something to another person as a type of giving (as in *give a lecture to an audience, give a verdict* etc.), but unnatural to think of that as a type of taking. TAKE, on the other hand, is possible as a way of construing the reception of a message, as in *take a message* (in order to pass it on to someone else), *take a letter* (with the meaning of "write down a letter being dictated"), *take advice*. Notice that the expression *take advice* does not refer to listening to advice being given, but refers rather to accepting the advice and actually acting on the advice. The thing being taken in this case is understood then as not just coming into the sphere of interest of the person but is internalized by the receiver and made part of the receiver's new behaviour.

There are some acts relating to communication for which TAKE is quite an inappropriate source domain. This is particularly true of performative expressions such as *give one's blessing, give thanks* etc. One can speak of *receiving a blessing, receiving thanks*, but not *taking a blessing* or *taking thanks*. Recall that literal TAKE does not presuppose a GIVER or indeed any other person apart from the TAKER, whereas *receive* does presuppose a GIVER. Consistent with this, the figurative extension of *receive* (but not *take*) usually complements the figurative extension of *give* in such expressions.

When we consider GIVE and TAKE in terms of the control exercised over a thing, the differences between GIVE and TAKE are striking. With GIVE, control over the thing is passed to another person and it is this feature which underlies the figurative extensions of GIVE relating to the transfer of control. These are the permissive, manipulative, causative, purposive senses of GIVE found in many languages, as discussed in this chapter. Just as literal GIVE involves a transfer of control over a physical object (in its prototypical sense), figurative GIVE involves a transfer of control over an event to some other party. With

TAKE, on the other hand, control over the thing comes to reside in the TAKER, without any necessary implication that control was passed to that person from someone else. Consequently, TAKE is inappropriate as a way of construing the granting of permission to perform some act, or causing another person to do something etc. and TAKE predicates have not developed these senses, as far as I am aware. On the other hand, TAKE is compatible with complements relating to an assumption of control as in *take responsibility, take charge, take courage, take care, take on something* etc. Note that GIVE and TAKE can both appear in expressions involving a transfer of responsibility, but with different nuances. Thus, *give oneself responsibility for something* implies that the subject had the authority to assign the responsibility in the first place, whereas *take responsibility for something* does not carry that implication and could well be used to describe taking responsibility away from someone else without there being any orderly transfer of control. Once again, these figurative extensions of GIVE and TAKE reflect properties of their literal senses.

It was observed earlier in this chapter that the force dynamics of GIVE involved a relatively clear "energy flow" from one person to another and this would appear to make GIVE a suitable source for extensions where GIVE functions as a kind of schematic transitive verb, as in *give the car a wash*. Since the energy flow in the case of TAKE proceeds from a person (the one who initiates the taking) back to the same person, the beginning and end points in the TAKE scene are one and the same. This means that TAKE is not such an obvious image as a way of understanding a flow of energy from one point to another. On the other hand, there is an obvious sense in which there is a movement to the taker in a TAKE scene. While the act of taking is initiated by a person, the movement of the thing to that person is the most obvious change brought about by the act of taking. TAKE is thus appropriate as a way of visualizing more abstract kinds of energy flow to a person, especially where the energy source is indeterminate. So, for example, one finds expressions such as *take a beating, take a hiding, take a battering, take a punch, take a knock, take a catch,* etc., all of which are, semantically, like passives. TAKE, for example, functions as a kind of passive counterpart to an active GIVE in a pair of sentences such as *The thugs gave Harry a beating* and *Harry took a beating (from the thugs)*, parallel to *The thugs beat Harry* and *Harry was beaten (by the thugs)*.

A commonality between the energy flows of GIVE and TAKE which may be noted is that they both lead to a point where the act is seen to be completed. This makes both predicates perfective in nature and this was commented on with respect to GIVE earlier in this Chapter. Note that Middle High German *nemen* 'take' behaves like *geben* 'give' with respect to the *ge-* prefix, an indication of an inherent perfectivity in both these verbs (Section 4.9). Lord (1993: 124–125, 128–129) discusses a number of examples where a TAKE morpheme is closely associated with a perfective aspect. This is the case, for example, in Dagbani (Gur, Ghana). In (98a), the TAKE morpheme *zang* is used in a construction which looks like a serial verb construction, but where the use of *zang* does not imply any actual taking. Instead, *zang* reinforces a sense of perfectivity to the event. The semantics of *zang* are brought out nicely by contrasting (98a) with the imperfective sentence (98b), in which *mala*, literally meaning "have", is required in place of *zang*.

(98) a. *M   zang   m   suu   nmaai   nimdi.*
     I   take   my   knife   cut:PERF   meat
     'I cut the meat with my knife (the knife may already be in
     my hand).'   (Dagbani, Lord 1993: 128)

   b. *M   mala   m   suu   nmaara   nimdi.*
     I   have   my   knife   cut:IMPERF   meat
     'I am cutting the meat with my knife.'
                                                   (Dagbani, Lord 1993: 128)

There is more to the meaning of *zang* than just the reinforcement of perfective aspect. As noted by Lord (1993: 129), the *zang* construction also requires that the direct object of the clause be something movable.

One significant point of difference between GIVE and TAKE concerns the way in which the thing given or taken is further utilized. In an act of giving, it is natural for the RECIPIENT to go on to do something with the thing newly acquired, whereas in the act of taking something, it is the TAKER who may be expected to do something with the thing ac-

quired. Consequently, we find different natural elaborations of GIVE
and TAKE clauses, along the lines of (99).

(99) a. *X gave Y to Z in order for Z to do something with Y.*
          (I gave Kim the book to read, I gave Kim the book for her
          to have a look at etc.)
      b. *X took Y in order for X to do something with Y.*
          (I took the book to read etc.)

It is the frame encoded in (99a) which is most relevant to an understanding of the extension of GIVE predicates to enablement and permission, as discussed earlier in this chapter. The semantics of TAKE,
however, make it less suitable as a source for such extensions. On the
other hand, the semantics of TAKE make it (rather than GIVE) suitable
as the first predicate in a serial verb construction, along the lines of "X
took Y (and) read (it)", where the subject referent of each predicate is
the same. Where a language has serial verb constructions involving
TAKE as the first predicate, it is possible for TAKE to develop into an
adposition, marking an object of the second verbal predicate. This kind
of reanalysis is well documented by Givón (1975) in African languages.
So, for example, in the Yatye (100a) sentence below, the literal sense of
TAKE is still present, but it is less so in the (100b) sentence, where it
may be analyzed as a marker of the direct object:

(100) a. *Ìywi   awá   òtsi   ikù   utsì.*
          child   took stick shut   door
          'The child shut the door with a stick.'
                  (Yatye, Stahlke 1970, quoted in Givón 1975: 83)
      b. *Ìywi   awá   utsì   ikù.*
          boy   took door   shut
          'The boy shut the door.'
                  (Yatye, Stahlke 1970, quoted in Givón 1975: 83)

A similar reanalysis is evident in the history of Mandarin *bǎ*, which in
earlier periods could be used as a full verb "take, hold", but now functions as a marker of a direct object (cf. Li—Thompson 1981: 356–369,
463–491). Sometimes, the sense of physically taking something may be

present, but this is not necessarily so. Compare (101a) and (101b) below, where the sense of taking is present in the former but not in the
latter.

(101) a. *Bǎ   nèi   ge   bēi   dì   gěi   wǒ.*
           DO   that   CL   cup   hand   give   me
           'Hand me that cup!' (Mandarin, Li—Thompson 1981: 359)
       b. *Nǐ   bǎ   tā   de   yìsi   jiǎng*
           you   DO   3SG   GEN   meaning   talk
           chū   lái   le.
           exit   come   PARTICLE
           'You have explained what (s)he meant.'
                              (Mandarin, Li—Thompson 1981: 463)

Surprisingly, Mandarin *gěi* 'give' may also function as a marker of the
direct object as shown below, although *bǎ* remains the preferred alternative. (My Mandarin informants disagreed about the acceptability of
sentences with *gěi* used in this way, some claiming the constructions
with *gěi* were quite unacceptable.)

(102)   *Tāmen   gěi   nèi   běn   shū   ná   zǒu   le.*
          they   give/DO   that   CL   book   take   go   PARTICLE
          'They took away that book.'   (Mandarin)

I say "surprisingly" here, since it is difficult to reconcile an extension of
GIVE in this way with the semantics of literal GIVE.[12] As discussed
above, when something is given to a RECIPIENT it is the RECIPIENT
who is expected to go on to do something with the thing passed, rather
than the GIVER. Nor have I encountered examples in other languages
of a GIVE predicate being extended to direct object marking. Note also
that in Lord's (1993: 65–138) overview of verbs extending to object
markers, it is only TAKE, not GIVE, which is the source for such
extensions. Possibly, other points of similarity between GIVE and
TAKE (e.g. both involving the movement of a THING) may have been
a reason for the extension of direct object marking from *bǎ* to *gěi*.[13]

4.13. Summary

Literal GIVE is a rich source of figurative extensions and it is necessary to establish some major categories within the extensions in order to deal with the data effectively. These areas of semantic extension are summarized in Figure 38 above. The categories of extensions employed in our discussion reflected semantically close groupings of meanings. While I found it convenient to work with eight major categories, it must be admitted that other categorizations of the data may also have been possible.

While there are often multiple motivations for any one extension, the discussion has focused on the most obvious motivation for each extension, as summarized below:

(i)   The *interpersonal communication* group of extensions is motivated by an extensive and robust metaphorical mapping between the giving act (involving GIVER, THING, and a RECIPIENT) and interpersonal communication (involving a speaker, a message, and a listener).

(ii) *Emergence/manifestation* extensions are relatable to the movement of a THING out of the sphere of control of the GIVER. The movement out of a region in the case of literal GIVE is both concrete (the THING moves physically from the GIVER to the RECIPIENT) and abstract (the THING moves out of an intangible sphere of control into a new sphere of control). The emergence/manifestation extensions may likewise be relatively concrete (as in land "giving" good crops) or abstract (e.g. an event manifests itself by "giving itself").

(iii) *Causation* extensions are motivated by the fact that the GIVER may be construed as the causer of the RECIPIENT coming to have control over the THING, the volitional nature of giving, and the strong sense of a flow of action from GIVER to RECIPIENT.

(iv) *Enablement* extensions have their source in the typical larger frame of giving, whereby the GIVER enables the RECIPIENT to be in control of the THING and to do with the THING what the RECIPIENT wishes to.

(v)   *Schematic interaction* refers to those extensions like *give the car a wash*, where the GIVE verb provides a kind of skeletal structure with a relatively schematic meaning having to do with an agent-patient type of interaction. Such extensions, in English and other languages, preserve the overall force dynamics of literal GIVE.

(vi)   The *recipient-benefactive* group of extensions includes GIVE morphemes used to mark both RECIPIENTs with verbs of transfer, exchange etc. and benefactives. This group of extensions has its source in the characteristics of a typical RECIPIENT entity in literal GIVE.

(vii)   *Movement* extensions involve GIVE morphemes which refer to movement and have their origin in the physical movement of the THING in an act of giving. An abstract kind of motion is arguably present in many of the other extensions of literal GIVE.

(viii) *Completedness* extensions refer to GIVE morphemes used to impart or reinforce a sense of completion or perfectivity or abruptness within a clause. These extensions are relatable to an inherent perfectivity in the semantics of literal GIVE.

In addition to these main categories, there are miscellaneous extensions, some of which have been briefly discussed but which have not been fully documented here.

It is rarely the case that an extension is relatable to one and only one component of the meaning of literal GIVE. In seeking a motivation for an extension, one must be prepared to find multiple aspects of literal GIVE which provide some basis for the extension. Although the discussion in this chapter has tried to identify an aspect of literal GIVE most relevant to motivating an extension, this should not obscure the fact that often there are other co-existing motivations to be considered.

When confronted with such diversity in the range of semantic extensions, as has been documented in this chapter, one might be tempted to declare that literal GIVE may be extended to absolutely anything! This would be wrong. While there is indeed a great diversity within the extensions, the extensions remain compatible with aspects of literal GIVE. Here, as in previous chapters, it is instructive to compare GIVE and TAKE with respect to the figurative extensions they exhibit. There are some clear differences in the kinds of extensions which these two predicates support, reflecting the different dynamics of the source predicates. A comparison of GIVE and TAKE helps us to better appreciate the constrained nature of the semantic extensions in each case.

Chapter 5. Conclusion
and prospects for future research

5.1. Conclusion

In this final chapter I shall review the whole enterprise which has been undertaken in the preceding pages. The study of GIVE is an attempt to bring
together various guiding principles of cognitive linguistics, as defined in
the Preface, into a unified case study of one concept and its linguistic realization. The study is not intended to be a model which other linguists
should follow, and, indeed, the rather special nature of GIVE means that
the present study could not be simply replicated for just any verbal concept
with comparable results. Nevertheless, the study may serve to illustrate
some of the richness and freshness which a cognitive linguistic approach
brings to the study of language.

The parts which make up this study of GIVE are integrated and interrelated in important ways which may not have been fully appreciated in the
discussions which constitute the individual chapters. I see this chapter,
therefore, as helping to impress upon the reader the unified nature of the
study. The interrelatedness of the topics raised in the preceding chapters,
e.g. the connections between literal and figurative GIVE, underscores an
important aspect of a cognitive linguistic approach to language study, as
outlined in the Preface.

In this chapter I shall also venture some thoughts on how the present
study points towards future research. With a focus on one verb and its associated structures, the findings from this study might appear to have a relatively limited significance. I suggest the findings do have a wider significance than might first appear to be the case and in Section 5.2 I offer some
thoughts on this. More specifically, I will discuss how the present study
naturally leads to further research focusing on GIVE in particular languages, diachronic studies investigating the stages by which semantic extensions and grammaticalizations of GIVE come about, and basic
vocabulary.

5.1.1. Giving as a basic and complex act

Two significant properties of the act of giving need to be distinguished and kept firmly in mind in the discussion of GIVE morphemes: giving is experientially basic but conceptually complex. These two properties are independent of each other and different considerations are involved in establishing each of these properties.

The "basicness" of a concept may be argued for by appealing to various kinds of considerations, both non-linguistic and linguistic. It is pertinent to observe, as was done at the very beginning of this study, that the act of giving something to someone (in the most literal sense of *give*) is a common and functionally significant act within the sphere of human activity. One gives things, one receives things which have been given by others, one observes others giving and receiving. The very idea of a human community functioning as an interactive group working towards some common goals seems almost to require that some form of transferring of things from one person to another be an integral and salient part of human activity. This observation may strike some as an unusual way to open a discussion of linguistic phenomena, including a good deal of syntax, coming as it does from a "naive" understanding of our everyday experiential reality rather than a technical theory of formal syntax. I would maintain, however, that it is a sensible starting point for a discussion of basic vocabulary and a discussion of giving which did not acknowledge the everyday reality of such acts would seem to be seriously flawed. It is, furthermore, appropriate to begin the discussion with this particular kind of basicness, since it locates the discussion within the context of broader human considerations. In cognitive linguistics, we do not seek to exclude the human experience from a discussion of human language. On the contrary, we seek, where possible, to see a relevance for human experience in attempts to elucidate language and its structures.

The linguistic facts which reflect the basicness of giving are of various sorts. These are facts which point to a GIVE morpheme in a language as basic vocabulary, according to some criterion. The evidence which has been appealed to in this study has included data from first language acquisition, restricted vocabularies in certain natural language systems, and the restricted vocabulary of "artificial" languages such as Basic English. A

GIVE morpheme has some privileged status in the discussion of each type of data. First language acquisition studies tell us that GIVE constructions are amongst the earliest ones understood. The early comprehension of GIVE constructions is matched by the early use of verbal requests to be given things, with the verbal request often amounting to no more than the use of the noun referring to the thing desired. In the child's use of language, the use of such nouns may, and often does, carry with it the pragmatic function of a request to be given that object. A language such as Kalam illustrates an extremely restricted core set of verbal morphemes which nevertheless serve as the basis for expressing the extensive range of meanings natural language typically conveys. The core verbal morphemes, of which GIVE is one, enter into a great variety of combinations with other morphemes to produce this result. Kalam is an extreme example of a language making highly productive use of limited verbal resources and would seem to be especially relevant to a discussion of basic vocabulary in natural languages. Dyirbal provides yet another type of core vocabulary in the way in which the taboo variety contains just a relatively minimal set of verbs, including a GIVE morpheme, which combine with other lexical items to convey the same range of meanings which the much larger set of verbs in the everyday language describes. Kalam and the taboo variety of Dyirbal are "naturally" occurring basic vocabularies which permit the expression of an extensive set of meanings. An example of an artificially constructed basic vocabulary is the set of words which constitute Basic English and other comparable, simplified vocabularies for purposes such as teaching a language or writing definitions for learners' dictionaries. In such cases we are dealing with proposals by individual thinkers, reformers, lexicographers etc. for ways of reducing vocabulary to a functionally significant minimal set of morphemes or words. Such attempts are worthy of attention in studies of basic vocabulary. Basic English was a carefully thought-out system, created by a thinker of some stature, and designed without any specific modern linguistic theory in mind. The fact that Basic English was able to rely on very few verbal words is an interesting result and one which is consistent with what is found with naturally occurring examples of core vocabularies. Again, the GIVE morpheme is one of the privileged few verbal words included in Basic English.

"Basic vocabulary" is something which can be approached in different ways, as suggested above. When various approaches nevertheless throw up GIVE as one of the basic items of vocabulary, as is true for the most part, then we would appear to be dealing with an exceptionally basic verb.

There is another property of the act of giving which is relevant and that is its relative complexity. Since this study has GIVE morphemes in natural languages as its focus, rather than giving-behaviour as such, it is more accurate in the present context to speak of the semantic complexity of a GIVE morpheme. The semantic complexity of the typical GIVE morpheme comes from the presence of three key participants (GIVER, THING, and RECIPIENT), their peculiar characteristics, and the interactions between them. It is a complexity which is not adequately characterized merely in terms of semantic roles or semantic features. It seems much more helpful to describe the semantics of GIVE by patiently and thoroughly describing all the components, which is what I hope to have achieved in this study.

As a way of managing the discussion of the meaning of GIVE, it is convenient to distinguish various domains which are involved in the semantics. For the purpose of characterizing the semantics of GIVE, four domains may be invoked: the spatio-temporal domain, the control domain, the force-dynamics domain, and the domain of human interest. Domains such as these enable us to separate out observations about the meaning of GIVE into subgroups, each of which has some conceptual coherence to it. Different predicates require different kinds of domains to elucidate meaning. The particular domains posited for the discussion of GIVE seem to capture, between them, the full complexity of GIVE. In the spatio-temporal domain GIVE is seen as involving a change in the location of a THING, originating with a GIVER, and terminating with the RECIPIENT. With prototypical GIVE there is a close proximity between the GIVER and the RECIPIENT and the transference of the THING is accomplished through the use of hands. In the control domain, it is the change in control over the THING which is central to the discussion. At the commencement of the giving act, the THING falls within the sphere of control of the GIVER, but eventually the THING comes to reside within the sphere of control of the RECIPIENT. The force-dynamics domain refers to the components of GIVE which involve the different kinds of forces felt to be present in the interactions between the three participants. There is a clear directionality and assymetry in the flow of action, in so far as it is the GIVER who initiates the flow of action, which then passes through to the RECIPIENT. The domain of human interest calls attention to the fact that the RECIPIENT is not some unaffected bystander witnessing some event. Rather, the RECIPIENT is most typically advantaged by receiving the THING and subsequently makes some use of the THING. The experiential reality behind this aspect of GIVE is the tendency for humans to interact with one another in meaningful and positive ways. We can be harmful to others and we can give them useless things, but most of our interactions are, thankfully, not like this.

These two properties of GIVE, its basicness and its semantic complexity, are not contradictory. The basicness of GIVE reflects the functional significance of the act of giving in human society; the semantic complexity refers to the internal structure of the act of giving. Each of these properties needs to be appreciated in order to understand various facts about GIVE morphemes. The basicness of GIVE may manifest itself in minimal forms in language. This is evident in a dramatic way in Amele, where GIVE appears as a zero morph, so that the sense of giving is conveyed by the presence of the appropriate nominals (representing GIVER, THING, and RECIPIENT) and concomitant verb marking. It is as though the sense of GIVE is self-evident from the presence within a clause of a human subject, an inanimate object, and a human object. In Woods Cree, GIVE verbs contain less morphology than is found with other three-place predicates, reflecting the basicness of GIVE as compared with these other verbs. The semantic complexity of GIVE, on the other hand, manifests itself in quite different ways. In Ainu, the GIVE word is analyzable as the causative of "have", highlighting some crucial components present in the meaning of GIVE. In Japanese, the relative social status of the GIVER and RECIPIENT is a key factor in selecting the appropriate form of GIVE, making the construction of GIVE clauses an especially complex matter. The range of constructional possibilities of literal GIVE clauses across languages is further evidence of the internal complexity of the act of giving. Thus, languages might utilize directional morphemes to integrate the RECIPIENT into the construction, or they might use benefactive morphemes, possessive morphemes etc. Each of these construction types is motivated by some component of the meaning of GIVE, and seeing the full range of the constructional possibilities gives some insight into the complex nature of the GIVE morpheme.

The abundance and the diversity of figurative uses of GIVE, as documented in the preceding pages, have their source in the two properties of literal GIVE which we have drawn attention to: its basicness and its semantic complexity. The experiential or conceptual basicness of a morpheme makes the morpheme an attractive candidate as a source for metaphorical understanding of more complex notions. It is typical of basic vocabulary that it gives rise to metaphorical uses. In the case of GIVE, we have, in addition to its experiential basicness, an impressive constellation of elements and forces which can "sponsor" new, figurative uses of the morpheme. That is, the semantic complexity inherent in literal GIVE is a rich source for figurative extensions, allowing many different directions for such extensions. Literal GIVE contains within it human interaction, human-thing interaction, handling of a thing, concrete motion, abstract motion, movement from a person, movement to a person, causation, initiation, purposefulness, change in control over a thing, a beneficiary, and completion of a change. Each of these characteristics of literal GIVE can motivate a figurative use of GIVE and a cross-linguistic survey of the sort carried out in this study reveals this diversity. That is, the diversity of figurative extensions correlates with the internal complexity of the basic morpheme. Basic vocabulary, regardless of the degree of semantic complexity associated with the morpheme, will tend to be exploited for the purposes of metaphorical ways of understanding more complex concepts. The combination of basicness and semantic complexity in a morpheme makes the morpheme an exceptionally productive source for metaphorical extensions.

I see a discussion of the nature of the act of giving and the semantics of the typical GIVE morpheme as laying the groundwork for the subsequent discussion of the syntax and semantics of GIVE constructions. I do not take the position that everything in the syntax of GIVE constructions can be successfully explained away by referring back to the meaning of GIVE. Some aspects of syntax may not be easily motivated by semantic or broader cognitive considerations. In this study, however, I have made a concerted effort to understand, as far as possible, the form and meaning of GIVE constructions by reference to properties of the literal GIVE morpheme and the act it encodes. This applies equally well to both literal and figurative GIVE constructions. In a very real way, the semantics of GIVE constitute an everpresent backdrop to the whole of the preceding discussion. In this study, vocabulary and "word semantics" are not perceived as separate fields of study, removed from the study of syntax and the semantics of clause level constructions. Rather, the semantics of individual items, such as a GIVE morpheme, motivates much of the syntax and semantics of the constructions which GIVE enters into.

5.1.2. Literal GIVE

Constructions which involve literal GIVE show considerable diversity in their grammatical structure. In this study the focus of attention has been on the ways in which the GIVER, THING, and RECIPIENT are integrated into clause structure, and the diversity shows itself in the variety of case marking, adpositions, and other relational morphemes which are utilized in GIVE clauses cross-linguistically. The grammatical diversity associated with GIVE clauses is a reflection of the complexity inherent in the semantics of GIVE. Unravelling the meaning of GIVE and separating out the components which contribute to its overall meaning are prerequisites for understanding much of the syntax that accompanies GIVE morphemes in languages.

As a first step in documenting the syntax of GIVE morphemes, one should note the alternative ways in which the AGENT-PATIENT model of interaction may be imposed upon the GIVE scene. The AGENT-PATIENT schema of interaction may be mapped onto the GIVER-THING pair or the GIVER-RECIPIENT pair of participants, correlating with the syntactic fact that either the THING or the RECIPIENT may be encoded as the direct object in active, transitive GIVE constructions. There is no good reason to assume that either one of these ways of construing the GIVE scene is more basic than the other way. The THING, being inanimate in the prototypical case, is more obviously like a PATIENT than a RECIPIENT is. On the other hand, the RECIPIENT is affected by the act of giving and is the entity to which the action finally flows, making it, too, a good candidate for the PATIENT in mapping AGENT-PATIENT onto the GIVE scene. Languages may conventionalize one of these ways of imaging the GIVE scene as the sole way of constructing a GIVE clause. In French, for example, a nominal THING must function as the direct object in the active, transitive GIVE construction. In Tzotzil, a RECIPIENT, when present, must appear as the direct object in the active, transitive GIVE clause. Furthermore, both the THING and the RECIPIENT are less like an AGENT than the GIVER, which makes them both appear PATIENT-like with respect to the GIVER. The syntactic corollary to this is the fact that GIVE may feature in a ditransitive construction in which both the THING and the RECIPIENT have some object-like properties, even though one is typically more like a direct object than the other.

Usually, GIVE constructions involve oblique phrases which serve to integrate the THING or RECIPIENT into the clause structure. Consistent with the approach taken in cognitive linguistics generally, so here the grammatical morphemes which are utilized for these purposes are viewed as having their own interesting semantics. This includes a degree of polysemy amongst the meanings, similar to the polysemy typical of full-blown lexical items. An investigation into the syntax of GIVE constructions inevitably turns upon these grammatical morphemes and their meanings. A particularly common grammatical device to integrate the RECIPIENT into clause structure is a dative case. Although the term "dative" is used in a variety of ways in linguistic descriptions of languages, the term has a special relevance to GIVE. For many linguists, the prototypical basis for labelling a case "dative" is its use to mark the RECIPIENT in a GIVE clause. Where a dative case has additional uses, it is often the case that the additional uses are naturally understood as being extensions from the central, RECIPIENT-marking use. Perhaps more so than any other oblique case, the dative shows extensive polysemy and to some extent this may be a reflection of how easily the notion of RECIPIENT may be extended metaphorically to other semantic categories, such as an addressee, a person to whom something is served etc.

It is possible for the RECIPIENT to be integrated into clause structure through the use of relational morphemes which have other quite distinct and well-entrenched uses, apart from marking the RECIPIENT. In the overview of such morphemes in this study, the RECIPIENT could be integrated into the GIVE clause in the same way as a goal, locative, benefactive, and possessor. These alternatives are made possible by the fact that the RECIPIENT can be understood as functioning simultaneously in various ways, depending upon which domain one chooses to focus upon. It is an end-point for the movement of the THING when one considers the spatio-temporal domain, making it like a goal to which something moves. Hence, one finds that the RECIPIENT is marked by the same morpheme that marks a goal or locative in some languages. The RECIPIENT is typically a beneficiary of the act of giving who goes on to make some use of the THING transferred. Not surprisingly, the RECIPIENT may be marked by the same morpheme that marks benefactive phrases. The RECIPIENT comes to have control over the THING transferred and, consistent with this, the RECIPIENT may be marked in the same way as possessors of things. In other words, the syntax which accompanies GIVE is not a bizarre collection of random grammatical morphemes. The grammatical morphemes which are utilized are ones which are motivated by the components of meaning of GIVE. Similarly, when the THING is taken to be the direct object, the RECIPIENT needs to be integrated into the clause structure. Again, the oblique marker which is used for this purpose, the instrumental marker, is well motivated. The THING, as an inanimate entity handled in the course of the act, can be easily construed as a metaphorical instrument.

In characterizing the meanings of these grammatical morphemes, it is convenient to rely upon the idea of a schematic network, which expresses the commonalities between the submeanings. Until one has properly investigated native-speaker judgements about the relationships between the submeanings, proposals for such schematic networks remain somewhat hypothetical. Even without the benefit of detailed psycholinguistic support for particular schematic networks, however, it is possible to sketch some of the more important interconnections which hold between the submeanings. In doing this, considerations about the naturalness of semantic extensions and the directionality of such extensions arise. Thus, when a language marks the RECIPIENT and a beneficiary by means of the same grammatical morpheme, should one think of the central meaning of the morpheme as marking RECIPIENT (and extended to beneficiaries), or should one think of it as basically marking a beneficiary (and extended to RE-

CIPIENTs)? Such questions are not easily answered in the absence of psycholinguistic experiments designed explicitly to answer such questions.

5.1.3. Figurative GIVE

Cognitive linguistics does not exclude figurative language from its field of inquiry. On the contrary, the study of semantic extensions and the relationships between meanings at the word level and at the clause level has been a prominent feature of this approach to language study. Metonymy and metaphor, in particular, are seen to play a pervasive and central role in natural language. This contrasts sharply with the approach found in some modern linguistic theories which view figurative language as outside the scope of inquiry.

In the present study, an attempt has been made to describe and explicate a large selection of GIVE constructions, including both literal and figurative uses of the GIVE morpheme. The figurative uses of GIVE involve the use of a GIVE morpheme to mean something other than "to transfer control of a thing from one person to another" and there is a plethora of such uses. As noted above, this situation correlates with the basicness of literal GIVE, as well as the considerable semantic complexity which resides in literal GIVE. These two properties make GIVE an ideal candidate for use in metaphorical ways of understanding other acts and events. The metaphorical uses of GIVE to image some other event are not seen as some decorative "add-on" in language. As linguistic phenomena, they are just as natural as the literal use of GIVE and are just as worthy of serious study.

Amongst the figurative uses of GIVE which are considered in this study are those uses which might be called grammaticalizations and there are a number of such cases. As is the case with motivating other extensions of GIVE, so too with grammaticalizations one seeks the basis for the extension in one or more of the semantic components which are present in literal GIVE. Grammatical morphemes lie at one end of a continuum which connects grammatical morphemes with full lexical items, and grammaticalized uses of GIVE may be related in various ways to properties of the full verb GIVE.

In order to give some order to the discussion of the figurative extensions of GIVE, eight main classes of extensions may be distinguished, each one containing further subclasses. One of the most common types of extension of GIVE morphemes is in the area of interpersonal communication, as in *give a talk (to some audience)*. The conceptual mapping between the components of literal GIVE and such acts of interpersonal communication seems a particularly easy one to make and we see this kind of extension of GIVE in many languages. A second group of extensions involves meanings relating to the emergence of some entity from another, or simply the manifestation of some entity. This is the use of GIVE to mean "produce (fruit, crops etc.)" as well as a large number of other closely related meanings pertaining to growth, production, and reproduction. The manifestation meaning is similar to emergence but without any obvious AGENT-like entity responsible for the appearance of a thing. Reflexive, impersonal, passive, and intransitive construction types are the natural syntactic devices to carry this kind of sense, as in the German *es gibt* construction. A third group of extensions relates to causation. It is possible for the morpheme GIVE to be used as a causative verb or as a causative affix in some languages. The fourth group of extensions involves enablement which is similar to causation but is nevertheless distinct. The fifth group involves schematic interaction, which refers to the use of GIVE in constructions such as *give the car a wash*. In such cases, the GIVE verb provides the basic skeletal structure of an interaction between two entities, with the main semantic verb-like content being contributed by the deverbal. The sixth group is made up of extensions of GIVE to mark benefactives or more generalized kinds of recipient phrases. These uses are especially common in serial verb languages. The seventh group involves movement, as in German *sich begeben*. Some uses of GIVE can be thought of as involving relatively abstract kinds of motion and they, too, may be included in this group. Finally, one may classify some uses of GIVE as having some connection with perfectivity in an aspectual sense. This subdivision into eight major semantic areas is convenient and helps to bring out the diversity of the possible extensions of GIVE morphemes cross-linguistically, though there is some overlap between the various classes. Thus, concrete or abstract motion is present in a number of these subgroups, such as interpersonal communication, emergence, manifestation, and causation.

For each of these extension types, one may find some motivation for the extension in one or more of the components which constitute the meaning of literal GIVE. The key word in this part of the discussion is *motivation*. The facts of literal GIVE motivate the figurative extensions rather than predict them. The prior analysis of the semantics of literal GIVE is particularly necessary here, since it is that analysis which lays bare the component parts of the source predicate. Just as the components of literal GIVE motivate the various kinds of oblique marking which can appear in literal GIVE constructions, so too these components motivate the different extensions of GIVE which may be observed in figurative GIVE constructions. The extensions are not all equally easy to motivate. Sometimes, there are multiple connections one can make between components of literal GIVE and the extension. The use of *give* in *give a lecture to a class*, for example, preserves quite a lot of the cognitive topology of literal GIVE. One can associate the GIVER with the lecturer, the THING with the lecture, and the RECIPIENT with the class. The flow of action in the case of literal GIVE is matched by the flow of action in delivering a lecture. With some other extensions, however, the connection with literal GIVE may not be at all obvious and the suggestions concerning the motivations for the extension must be more tentative. When one is dealing with just the synchronic facts, there is necessarily a degree of speculation involved in any attempt to explain away the precise nature of semantic relatedness.

At various points throughout the discussion of GIVE, comparisons have been drawn with TAKE. As collocations like English *give and take* suggest, the concepts GIVE and TAKE are semantic opposites in a number of ways. With GIVE, there is movement of a THING away from the subject referent, whereas with TAKE there is movement of a THING to the subject referent. A further significant point of difference between literal GIVE and TAKE concerns the way the thing given or taken is further utilized. With GIVE, it is the RECIPIENT who has the opportunity to further utilize or interact with the THING transferred. In the case of TAKE, it is the one who does the taking who might proceed to utilize the THING. These differences in the semantics of the predicates correlate with differences in both literal and figurative constructions involving these predicates. The differences between GIVE and TAKE are particularly evident in the case of figurative extensions. As noted above, literal GIVE involves a transfer of control over a THING to another person and this aspect of GIVE motivates extensions to meanings of causation, enablement, and permission. Literal TAKE concerns one person exercising control over a THING, rather than passing control over it to someone else. Consequently, TAKE is an inappropriate source for metaphorically construing causation of events involving others, enabling of others to act, and the granting of permission to others. On the other hand, TAKE is an obvious source for extensions to meanings relating to assumption of control, as in *take care of something, take on some responsibility, take over a job* etc. The comparisons between GIVE and TAKE enable one to better appreciate the constrained nature of the figurative extensions of GIVE. One might well form the impression that there are no limits to the figurative meanings which GIVE morphemes evidence. It is precisely through a comparison with TAKE morphemes that the limits become clearer.

Cognitive linguistics does not predict that the GIVE morpheme will necessarily be extended in any particular direction in a language. Indeed, it may be the case that the GIVE morpheme in some language has no conventionalized figurative extensions at all (although I have yet to find such a language). Where a language does show figurative extensions of GIVE, however, then those extensions invariably follow certain paths. Cognitive linguistics provides us with the conceptual framework to understand why this should be the case.

5.2. Prospects for future research

The present study has been devoted mainly to one verb and its associated syntax and semantics. The study is offered as an illustration of the cognitive linguistics approach to the study of language and it is hoped that the study has shown something of the range and depth of this approach. In addition, the study points the way to future research undertakings which might consolidate and further extend the findings from this study. Three broad areas suggest themselves: studies of the full range of uses of GIVE verbs in a particular language, research into diachronic aspects of extensions and grammaticalizations of GIVE verbs, and investigation into basic vocabulary. To complete this discussion of GIVE, I shall say a few words about each of these directions for future research.

5.2.1. *Studies of individual languages*

The full diversity and complexity of GIVE constructions only become evident when one takes a broad cross-linguistic view. No one language could be relied upon for supporting evidence for each of the literal or figurative constructions which occur cross-linguistically. The extent to which GIVE morphemes are utilized in a language for imaging acts, events, and states varies considerably, and it is only a cross-linguistic investigation, drawing upon a rich database of many genetically unrelated languages, that enables the researcher to see the complete picture. The present study confirms the desirability, indeed, the necessity for such an approach. In addition to this kind of broadly-based research undertaking, there is a place for in-depth research into the manifestations of GIVE within a particular language. Such research would complement the present study which has not attempted to document all the facts from any one language. One might investigate either literal or figurative uses of GIVE within a particular language. Such studies would show the range of "work" which may be done by GIVE morphemes in different languages.

If one considers the expression of literal GIVE, it is interesting to consider how many alternative constructions a single language might make available and what different nuances are carried by each of the constructions. There can be a number of GIVE constructions in a particular language, though I have not found any language which has all the possible construction types documented in this study. Sochiapan Chinantec is somewhat unusual in having three distinct GIVE constructions all occurring with one and the same verb stem, as illustrated in (1).

(1) a. *Cuéh³²*   *tsú²*   *jon²*   *quie³*   *tsa³ háu².*
        give:FUT:3 he/she child:his/her money tomorrow
        'He/she will give her/his child money tomorrow.'
                           (Chinantec, Foris 1993: 378)

    b. *Cuéh³²*   *tsú²*   *quie³*   *ñí¹con²* *jon²*   *tsa³ háu².*
        give:FUT:3 he/she money to child tomorrow
        'He/she will give his/her child money tomorrow.'
                           (Chinantec, Foris 1993: 378)

    c. *ñí¹-cue¹*   *jná¹³* *Pé¹*   *quioh²¹*   *cá¹háu².*
        intend-give:ISG I Peter have:3 chicken
        'I intend to give Peter some chicken.'
                             (Chinantec, Foris p.c.)

(1a) illustrates a ditransitive construction. (1b) is a monotransitive construction with the RECIPIENT encoded as an oblique (benefactive) phrase. (1c) contains an embedded clause which literally expresses the possession of the THING. Each of these constructions has its own additional nuances. The construction in (1a) is used when the act of giving is irrevocable and the THING truly becomes the possession of the RECIPIENT. The (1b) construction lacks this connotation. Rather, it is used when the THING is entrusted to the RECIPIENT for the RECIPIENT to utilize in some way, but without the THING forever being in the possession of the RECIPIENT. In (1b), the understanding is that the money is given to the child to purchase something for the GIVER. In (1c), which is described as an antipassive by Foris, the THING is understood as partitive, i.e. the implication is that some chicken, rather than all the chicken, was given to the RECIPIENT. More detailed studies of individual languages are needed in order to establish just what possibilities for encoding the GIVE scene may coexist within a language.

Figurative extensions may be investigated from a similar point of view. So, for example, one could map out the metaphorical territory occupied by a GIVE morpheme in a particular language. Comparing results from this approach across languages might reveal significant patterns in the ways in which GIVE participates in figurative constructions. Certainly, some languages make very copious use of GIVE in its metaphorical extensions, while other languages make relatively little use of it. A good start in this direction is Salomao (1990) with its focus on GIVE in Brazilian Portuguese. Salomao maps out the extensive conceptual ground covered by Brazilian Portuguese GIVE. By focusing on one language in this way, she manages to bring out the internal coherence of the whole system, an aspect which, of course, does not reveal itself in the present study. In detailed studies of individual languages such as Salomao's, one really needs the judgements of native speakers in order to properly define the limits of GIVE extensions. This is something which is not very realistic when the researcher is working with dozens of languages, but could certainly be expected in a study confined to just one language. Including native speakers' judgements on possible extensions in the use of GIVE would add an important dimension to research on figurative GIVE.

A natural way to extend the present study of GIVE is to focus on words derived from a GIVE morpheme and to consider the effects of derivation in such cases. In the present study, most of the discussion has concerned a basic verb GIVE, with only occasional references to other forms derived by prefixation, suffixation, compounding, nominalization etc. German, for example, has a large number of words from various grammatical categories, all involving some form of the GIVE morpheme *geb(en)*. (2) lists some of these derivatives, as found in standard dictionaries, with an approximate English translation. Many of these forms have additional reflexive and impersonal uses which have been ignored in the glosses.

(2)   a.   Verbs:
abgeben 'deliver (up); hand in; transfer; give (an opinion)'
angeben 'declare, state, give an account of; estimate; specify; denounce'
aufgeben 'give up, deliver, surrender, abandon; ask; give notice of'
ausgeben 'give out, distribute; deal (cards); spend (money)'
begaben 'endow (with); bestow upon, give presents to'
begeben 'negotiate, transfer, sell; pass (a note)' (commercial language)
beigeben 'add, join to, attach; allot to, appoint'
eingeben 'insert, suggest, prompt, inspire; deliver, present'
ergeben 'produce, yield, deliver up; result in, amount to'

hergeben 'give up, deliver, hand over, give away'
hingeben 'give up; surrender, resign, sacrifice'
mitgeben 'give to a departing guest; impart; give as dowry'
übergeben 'hand over, give up (to), give in charge, commit to'
umgeben 'put on (a cloak); surround, encircle'
untergeben 'lay under; entrust to, submit'
vergeben 'give away; confer, bestow upon; forgive, pardon'
vorgeben 'give handicap, give points to, assert, advance, allege, pretend'
weggeben 'give away; let go; send away (to school)'
wiedergeben 'give back, return; reproduce; render'
zugeben 'add; grant, concede, admit; confess; follow suit (in cards)'
zurückgeben 'give back, return, restore, surrender, deliver up'

b. Adjectives:
angeblich 'alleged, ostensible'
ausgiebig 'plentiful, rich, abundant, productive, fertile'
begabt 'clever, talented, endowed'
ergeben 'devoted, loyal, attached; submissive, humble'
gegeben 'given, accepted, acknowledged; traditional, inherited'
vergeblich 'vain, idle, fruitless, futile'
vorgeblich 'pretended, supposed, so-called'
zugegeben 'granted, admitting'

c. Nouns:
Angabe 'declaration, statement'
Ausgabe 'expenses, outlay; issue, publication'
Begabung 'gift, talent, ability'
Beigabe 'supplement, addition, free gift'
Begebung 'renunciation; negotiation (commerical language)'
Eingabe 'petition, application, memorial'
Eingebung 'presentation; inspiration, suggestion'
Ergebung 'submission, resignation, surrender'
Gabe 'gift, present, donation; alms, offering; talent'
Gegebenheit 'reality, actuality, conditioning factor'
Gift 'poison, toxin, virus'
Mitgift 'dowry'

Übergabe 'delivery, transfer; surrender, capitulation'
Umgebung 'surroundings, environs, environment'
Vergebung 'giving, granting; allocation of work;
misdeal (cards); pardon'
Vorgabe 'points given; handicap (sport)'
Zugabe 'addition, extra; overweight; adjunct, supplement'
Zurückgabe 'returning, return, restoration, surrender'

Taken together, these forms show considerable diversity in the directions in which the semantics of GIVE have been modified as part of a derivation. A close examination of such forms would be rewarding, not only as a way of further understanding the GIVE morpheme, but also as a way of better understanding the semantic effects of the affixes involved.

5.2.2. *Diachronic case studies*

GIVE morphemes participate in a great variety of semantic extensions and grammaticalizations, resulting in the extensive polysemy and heterosemy evident synchronically. The present study has suggested connections between some of these additional meanings associated with GIVE, without, however, attempting to document the full history of any one development. Providing historical accounts of these extensions, particularly the grammaticalizations, is, however, necessary in order to fully substantiate claims and hypotheses concerning the interrelatedness of the extensions. Thus, I see detailed historical research on GIVE and its extensions as a way to follow up the results derived from the present study which has been solely concerned with synchronic facts. The studies of GIVE in individual languages, advocated in the preceding section, should be seen as encompassing the diachronic dimension as well as the synchronic. It would be interesting to trace the paths of development of a GIVE morpheme in a particular language and to consider the conditions under which new meanings and grammaticalizations arise.

Some studies have already dealt with historical developments with a focus on GIVE morphemes. Lichtenberk (1985) discusses a range of historical developments in Oceanic languages affecting a reconstructed Proto-

Oceanic *pa(nñ)i* 'give'. Lichtenberk pays special attention to the development of grammatical reflexes of this proto-form, which include the familiar ones of marking a goal, beneficiary, and purpose, as well as certain intriguing developments of GIVE specific to some of the Oceanic languages. In certain Southeast Solomonic languages, for example, the GIVE morpheme appears in a modified form as the noun-like head of a possessive construction and to which possessive suffixes may be attached. A benefactive phrase such as "for me" may be rendered in these languages as a phrase which is literally "for GIVE-my" (Lichtenberk 1985: 32–33). This is not a development found outside Oceanic, as far as I am aware, and indeed, Lichtenberk (1985: 63–68) convincingly argues that the development is closely tied to certain structural ambiguities in GIVE forms in these languages. The facts are complex and I shall not try to summarize them all here, but, clearly, the development relies on coincidences in the shapes of historically unrelated forms in these languages. As such, one would not expect such developments outside of these particular languages. Inevitably, and despite Lichtenberk's careful argumentation, a certain amount of the discussion of the history of the Oceanic reflexes remains somewhat speculative, based as it is on earlier stages for which there are no written records. A relevant study involving a GIVE morpheme and its historical developments, based on attested earlier stages, is Peyraube (1988). Peyraube's study focuses on the stages in the evolution of GIVE-type constructions in early Chinese, from 475 B.C. to 581 A.D. Peyraube carefully documents the range of possible GIVE-type constructions for each of the periods he looks at and succeeds in showing the multiplicity of factors which may contribute to the emergence of a new construction type.

It is particularly interesting to consider the historical developments which give rise to uses of GIVE which, at least on the surface, seem far removed from the meaning of literal GIVE. A case in point would be the evolution of the German *es gibt* construction, discussed in synchronic terms in Chapter 4. The *es gibt* construction is quite distinct, both in form and meaning, from the literal GIVE construction in German. *Es gibt* is followed by an accusative object, without the possibility of a dative phrase, whereas the literal GIVE construction in German requires an accusative object (for the THING given) as well as a dative indirect object (for the RECIPIENT phrase). *Es gibt* functions as an existential construction, without there being any transfer of control over anything. How, then, could the *es gibt* construction develop out of a literal GIVE construction? In Newman (ms.) I discuss the early history of this construction. Conveniently, the construction does not appear at all before the fourteenth century and only becomes common in the course of the sixteenth century. Since we have extensive written records of German going back to this period and well before it, we are in a good position to observe this historical change. Without attempting to write the full history of *es gibt* here, I shall just cite some of the key points which are relevant to understanding the historical connection between the literal GIVE sense and the existential GIVE construction.

The first significant author to make extensive use of the *es gibt* construction is Johann der Täufer Friedrich Fischart (1546/7-1590). When one examines the instances of *es gibt* in his major work, *Geschichtklitterung*, one finds that there is a particular context in which *es gibt* frequently appears. This is the context of antecedent clause followed by consequent clause, with the *es gibt* construction appearing in the consequent clause. Examples of this are given in (3).

(3)　　a.　　*wann nur alte Weiber unnd die Hund dran seychten, so gebs guten Burgundischen Saltpeter...* (Fischart 1590 [1963]: 125, lines 37–38).
　　　　　　 'if just old women and dogs urinate on it, one would get good Burgundy saltpetre...'
　　　　b.　　*da schneiet und hagelt es mit Gelt zu, das es Beulen gibt...* (Fischart 1590 [1963]: 106, lines 17–18)
　　　　　　 'it will snow and hail with money, so much so that there will be bumps...'

The consequent clauses in (3) refer to what will eventuate, as a result of the event referred to in the antecedent clause. The *es gibt* clause does not simply assert the existence of some entity in these examples. Rather, there is a dynamic, evolutionary sense associated with its use. One could just as well translate the consequent clause in (3a) as "this will produce good Burgundy saltpetre" and the consequent clause in (3b) as "this will cause bumps". Understood in this way, the *es* of *es gibt* in these early examples could be taken to be referring to the antecedent clause, rather than being semantically empty. Regardless of just how much one should analyze the *es* as referring to an antecedent clause or some other phrase in the linguistic context, the examples show, in any case, that a "produce, cause, lead to" sense could be associated with the *es gibt* construction from the very earliest period of its use. This observation is important as it helps to bring into focus a connection between *es gibt* and the use of *geben* as a two-place predicate meaning "yield, produce", illustrated in (4).

(4)   a.   *verzicht mir, daß ich euch den Säuen vergleich, sie geben dan-
            noch guten Speck...* (Fischart 1590 [1963]: 56, lines 30–31)
            'pardon me that I compare you to sows, but they do produce
            good bacon...'
      b.   *als vil all Berge Trauben geben...* (Fischart 1590 [1963]: 82,
            lines 22–23)
            'as much as all mountains produce grapes...'

The *es gibt* construction as used in (3) is not at all far removed, semantically, from the use of *geben* in (4). In both uses, there is the idea that some entity (a thing, or a previous event) leads to some other entity. The difference resides mainly in the fact that in the case of *es gibt*, there is no explicit reference to the entity which causes the change. By comparing the uses of *geben* in (3) and (4), then, we see the key to understanding the origin of the impersonal *es gibt* construction. The transition from literal GIVE to the existential construction does not take place in one cataclysmic episode. The transition breaks down into a series of smaller, more easily understandable stages: (i) the meaning of *geben* is extended from "transfer of possession" to "produce, yield", evident already in the period prior to the first occurrences of *es gibt*; (ii) *geben* in the "produce, yield" sense comes to be used impersonally, introducing the consequent in an antecedent-consequent structure; (iii) *es gibt* is used to refer not just to entities which come about as a result of some event, but is also used to refer to the present existence of entities.

These brief observations about *es gibt* fall far short of a complete history, but they point the way to solving what seems at first a linguistic puzzle. The example also serves as a reminder that one must not assume that all developments affecting a GIVE morpheme must have their source in the "transfer of possession" sense of literal GIVE. This sense may be a central, prototypical sense of a GIVE morpheme in a language, but it is typically part of a network of related senses and any one of the senses in this network may be the source for a new extension of meaning. In the case of the *es gibt* construction, it is not the "transfer of possession" sense, but one of its extensions, which is the more immediate starting point for the emergence of the new construction. In other words, what appears to be the most obvious, central meaning of a morpheme may not be the meaning which one should start with in tracing the diachronic developments affecting the morpheme.

5.2.3. *Basic vocabulary*

There is a further area of research which the present study leads to and that is the whole field of basic vocabulary and the way in which it is used, metaphorically, to conceptualize the world around us. Basic vocabulary could be understood in many different ways, though this should not be taken to mean that there is no point in trying to identify such vocabularies. Clearly, there are different criteria for basicness in vocabulary. Criteria which one might appeal to include: *frequency of occurrence* of items in discourse, noting of course that there will be different frequencies depending upon the types of discourse involved; early items in *first language acquisition*; early items acquired as part of *second language acquisition*, especially where the second language is acquired in a natural setting, outside of controlled, formal instruction; the *conceptual simplicity* of an item; *artificial language systems* designed around vocabularies of minimal size, such as Ogden's Basic English, the vocabulary built into computer games involving language input etc.; natural languages which utilize a *minimal set of morphemes* which nevertheless provide the means for the expression of a rich array of concepts, such as Kalam; the morphemes which are used most extensively in *metaphorical expression* in a language. Each of these approaches to basic vocabulary will produce different results, though there will be some items which are part of more than one basic vocabulary, such as GIVE. It is these recurring items which are arguably the "most basic" and which would be the most obvious candidates for specific research projects.

One important consideration in cognitive linguistics affecting many areas of research is the role of human experience in shaping and, at the same time, constraining our conceptual and linguistic patterns. The relevance of human experience in the study of human language and thought has been discussed in such works as Lakoff—Johnson (1980: 56–60), Johnson (1987), Lakoff (1987: 260–268), Lakoff—Turner (1989: 112–114), and Sweetser (1990: 28–32). Lakoff (1987: 266) describes an experientialist approach as involving the attempt "to characterize meaning in terms of *the nature and experience of the organisms doing the thinking*" and there is a strong interest in pursuing this kind of experientialist approach in the cognitive linguistics movement. One very obvious way in which "the human experience" manifests itself is the extensive role which the human body and body parts play in the conceptualization of the world around us. Concepts such as "head", "face", "eye", "mouth", "back", "belly", "leg", "foot" etc. may be described as "experientially basic" and these items of vocabulary may play an important role in a language, especially in their metaphorical and grammaticalized uses. As is well known, such terms are often sources of locative adpositions as well as other preposition-like morphemes.[1] The research into basic vocabulary which I advocate would certainly include further studies into the language of body parts, including, of course, the figurative uses of such terms.

In my study of GIVE, however, I have tried to go beyond the study of basic "thing-like" concepts such as body parts, choosing, instead, to focus on a basic action concept, i.e. GIVE. A vocabulary item like GIVE is as much rooted in everyday, ordinary human experience as are terms for body parts and it is equally deserving of attention. It is not just our bodies, but what we *do with* our bodies and what *happens to* our bodies, which constitute some of our most basic human experiences. One expects that an experientially realistic approach to language study would include an analysis of a large range of basic human actions and their linguistic realization. More generally, basic human experiences and conditions, and their linguistic expression, would be obvious areas of research for linguists who adopt the experientialist strategy described above.[2]

Notes

Chapter one

1. I will use capital letters, as in GIVE, GIVER, etc. to refer to the semantically defined categories which are the focus of this study. As usual, italicized forms such as *give* refer to the forms rather than meanings.

2. In Lakoff's discussion of basic level categories, certain linguistic facts are also used to help establish that level of category, e.g. "people name things more readily at that level" and "languages have simpler names for things at that level" (Lakoff 1987: 33). The range of linguistic facts which I present as correlates of the basic level nature of the act of giving in the following sections goes somewhat beyond these two types.

3. Note also that the phrase *Give me* is subject to a phonological simplification to *Gimme*. Presumably, this is related to the frequency of occurrence of the phrase. Phrases such as *Love me* and *Leave me* are not similarly reduced.

4. It can happen that the set of basic verb stems of a Papuan language does not include a GIVE morpheme. Foley (1986: 120) lists the basic verb stems of Enga as the verbs corresponding to "say", "do", "hit", "hear", "get", "hold", "be", "lie", "stand", "go", "eat", and "burn". There is no GIVE morpheme in this list.

5. Chamorro is not unique in having a GIVE word which has a causative as part of its makeup. In Ainu, the GIVE verb *kore* is morphologically a causative of the verb *kor* 'have'. Chamorro, however, is unusual in having a GIVE word which morphologically contains a causative of a zero morph. That is, one could think of Chamorro *na'i* as *na-∅-'i* = 'cause-have-referential marker', where 'have' is realized as a zero morph.

6. The verb *waiho* 'put, place, leave' is similar. One can analyze this form as containing the adverb *iho* 'down'. There is no distinct passive form for *waiho*. It has been reported to me that passive endings do sometimes occur on *hōmai*, *hōatu*, and *waiho* in present-day usage.

7. Younger speakers allow *ageru* as an alternative where older speakers would insist on *sashiageru* (*sasageru* when giving to a deity). Younger speakers also allow *ageru* as an alternative to *yaru* in the case of a person giving things to animals. Thus, *ageru* is taking on the status of a general verb for giving when the Speaker

identifies with the GIVER. However, *yaru* is always required when the RE-
CIPIENT is inanimate, as in figurative extensions of GIVE:

(i) *Kono*   *mondai*   *ni*   *me*   *o*   *yaru/*ageru.*
     this   problem   DAT   eye   ACC   give
     '(I) will give my attention to this problem.'   (Japanese)

8. Two other verbs which are exceptionally simple in formal structure are the verbs
    "to say" and "to eat". Both these verbs lack one or more morphemes which would
    normally appear after the verb stem.

Chapter two

1. Rudzka-Ostyn (1988: 518) suggests the term *agentive trajector* for the trajector
    which causes movement, as opposed to *trajector* for the entity which executes the
    movement.
2. I am grateful to Sally Rice for providing me with the Chipewyan data.
3. Compare the discussion of the dative in Paamese in Section 3.2.1, where a
    distinction is made between a "punctual" and "areal" dative. It should not be
    thought, therefore, that all languages tolerate this vagueness about the RE-
    CIPIENT and the RECIPIENT's sphere of control in the GIVE construction.
4. This also applies to the English of some speakers who have Chinese as their first
    language.
5. A useful discussion of such phenomena may be found in Kretschmer—Wahrmann
    (1931: 207–209). This is a summary of a Vienna dissertation by Katharine
    Wlaschim (1927) entitled *Studien zu den indogermanischen Ausdrücken für
    Geben und Nehmen.*

Chapter three

1. Alternatively, one might seek a difference in the meanings associated with the two
    constructions, independent of discourse factors, an approach to which I return in
    Section 3.1.2.
2. Some donatory verbs in English have additional restrictions on the syntactic
    frames they occur in, compared with *give*. So, for example, only the THING
    occurs as the direct object with *donate*:

(i)   *We donated money to the hospital.*

(ii)   **We donated the hospital money.*

See Green (1974) for further discussion of the syntactic frames and semantics associated with various donatory verbs in English. There has been an extensive debate about the syntax of such verbs in English which I will not attempt to review here. Givón (1984b) is an interesting account of some cross-linguistic facts about alternative syntactic frames with GIVE-type verbs.

3.   The facts concerning the GIVE verb *beri* in Malay/Indonesian are complicated on account of some variation amongst speakers. Also, in casual conversation, the *-kan* suffix tends to be omitted.

4.   Baker (1988: 12–13) summarizes the situation as follows: "[Grammatical Function changing rules] all tend to include the *addition* of the characteristic morpheme as a "side effect" of the change. This morpheme then registers to a language perceiver that a particular [Grammatical Function] change has taken place, so that he or she can undo the change." (my italics) The "Mirror Principle", as formulated by Baker (1988: 13), insists on a very close parallel between morphology and syntax: "morphological derivations must directly reflect syntactic derivations (and vice versa)". The Mirror Principle would appear to require that some syntactic process has applied just in those cases where an affix has been added to the verb stem.

5.   The Malay/Indonesian suffix *-kan* bears a similarity to a preposition *akan* 'to', although this preposition is not normally used for the "to" phrase in the GIVE construction. Instead, the preposition *kepada* is used.

6.   Indeed this seems to be what Lewis (1972: 191) has in mind in a brief allusion to the use of *-kan* in the variety of Malay described above when he says: "With such verbs [i.e. verbs which take two objects] the suffix *-kan* is the remnant of a preposition, the word *akan*, denoting 'towards' or 'to'. For this reason, an indirect object which would have been governed by the preposition *akan* in the original construction must be placed immediately after the suffix, i.e. between the verb and its direct object."

7.   As pointed out by Killingley (1993: 37–39), Cantonese word order involving double objects is subject to some variation. When the THING is a simple noun phrase and the RECIPIENT is a pronoun, the preferred order is THING RECIPIENT, as in (14). But the order RECIPIENT THING is possible in some other cases. For example, a lengthier noun phrase for the THING, such as *hóu dō chín* 'a lot of money' would be positioned after a pronominal RECIPIENT.

8. Avery Andrews (1985: 123), in a discussion of double object constructions, observes that where one of the NPs functions like a direct object that NP will always be the RECIPIENT-like NP. In Dryer's terms, this is tantamount to claiming that double object constructions always follow the primary objectivity pattern. The Cantonese construction illustrated here (and the Sochiapan Chinantec double object construction discussed later in the text) would appear to fall into the category of a double object construction where it is the THING, rather than the RECIPIENT, which functions as the direct object.

9. See, for example, the discussion of the passive test as it applies to Korean GIVE sentences in O'Grady (1991: 55–65). The test, along with some others, fails to distinguish between the two objects.

10. If the THING in the English double object construction is indeed analyzed as the primary object, as suggested by Hudson's review of the evidence, then English too would be a counter-example to Avery Andrews' (1985: 123) claim that it is always the RECIPIENT which functions like the primary object.

11. Dahl (1987) is an interesting discussion of how an account of meanings of cases and adpositions needs to invoke the notion of prototypes and their extensions to other less prototypical instances. Dahl's discussion is also pertinent in so far as it makes a number of points with reference to GIVE constructions. Rudzka-Ostyn (to appear, b) is a useful overview of polysemy in the Polish dative case, again making crucial reference to the notion of prototype. Heine (1990) discusses some of the typical semantic extensions which are found in dative cases.

12. I use *t'* to indicate the palatalized *t* which appears as part of the infinitival suffix in Russian.

13. See, for example, the discussion of the use of the label "dative" in relation to Kalkatungu later in this Chapter. Compare also Dixon's cautionary advice about the names of cases in Australian linguistics (Dixon 1980: 292) and his remarks concerning the label "dative":

    Cases that we label "dative" in different Australian languages will have a common semantic core but also important differences. In both Warlpiri and Warrgamay dative is used to mark the indirect object "the child" in "the man is speaking to the child"; but for "the child" in "the man gave food to the child" Warlpiri again uses dative while Warrgamay prefers genitive. (Dixon 1980: 293)

14. Note also that GIVE may be a source for the marker of the dative in a language. For example, the use of *gěi* 'give' as a kind of preposition in Mandarin marking

the RECIPIENT is similar to the typical function of a dative case, rather than as a marker of a goal or a "to" morpheme as it is often glossed. So, for example, the preposition is used to mark the RECIPIENT with verbs such as "to give, to pass on, to hand over, to mail, to sell, to lose, to promise, to teach, to bestow" etc. It can not be used to mark the goal. Cf.:

(i) *Wǒ*   *chuán-le*   *zhèi*   *běn*   *shū*   *gěi*   *tā.*
     I   pass on-ASP   this   CL   book   give   him/her
     'I passed on this book to him/her.'   (Mandarin)

(ii) **Wo*   *qù-le*   *gěi*   *New York.*
     I   go-ASP   give   New York   (Mandarin)

15. The transcriptions used by Scott and Asmah Haji Omar have been slightly modified to show a phonemic level.

16. Unfortunately, the only example of the use of *nu* in Asmah Haji Omar (1983) is the GIVE sentence cited here. As such, it would be consistent with the label "dative", specifically marking the RECIPIENT in a GIVE construction. Presumably, the label "benefactive" was chosen on account of benefactive uses of the preposition apart from its use in the GIVE construction.

17. Dixon's discussion of GIVE constructions in Dyirbal leaves it unclear to me whether one finds the general genitive in a GIVE construction, contrasting with the simple genitive.

18. See Heine (1990) for some discussion of the directionality in the extensions of meaning found with Kanuri *rò*.

19. This does not appear to be the case, however, in West Greenlandic. The instrumental case marking on nouns (as used with the GIVE construction) only means instrumental; a verbal affix attached to verbs, on the other hand, may carry either an instrumental or comitative meaning (Fortescue 1984: 214–215).

Chapter four

1. When I cite simple phrases or clauses from other languages in this chapter, I will refrain from detailing the bibliographic reference for every cited form. The phrases/clauses are generally simpler than the clauses dealt with in Chapter 3 and, for the most part, can be easily verified in the standard dictionaries of the languages concerned. Where this is not the case, the relevant source in the literature will be provided.

2.   I cite the Bulgarian verb GIVE in a 1st Singular Perfective form.

3.   One instance where GIVE does appear to have taken on the sense of "relate, tell" is *geben* in the Frankfurt dialect of German:

    (i)   *Geb's   von   der!*

            give:it   of   that

            'Tell me what you know!'

                     (1938 example of Frankfurt dialect, Frankfurter Wörterbuch 1971: 809)

It is not clear from the source of this example, however, whether this usage of *geben* is restricted to just this one expression or has a wider distribution. The use in (i) may be comparable to the use of English *Give!*, which, as an imperative, may be used to mean "tell me about it", but this use is restricted to the imperative.

4.   It is worth noting that, at least in the Luxembourg dialect, there is some overlap in the forms for the verbs meaning "give" and "go" (cf. Schanen 1987) and this may facilitate the extension to abstract motion senses of GIVE. Also, in at least some of these dialects, GIVE is used as the auxiliary in the dynamic passive, comparable to the use of *werden* in standard German.

    (i)   *Gŏffs   gehol.*

            give:you fetch:Past Participle

            'You will be fetched.'

                     (19th century Trier dialect, DWB, Vol.4, [1984]: 107)

    (ii)   *D' Grompere   gi   geschielt.*

           the potatoes   give   peeled

           'The potatoes are being peeled.'

                     (Luxembourg dialect, Schanen 1987: 39)

    (iii) *Sonndës gët   bei   us   nët   geschafft.*

           Sundays gives at   us   NEG done

           'On Sundays, nothing is done in our house.'

                     (Luxembourg dialect, Schanen 1987: 39)

Presumably, the extension of standard German *werden* to a passive auxiliary has played a part in motivating a similar extension of *gin* 'give, become' in Luxembourg dialect.

5.   Note, however, that Talmy (1976: 55–58) argues that a structure like "event B results from event A" is more appropriate as a characterization of the basic causative situation. Talmy argues on the basis of syntactic facts for this position. He notes that the caused event may function as the main clause in English as in *The window broke as a result of a ball's sailing into it*, whereas the causing event

does not function as a main clause in a structure such as *I threw a ball at the window to the point of breaking it.* Talmy sees this as lending support to the resulting event as being a more natural "figure" and the causing event as being a more natural "ground".

6. Only the RECIPIENT object "him" morpheme is shown in the verb form *bi-wo-ŋ*, although a 3rd Singular pronoun is understood for the GIVER as well. The omission of the subject pronominal prefix relates to a constraint in Kunwinjku which disallows the presence of both subject and object pronouns when both are singular (Oates 1964: 45).

7. English *give* in fact shows up in a RECIPIENT sense in some English-based pidgins and creoles of Africa, parallel to the way *fún* is used in Yoruba (cf. Hall 1966: 78–79).

8. See Newman (1993a, 1993b) for more detailed discussion of Mandarin *gěi* 'give', including the extension of *gěi* to RECIPIENT marking.

9. Although there is no extensive discussion of the syntactic status of RECIPIENT-marking *gěi* in Chao (1968), the construction with RECIPIENT-marking *gěi* is (contra Liang 1971) referred to as containing "two verbs, each with an object to itself" (Chao 1968: 317).

10. See Shibatani (to appear) for an insightful discussion of this use of GIVE in Japanese and Korean.

11. Cf., for example, the use of the genitive for the landmark *Amt* 'office' with the verb *entheben* 'to relieve of, remove from' in the following example:

(i) | *Man* | *enthob* | *ihn* | | *des* | *Amtes.* |
     | one | relieved | him:ACC | | the | office:GEN |

   'He was relieved of the office.'   (German)

12. See Xu (1994) for some discussion of the use of GIVE to mark the direct object in Mandarin and Chinese dialects.

13. Compare this with the extension of German *geben* 'give' to a construction *es gibt mich/mir wunder* 'it surprises me', attested in the period 1600–1800, presumably by analogy with the use of *nehmen* 'take' as used in the older and more firmly entrenched construction *es nimmt mir/mich wunder* 'it surprises me'.

Chapter five

1. For some recent discussion on the role of body parts in language, see Heine et al. (1991a: 124–131) and Heine et al. (1991b: 151–153). Rubba (1994) is a detailed study of the metaphorical extension and grammaticalization of certain body part words in Aramaic languages, couched within Langacker's Cognitive Grammar.
2. Sweetser's (1990: 32–48) study of sense-perception verbs and their significance in our conceptualization of knowledge is a good example of linguistic research grounded in an experiential realism.

References

Aissen, Judith L.
  1987   *Tzotzil clause structure*. Dordrecht: Reidel.
Akatsuka, Noriko (ed.)
  to appear *Japanese/Korean linguistics*. Vol. 4, CSLI. Stanford: Stanford University.
Andrews, Avery
  1985   "The major functions of the noun phrase", in: Timothy Shopen (ed.), Vol. I, 62–154.
Andrews, Lorrin
  1985   *A dictionary of the Hawaiian language*. Tokyo: Charles E. Tuttle Company.
Axmaker, Shelley—Annie Jaisser—Helen Singmaster (eds.)
  1988   *Proceedings of the Fourteenth Annual Meeting, Berkeley Linguistics Society*. Berkeley, California: Berkeley Linguistics Society.
Baker, Mark C.
  1988   *Incorporation: a theory of grammatical function changing*. Chicago: The University of Chicago Press.
  1989   "Object sharing and projection in serial verb construction", *Linguistic Inquiry* 20: 513–553.
Beach, Woodford A.—Samuel E. Fox—Shulamith Philosoph (eds.)
  1977   *Papers from the Thirteenth Regional Meeting, Chicago Linguistic Society*. Chicago: Chicago Linguistic Society.
Benedict, Helen
  1979   "Early lexical development: comprehension and production", *Journal of Child Language* 6: 183–200.
Blake, Barry J.
  1979   "Australian case systems: some typological and historical observations", in: Stephen A. Wurm (ed.), 323–394.
  1990   *Relational grammar*. London: Routledge.
  1994   *Case*. Cambridge: Cambridge University Press.
Blansitt, Edward L.
  1984   "Dechticaetiative and Dative", in: Frans Plank (ed.), 127–150.

1988   "Datives and Allatives", in: Edith A. Moravcsik—Jessica R. Wirth—
          Michael Hammond (eds.), 173–191.

Boas, Franz
1911   "Kwakiutl", in: Franz Boas (ed.), 427–557.

Boas, Franz (ed.)
1911   *Handbook of American Indian languages*. Washington: Government
          Printing Office.

Borg, Albert J.—Bernard Comrie
1984   "Object diffuseness in Maltese", in: Frans Plank (ed.), 109–126.

Braunwald, S.
1978   "Context, word and meaning: towards a communicational analysis of
          lexical acquisition", in: Andrew Lock (ed.), 485–527.

Brugman, Claudia M.
1981   Story of *over*. [M.A. thesis, University of California, Berkeley.] Also
          published, 1989, as *The story of 'over': polysemy, semantics, and the
          structure of the lexicon*. New York: Garland.
1990   "What is the Invariance Hypothesis?", *Cognitive Linguistics* 1: 257–
          266.

Bynon, Theodora
1977   *Historical linguistics*. Cambridge: Cambridge University Press.

Capell, A.
1979   "Classification of verbs in Australian languages", in: Stephen A.
          Wurm (ed.), 229–322.

Carlson, Robert
1991   "Grammaticalization of postpositions and word order in Senufo lan-
          guages", in: Elizabeth Closs Traugott—Bernd Heine (eds.), 201–223.

Carter, Ronald
1987   "Is there a core vocabulary? Some implications for language teach-
          ing", *Applied Linguistics* 8: 179–193.

Chao, Yuen Ren
1968   *A grammar of Spoken Chinese*. Berkeley: University of California
          Press.

Chapman, Robin S.
1981   "Cognitive development and language comprehension in 10–21-
          months-olds", in: Rachel E. Stark (ed.), 359–391.

Chatterjee, Ranjit
1988 *Aspect and meaning in Slavic and Indic.* Amsterdam: Benjamins.
Chung, Sandra
1976 "An object-creating rule in Bahasa Indonesia", *Linguistic Inquiry* 7: 41–87.
Coate, H.H.C—A.P. Elkin
1974 *Ngarinjin-English dictionary.* Oceanic Linguistic Monographs No. 16. Sydney: University of Sydney.
Cogen, Cathy *et al.* (eds.)
1975 *Proceedings of the First Annual Meeting of the Berkeley Linguistics Society.* Berkeley, California: Berkeley Linguistics Society.
Cole, Peter—Jerrold M. Sadock (eds.)
1977 *Grammatical relations. Syntax and semantics.* Vol. 8. New York: Academic Press.
Collins, Wilkie
1966 *The moonstone.* First published 1868. Penguin Books.
Comrie, Bernard
1982 "Grammatical relations in Huichol", in: Paul J. Hopper—Sandra A. Thompson (eds.), 95–115.
Comrie, Bernard (ed.)
1987 *The world's major languages.* New York: Oxford University Press.
Craig, Collette G.
1976 "Properties of basic and derived subjects in Jacaltec", in: Charles N. Li (ed.), 99–123.
1977 *The structure of Jacaltec.* Austin: University of Texas Press.
Craig, Colette G.—Ken Hale
1987 "Oblique relations and reanalysis in some languages of the Americas", in: Paul D. Kroeber—Robert E. Moore (eds.), 19–52.
Croft, William—Keith Denning—Suzanne Kemmer (eds.)
1990 *Studies in typology and diachrony.* Papers presented to Joseph H. Greenberg on his 75th birthday. Amsterdam: Benjamins.
Crowley, Terry
1982 *The Paamese language of Vanuatu.* Pacific Linguistics Series B, No. 87. Australian National University, Canberra: Department of Linguistics.

Dahl, Östen
    1987   "Case Grammar and prototypes", in: René Dirven—Günter Radden (eds.), 147–161.
Dakubu, M. E. Kropp (ed.)
    1988   *The languages of Ghana*. London: Kegan Paul International.
Davidse, Kristin
    to appear   "Functional dimensions of the Dative in English", in: William Van Belle and Willy Van Langendonck (eds.).
Davies, William D.
    1986   *Choctaw verb agreement and Universal Grammar*. Dordrecht: Reidel.
Dirven, René—Günter Radden (eds.)
    1987   *Concepts of case*. Tübingen: Gunter Narr Verlag.
Dixon, R. M. W.
    1971   "A method of semantic description", in: Danny D. Steinberg—Leon A. Jakobovits (eds.), 436–471.
    1972   *The Dyirbal language of North Queensland*. Cambridge: Cambridge University Press.
    1973   "The semantics of giving", in: Maurice Gross—Morris Halle—Marcel-Paul Schützenberger (eds.), 205–223.
    1980   *The languages of Australia*. Cambridge: Cambridge University Press.
    1991   *A new approach to English grammar, on semantic principles*. Oxford: Clarendon Press.
Dryer, Matthew S.
    1986   "Primary objects, secondary objects, and antidative", *Language* 62: 808–845.
DWB. Jacob Grimm—Wilhelm Grimm
    1878   Deutsches Wörterbuch. Leipzig: Hirzel.
    [1984]   [Reprinted München: Deutscher Taschenbuch Verlag.]
Echols, J.M.—H. Shadily
    1963   *An Indonesian-English dictionary*. 2nd edition. Ithaca: Cornell University Press.
Eilfort, William H.—Paul D. Kroeber—Karen L. Peterson (eds.)
    1985   *Papers from the parasession on causatives and agentivity*. Chicago: Chicago Linguistic Society.

Embree, Bernard L. M.
    1973   *A dictionary of Southern Min*. Hong Kong: Hong Kong Language Institute.

Evans, Nick
    1994   Class material for "Topics in Mayali Grammar". Australian Linguistic Institute 1994, La Trobe University.

Filbeck, David
    1975   "A grammar of verb serialization", in: Jimmy G. Harris—James R. Chamberlain (eds.), 112–129.

Fillmore, Charles J.
    1988   "The mechanisms of *Construction Grammar*", in: Shelley Axmaker *et al.* (eds.), 35–55.

Firth, Raymond
    1985   *Tikopia-English dictionary*. Auckland: Auckland University Press.

Fischart, Johann
    1590   *Geschichtklitterung (Gargantua)*. Printed at Grenflug im Gänsserich.
    [1963]   [Reprinted Düsseldorf: Karl Rauch Verlag.]

Foley, William A.
    1986   *The Papuan languages of New Guinea*. Cambridge: Cambridge University Press.

Ford, Kevin C.
    1988   "Structural features of the Central-Togo languages", in: M. E. Kropp Dakubu (ed.), 126–154.

Foris, David Paul
    1993   A grammar of Sochiapan Chinantec. [Unpublished Ph.D. dissertation, University of Auckland.]

Fortescue, Michael
    1984   *West Greenlandic*. Beckenham, Kent: Croom Helm.

Foster, John
    1991   *He tuhituhi Maori*. Auckland: Reed Books.

Frankfurter Wörterbuch
    1971   Frankfurt am Main: Waldemar Kramer.

Geiger, Richard A.—Brygida Rudzka-Ostyn (eds.)
    1993   *Conceptualizations and mental processing of language*. Berlin—New York: Mouton de Gruyter.

Gibson, Jeanne D.
    1980   Clause Union in Chamorro and in Universal Grammar. [Ph.D. disser-
              tation, University of California, San Diego.] Also published, 1992, as
              Clause Union in Chamorro and in Universal Grammar. New York:
              Garland.

Gildersleeve, B.—G. Lodge
    1898   *Gildersleeve's Latin grammar*. Boston: D.C. Heath and Co.

Givón, Talmy
    1975   "Serial verbs and syntactic change: Niger-Congo", in: Charles N. Li
              (ed.), 47–113.

    1979   *On understanding grammar*. New York: Academic Press.

    1984a   *Syntax*. Vol. 1. Amsterdam: Benjamins.

    1984b   "Direct Object and Dative Shifting: semantic and pragmatic case", in:
              Frans Plank (ed.), 151–182.

Goldberg, Adele E.
    1992a   Argument structure constructions. [Ph.D. dissertation, University of
              California at Berkeley.]

    1992b   "The inherent semantics of argument structure: the case of the
              English ditransitive construction", *Cognitive Linguistics* 3: 37–74.

Goudaillier, Jean-Pierre (ed.)
    1987   *Aspekte des Lëtzebuergeschen*. Hamburg: Helmut Buske Verlag.

Green, Georgia M.
    1974   *Semantics and syntactic regularity*. Bloomington: Indiana University
              Press.

Grimshaw, Jane—Armin Mester
    1988   "Light verbs and theta-marking", *Linguistic Inquiry* 19: 205–232.

Gross, Maurice—Morris Halle—Marcel-Paul Schützenberger (eds.)
    1973   *The formal analysis of natural languages*. The Hague: Mouton.

Haiman, John
    1985   *Natural syntax: iconicity and erosion*. Cambridge: Cambridge Uni-
              versity Press.

Hall, Robert A. Jr.
    1966   *Pidgin and Creole languages*. Ithaca: Cornell University Press.

Hammer, A. E.
    1971   *German grammar and usage*. London: Edward Arnold.

Harris, Jimmy G.—James R. Chamberlain (eds.)

    1975   *Studies in Tai linguistics, in honor of William J. Gedney*. Bangkok: Central Institute of English Language.

Harrison, C. J.—Suwipa Sukcharoen

    ms   "The question of polysemy in the Thai lexeme *hay*", Australian National University.

Heine, Bernd

    1990   "The dative in Ik and Kanuri", in: William Croft *et al.* (eds.), 129–149.

Heine, Bernd—Ulrike Claudi—Friederike Hünnemeyer

    1991a   *Grammaticalization: a conceptual framework*. Chicago: The University of Chicago Press.

    1991b   "From cognition to grammar — evidence from African languages", in: Elizabeth Closs Traugott—Bernd Heine (eds.), 149–187.

Hijirida, Kyoko—Muneo Yoshikawa

    1987   *Japanese language and culture for business and travel*. Honolulu: University of Hawaii Press.

Hook, Peter E.

    1991   "The emergence of perfective aspect in Indo-Aryan languages", in: Elizabeth Closs Traugott—Bernd Heine (eds.), 59–89.

Hopper, Paul J.—Sandra A. Thompson

    1980   "Transitivity in grammar and discourse", *Language* 56: 251–299.

Hopper, Paul J.—Sandra A. Thompson (eds.)

    1982   *Studies in transitivity. Syntax and semantics*. Vol. 15. New York: Academic Press.

Huang, Parker Po-fei

    1970   *Cantonese dictionary*. New Haven—London: Yale University Press.

Hudson, Richard

    1992   "So-called 'double objects' and grammatical relations", *Language* 68: 251–276.

Hurford, James R.—Brendan Heasley

    1983   *Semantics: a coursebook*. Cambridge: Cambridge University Press.

Hutchison, John P.

    1981   *The Kanuri language: a reference grammar*. Madison: University of Wisconsin.

Ingram, David
    1989   *First language acquisition: method, description, and explanation.*
                Cambridge: Cambridge University Press.

Jackendoff, Ray
    1983   *Semantics and cognition.* Cambridge, Mass.: The M.I.T. Press.

Jacob, Judith M.
    1968   *Introduction to Cambodian.* London: Oxford University Press.

Janda, Laura A.
    1993a   "The shape of the Indirect Object in Central and Eastern Europe",
                Slavic and East European Journal 37: 533–563.
    1993b   *A geography of case semantics: the Czech dative and the Russian in-*
                strumental. Cognitive Linguistics Research 4. Berlin—New York:
                Mouton de Gruyter.

Johnson, Mark
    1987   *The body in the mind. The bodily basis of meaning, imagination, and*
                reason. Chicago: The University of Chicago Press.

Joseph, Brian D.—Irene Philippaki-Warburton
    1987   *Modern Greek.* London: Routledge.

Kabata, Kaori—Sally Rice
    1995   "Japanese *ni*: the particulars of a somewhat contradictory particle".
                Paper presented at the Fourth International Cognitive Linguistics
                Association Meeting, Albuquerque, New Mexico.

Katz, Jerrold J.
    1972   *Semantic theory.* New York: Harper and Row.

Kemmer, Suzanne—Arie Verhagen
    1994   "The grammar of causatives and the conceptual structure of events",
                Cognitive Linguistics 5: 115–156.

Killingley, Siew-Yue
    1993   *Cantonese.* Languages of the World, Materials 6. München—
                Newcastle: Lincom Eurpoa.

Kimball, Geoffrey D.
    1991   *Koasati grammar.* Studies in the Anthropology of North American
                Indians. Lincoln—London: University of Nebraska Press.

Kisseberth, Charles W.—Mohammad Imam Abasheikh
    1977   "The object relationship in Chi-Mwi:ni, a Bantu language", in: Peter
                Cole—Jerrold M. Sadock (eds.), 179–218.

Kövecses, Zoltán

1986 *Metaphors of anger, pride and love: a lexical approach to the structure of concepts*. Amsterdam: Benjamins.

1990 *Emotion concepts*. New York: Springer Verlag.

Kretschmer, P.—P. Wahrmann

1931 "Literaturbericht für das Jahr 1928", *Glotta* XIX: 153–231.

Kroeber, Paul D.—Robert E. Moore (eds.)

1987 *Native American languages and grammatical typology: Papers from a conference at the University of Chicago April 22, 1987*. Bloomington, Ind.: Indiana University Linguistics Club.

Lakoff, George

1977 "Linguistic gestalts", in: Woodford A. Beach *et al.* (eds.), 236–287.

1987 *Women, fire, and dangerous things*. Chicago: The University of Chicago Press.

1990 "The Invariance Hypothesis: is abstract reason based on image-schemas?", *Cognitive Linguistics* 1: 39–74.

Lakoff, George—Mark Johnson

1980 *Metaphors we live by*. Chicago: The University of Chicago Press.

Lakoff, George—Mark Turner

1989 *More than cool reason: a field guide to poetic metaphor*. Chicago: The University of Chicago Press.

Langacker, Ronald W.

1987 *Foundations of cognitive grammar*. Vol. 1. Stanford: Stanford University Press.

1991 *Foundations of cognitive grammar*. Vol. II. Stanford: Stanford University Press.

Lewis, M. B.

1972 *Malay*. London: Teach Yourself Books.

Li, Charles N. (ed.)

1975 *Word order and word order change*. Austin: University of Texas Press.

1976 *Subject and topic*. New York: Academic Press.

Li, Charles N.—Sandra A. Thompson
  1975   "The semantic function of word order: a case study in Mandarin", in:
            Charles Li (ed.), 163–195.
  1981   *Mandarin Chinese. A functional reference grammar.* Berkeley,
            California: University of California Press.

Liang, James Chao-ping
  1971   Prepositions, co-verbs, or verbs? A commentary on Chinese Grammar
            - past and present. [Unpublished Ph.D. dissertation, University of
            Pennsylvania.]

Lichtenberk, Frantisek
  1982   "Individual hierarchies in Manam", in: Paul J. Hopper—Sandra A.
            Thompson (eds.), 261–276.
  1985   "Syntactic-category change in Oceanic languages", *Oceanic
            Linguistics* XXIV: 1–84.
  1991   "Semantic change and heterosemy in grammaticalization", *Language*
            67: 474–509.

Liem, Nguyen Dang
  1979   "Cases in English and Southeast Asian languages", in: Nguyen Dang
            Liem (ed.), 43–66.

Liem, Nguyen Dang (ed.)
  1979   *South-east Asian linguistics.* Vol. 3. Australian National University,
            Canberra.

Lindner, Susan
  1981   A lexico-semantic analysis of verb-particle constructions with UP and
            OUT. [Unpublished Ph.D. dissertation, University of California, San
            Diego.]

Lock, Andrew (ed.)
  1978   *Action, gesture and symbol: the emergence of language.* London:
            Academic Press.

Longman
  1987   *Longman dictionary of contemporary English.* Harlow: Longman.

Lord, Carol
  1993   *Historical change in serial verb constructions.* Amsterdam: Ben-
            jamins.

Loveday, Leo
> 1986   *Explorations in Japanese sociolinguistics. Pragmatics and beyond.* VII:1. Amsterdam: Benjamins.

Matisoff, James
> 1991   "Areal and universal dimensions of grammatization in Lahu", in: Elizabeth Closs Traugott—Bernd Heine (eds.), 383–431.

Miller, J.—R. Chapman—M. Bronston—J. Reichle (eds.)
> 1980   "Language comprehension in sensorimotor stages V and VI", *Journal of Speech and Hearing Research* 23: 284–311.

Miller, Roy A.
> 1967   *The Japanese language.* Chicago: The University of Chicago Press.

Moravcsik, Edith A.—Jessica R. Wirth—Michael Hammond (eds.)
> 1988   *Studies in syntactic typology.* Amsterdam: Benjamins.

Newman, John
> 1993a   "The semantics of giving in Mandarin", in: Richard A. Geiger— Brygida Rudzka-Ostyn (eds.), 433–485.
> 1993b   "A Cognitive Grammar approach to Mandarin *gěi*", *Journal of Chinese Linguistics* 21: 313–336.
> ms.   "The origin of the *es gibt* construction". Massey University.

Noss, Richard B.
> 1964   *Thai reference grammar.* Washington, D.C.: Foreign Service Institute.

O'Grady, William D.
> 1991   *Categories and case: the sentence structure of Korean.* Amsterdam: Benjamins.

Oates, Lynette F.
> 1964   *A tentative description of the Gunwinggu language.* Oceanic Linguistic Monographs 10. Sydney: University of Sydney.

Ogden, Charles K.
> 1968   *Basic English: international second language.* New York: Harcourt, Brace and World.

Omar, Asmah Haji
> 1981   *The Iban language of Sarawak.* Kuala Lumpur: Dewan Bahasa dan Pustaka.
> 1983   *The Malay peoples of Malaysia and their languages.* Kuala Lumpur: Dewan Bahasa dan Pustaka.

Ortony, Andrew (ed.)
    1979   *Metaphor and thought*. Cambridge: Cambridge University Press.

Pagliuca, William (ed.)
    1994   *Perspectives on grammaticalization*. Amsterdam: Benjamins.

Paul, Hermann
    1969   *Mittelhochdeutsche Grammatik*. 20th ed. Edited by Hugo von Moser
              and Ingeborg Schröbler. Tübingen: Max Niemeyer Verlag.

Pawley, Andrew
    1966   The structure of Kalam: a grammar of a New Guinea Highlands lan-
              guage. [Unpublished Ph.D. dissertation, University of Auckland.]

Perlmutter, David (ed.)
    1983   *Studies in relational grammar 1*. Chicago: The University of Chicago
              Press.

Peyraube, Alain
    1988   *Syntaxe diachronique du chinois*. Paris: Institut des Hautes Études
              Chinoises.

Plank, Frans (ed.)
    1984   *Objects: towards a theory of grammatical relations*. London: Aca-
              demic Press.

Pulleyblank, Douglas
    1987   "Yoruba", in: Bernard Comrie (ed.), 971–990.

Pütz, Martin (ed.)
    1992   *Thirty years of linguistic evolution. Studies in honour of René Dirven
              on the occasion of his sixtieth birthday*. Amsterdam: Benjamins.

Reddy, Michael J.
    1979   "The conduit metaphor - a case of frame conflict in our language
              about language", in: Andrew Ortony (ed.), 284–324.

Rice, Sally Ann
    1987   Towards a cognitive model of transitivity. [Unpublished Ph.D. disser-
              tation, University of California, San Diego.]

Roberts, John
    1987   *Amele*. Beckenham, Kent: Croom Helm.

Rubba, Jo
    1994   "Grammaticalization as semantic change: a case study of preposition
              development", in: William Pagliuca (ed.), 81–101.

Rude, Noel

1991   "Verbs to promotional suffixes in Sahaptian and Klamath", in: Elizabeth Closs Traugott—Bernd Heine (eds.), 185–199.

Rudzka-Ostyn, Brygida

1988   "Semantic extensions into the domain of verbal communication", in: Brygida Rudzka-Ostyn (ed.), 507–554.

1993   "Introduction", in: Richard A. Geiger—Brygida Rudzka-Ostyn (eds.), 1–20.

to appear, a "The Polish dative", in: William Van Belle—Willy Van Langendonck (eds.).

to appear, b "The dative and its extension mechanisms", in: William Van Belle —Willy Van Langendonck (eds.).

Rudzka-Ostyn, Brygida (ed.)

1988   *Topics in cognitive linguistics.* Amsterdam: Benjamins.

Rumsey, Alan

1982   *An intra-sentence grammar of Ungarinjin North-Western Australia.* Pacific Linguistics Series B - No. 86. Australian National University, Canberra: Department of Linguistics.

Salomao, Maria-Margarida

1990   Polysemy, aspect and modality in Brazilian Portuguese: the case for a cognitive explanation of grammar. [Unpublished Ph.D. dissertation, University of California, Berkeley.]

Sandra, Dominiek—Sally Rice

1995   "Network analyses of prepositional meaning: mirroring whose mind—the linguist's or the language user's?" *Cognitive Linguistics* 6: 89–130.

Schachter, P.

1974   "A non-transformational account of serial verbs", *Studies in African Linguistics,* Supplement 5, 253–270.

Schanen, François

1987   "Grundzüge einer Syntax des Lëtzebuergeschen: die Verbalgruppe", in: Jean-Pierre Goudaillier (ed.), 3–90.

Schaub, Willi

1985   *Babungo.* London: Croom Helm.

Scott, N. C.
1956   *A dictionary of Sea Dayak.* London: School of Oriental and African Studies, University of London.

Serzisko, Fritz
1988   "On bounding in Ik", in: Brygida Rudzka-Ostyn (ed.), 429–445.

Shibatani, Masayoshi
1990   *The languages of Japan.* Cambridge: Cambridge University Press.
to appear "Benefactive constructions: a Japanese-Korean perspective", in: Noriko Akatsuka (ed.).

Shibatani, Masayoshi (ed.)
1976   *The grammar of causative constructions. Syntax and Semantics.* Vol. 6. New York: Academic Press.

Shopen, Timothy (ed.)
1985   *Language typology and syntactic description.* Cambridge: Cambridge University Press.

Smith, Michael B.
1985   "An analysis of German dummy subject constructions", in: *Proceedings of the Annual Meeting of the Pacific Linguistics Conference* 1, 412–425.
1987   The semantics of dative and accusative in German: an investigation in Cognitive Grammar. [Unpublished Ph.D. dissertation, University of California, San Diego.]
1993   "Cases as conceptual categories: evidence from German", in: Richard A. Geiger—Brygida Rudzka-Ostyn (eds.), 531–565.

Sperlich, Wolfgang
1993   Namakir: a description of a Central Vanuatu language. [Unpublished Ph.D. dissertation, University of Auckland.]

Stahlke, Herbert
1970   "Serial verbs", *Studies in African Linguistics* 1: 60–99.

Stark, Rachel E. (ed.)
1981   *Language behaviour in infancy and early childhood.* New York: Elsevier North-Holland.

Stein, Gabriele
1991   "The phrasal verb type 'to have a look' in Modern English", *International Review of Applied Linguistics* XXIX: 1–29.

Steinberg, Danny D.—Leon A. Jakobovits (eds.)

1971   *Semantics: an interdisciplinary reader in philosophy, linguistics and psychology*. Cambridge: Cambridge University Press.

Stubbs, Michael

1986   *Educational linguistics*. Oxford: Basil Blackwell.

Sweetser, Eve

1990   *From etymology to pragmatics. Metaphorical and cultural aspects of semantic structure*. Cambridge: Cambridge University Press.

Talmy, Leonard

1975   "Figure and ground in complex sentences", in: Cathy Cogen *et al* (ed.), 419–430.

1976   "Semantic causative types", in Masayoshi Shibatani (ed.), 43–116.

1985a   "Lexicalization patterns: semantic structure in lexical forms", in: Timothy Shopen (ed.), Vol. III, 57–149.

1985b   "Force dynamics in language and thought", in: William H. Eilfort *et al* (eds.), 293–337.

1988   "Force dynamics in language and cognition", *Cognitive Science* 12: 49–100.

Tarring, Charles J.

1886   *A practical elementary Turkish grammar*. London: Kegan Paul, Trench and Co.

Thomas, David D.

1971   *Chrau grammar*. Honolulu: University of Hawaii Press.

Thompson, Sandra A.

1989   *Information flow and 'Dative Shift' in English discourse*. Series A. Paper No. 259. Duisburg: L.A.U.D. (Linguistic Agency University of Duisburg).

Tomasello, Michael

1992   *First verbs: a case study of early grammatical development*. Cambridge: Cambridge University Press.

Topping, Donald M.

1973   *Chamorro reference grammar*. Honolulu: The University of Hawaii Press.

Topping, Donald M.—Pedro M. Ogo—Bernadita C. Dungca

1975   *Chamorro-English dictionary*. Honolulu: The University Press of Hawaii.

Traugott, Elizabeth Closs—Bernd Heine (eds.)

1991 *Approaches to grammaticalization Vol. II*. Amsterdam: Benjamins.

Tuggy, David

1989 "The Nahuatl verb *maka*. A cognitive grammar analysis", *Workpapers of the Summer Institute of Linguistics, University of North Dakota Session* 33: 121–147.

to appear "Dative-like constructions in Orizaba Nahuatl", in: William Van Belle—Willy Van Langendonck (eds.).

Turner, Mark

1990 "Aspects of the Invariance Hypothesis", *Cognitive Linguistics* 1: 247–255.

Vaid, Krishna Baldev

1970 *duusre kinaare se... (From the other shore...)*. Delhi: Radhakrishna Prakashan.

Van Belle, William—Willy Van Langendonck (eds.)

to appear, a *The dative. Descriptive studies*. Amsterdam: Benjamins.

to appear, b *The dative. Theoretical and contrastive studies*. Amsterdam: Benjamins.

Vilgelminina, A. A.

1963 *The Russian verb: aspect and voice*. Moscow: Foreign Languages Publishing House.

Weir, E. M. H.

1986 "Footprints of yesterday's syntax: diachronic development of certain verb prefixes in an OSV language (Nadëb)", *Lingua* 68: 291–316.

West, Michael

1953 *A general service list of English words*. First published in 1936 as *Part V, The general service list, of the interim report on vocabulary selection*. London: Longman.

Whistler, Kenneth *et al.* (eds.)

1977 *Proceedings of the Third Annual Meeting of the Berkeley Linguistics Society*. Berkeley, California: Berkeley Linguistics Society.

Wierzbicka, Anna

1972 *Semantic primitives*. Linguistische Forschungen 22. Frankfurt: Athenäum.

1980 *Lingua mentalis: the semantics of natural language*. Sydney—New York: Academic Press.

1988   *The semantics of grammar*. Amsterdam: Benjamins.

1992   "The search for universal semantic primitives", in: Martin Pütz (ed.), 215–242.

1993   "The alphabet of human thoughts", in: Richard A. Geiger—Brygida Rudzka-Ostyn (eds.), 23–51.

Wlaschim, Katherine

1927   Studien zu den indogermanischen Ausdrücken für Geben und Nehmen. [Unpublished Ph.D. dissertation, Vienna University.]

Woodbury, Anthony C.

1977   "The Greenlandic verbal suffix -*ut*- : interactions of linguistic form and grammatical function", in: Kenneth Whistler *et al.* (eds.), 251–269.

Wurm, Stephen A. (ed.)

1979   *Australian linguistic studies*. Australian National University, Canberra: Department of Linguistics.

Xu, Dan

1994   "The status of marker *gěi* in Mandarin Chinese", *Journal of Chinese Linguistics* 22: 363–394.

Zhang, Shi

1990   "Correlations between the double object construction and preposition stranding", *Linguistic Inquiry* 21: 312–316.

Index of languages

English is referred to throughout the discussion and specific references to English have not been included in this index.

African languages 237, 247
Ainu 13, 173, 257, 277
Akan 212, 218
Amele 17-19, 32, 257
Aramaic languages 284
Australian languages 280
Babungo 106-109
Bahasa Indonesia (*see* Malay)
Bantu 80
Barai 27
Basque 149-150, 152, 153
Bemba 69-70, 73, 74
Bengali 230
Brazilian Portuguese 150, 160, 164, 170-171, 207, 227, 238-239, 268
Bulgarian 137, 140, 141, 142-143, 146, 148, 149, 152, 158, 189, 195, 224-225, 241, 282
Cambodian 92, 151, 173, 180, 189, 217
Cantonese (*see* Chinese)
Chamorro 19-21, 116, 217, 277
Chinantec 77-78, 92-93, 99-100, 115, 267, 280
Chinese 1, 181, 237, 271, 278, 283
    Cantonese 55, 75-77, 219-220, 279, 280
    Fuzhou 215
    Hokkien 180, 220-221
    Mandarin xiv, 16, 120, 135, 174-175, 180, 182, 186, 189, 192, 196-201, 213-215, 217, 218, 221, 235, 247-248, 280, 283, 283, 283
    Teochew 214-215
Chipewyan 46
Choctaw 120-121
Chrau 96-97
Cree (*see* Woods Cree)
Czech 83, 86, 115, 117
Dagbani 246
Danish 159, 167
Dyirbal 1-2, 3, 4, 10-11, 32, 98-99, 255, 280
Enga 277
Eskimo (*see* Greenlandic)
Finnish 16, 89, 94, 118, 173, 187, 189, 194, 226, 228, 235, 242
French 58, 141, 158, 242
German 16, 22, 58, 84, 85, 86, 115, 117, 122, 126-128, 141, 158, 160, 161-164, 168, 186, 187, 213-214, 224-225, 226, 228, 235, 237, 241, 242, 243, 263, 268-270, 271-274, 282 283, 283
    Frankfurt 169, 282
    Hessen 169
    Luxembourg 169, 282
    Middle High 229, 246
    Old High 58, 229
    Trier 169, 282
Greek 86, 93, 94

Greenlandic 71-73, 105-106, 107, 281
Gunwinggu (*see* Kunwinjku)
Hawaiian 240
Hindi 229-231
Hokkien (*see* Chinese)
Hungarian 142, 195
Iatmul 89-90
Iban 90-91, 102-103, 281
Icelandic 158
Ik 23, 225
Indo-European 86, 87, 130, 278
Italian 58, 136, 142, 143, 146, 149,
        151, 152, 154, 158, 167, 183, 187,
        195, 228, 237, 241, 242
Jacaltec 160, 166, 175-176, 240, 241
Japanese 1, 23-27, 32, 103-105, 115,
        221-223, 229, 257, 277, 283
Javanese 137
Kalam 8-10, 32, 255, 274
Kalkatungu 112-114, 280
Kanuri 30-31, 101-102, 103, 105, 281
Klamath 74, 221
Koasati 19
Korean 279, 283
Kunwinjku 110, 135, 177-178, 283
Kwak'wala 111-112, 114
Kwakiutl (*see* Kwak'wala)
Latin 58, 86, 106-107
Malay 16, 31, 70-71, 73, 78-79, 183,
        184, 187, 189, 279, 279, 279
Maltese 28-29
Mandak 62
Mandarin (*see* Chinese)
Māori 22, 26, 93-95, 146, 150, 226, 277
Marathi 223, 226
Melanau 91-92

Murut 96, 281
Nahuatl 109-110, 178
Namakir 70
Nez Perce 135, 221
Norwegian 159, 166, 167
Oceanic languages 270
Old Irish 58
Orizaba Nahuatl (*see* Nahuatl)
Paamese 85-86, 277
Papuan languages 277
Polish 84, 85, 86, 116, 143-144, 149,
        154, 158, 167, 173, 187, 189, 240,
        241, 280
Portuguese (*see* Brazilian Portuguese)
Proto-Australian 17
Proto-Oceanic 270-271
Rumu 137, 141, 146
Russian 16, 62, 83-85, 86, 89, 137, 183,
        184, 187, 188-189, 195, 229, 235,
        280
Sahaptian 74, 221
Sahaptin (*see* Sahaptian)
Senufo 218
Siya 218
Sochiapan Chinantec (*see* Chinantec)
Southeast Asian languages 181, 218
Southeast Solomonic 271
Spanish 16, 152, 153, 158, 167, 224,
        226, 237
Sumambuq (*see* Murut)
Swahili 137, 183
Swedish 159, 228
Teochew (*see* Chinese)
Thai 135, 151, 173, 180, 189, 213, 218
Tikopia 240
Turkish 230

Twi 211-212
Tzotzil 68-70, 73
Ungarinjin 210
Urdu (*see* Hindi)
Veracruz Nahuatl (*see* Nahuatl)
Vietnamese 217
Warlpiri 280
Warrgamay 280
West Greenlandic (*see* Greenlandic)
Woods Cree 29-30, 257
Yatye 247
Yoruba 212, 213, 215, 283

Index of names

Abasheikh, M. 75, 80
Aissen, J. 68
Andrews, A. 280
Andrews, L. 240
Asmah Haji Omar (*see* Omar)
Baker, M. 218, 279
Benedict, H. 4-7
Berlin, B. 3
Blake, B. 86, 112-114
Blansitt, E. 62, 87, 94
Boas, F. 111-112
Borg, A. 21, 28-29, 32
Braunwald, S. 7
Brown, R. 3
Brugman, C. 36, 134
Bynon, T. 8
Capell, A. 178, 210
Carlson, R. 218
Carter, R. 8
Chao, Y. 198, 214, 283
Chapman, R. 5-6, 7
Chatterjee, R. 230
Chung, S. 31, 78-79
Claudi, U. 284
Coate, H. 210
Collins, W. 160
Comrie, B. 21, 28-29, 32, 75
Craig, C. 74, 164, 166, 175, 240, 241
Crowley, T. 85-86
Dahl, Ö. 280
Dancygier, B. xv
Davidse, K. 66
Davies, W. 120-121

Dirven, R. xii
Dixon, R. 1, 10-11, 17, 98, 202, 280, 281
Dryer, M. 62-63
Dungca, B. 19, 21, 116
DWB 169
Echols, J. 189
Eilfort, W. 171
Elkin, A. 210
Embree, B. 180
Evans, N. 110
Filbeck, D. 180
Fillmore, C. 68
Firth, R. 240
Fischart, J. 272-273
Foley, W. 8-10, 27, 87, 89-90, 277
Ford, K. 218
Foris, D. 77-78, 92, 99-100, 115, 267
Fortescue, M. 71, 105-106, 281
Foster, J. 22
Geeraerts, D. xii
Gibson, J. 19-20
Gildersleeve, B. 106-107
Givón, T. 65, 69, 159, 197, 247, 279
Goldberg, A. 68, 75
Green, G. 290
Grimshaw, J. 202
Grimm, J. (*see* DWB)
Grimm, W. (*see* DWB)
Haiman, J. 187
Hale, K. 74
Hall, R. 283
Hammer, A. 161-163

Harrison, C. 180
Heasley, B. 36
Heine, B. 119, 280, 281, 284
Hijirida, K. 1
Hirose, Y. xv
Hook, P. 223, 226, 229, 230, 231
Hopper, P. 205
Huang, P. 219
Hudson, R. 80
Hünnemeyer, F. 284
Hurford, J. 36
Hutchison, J. 30-31, 101
Ingram, D. 5, 7
Jackendoff, R. 35
Jacob, J. 92, 180, 217
Janda, L. 83, 86, 115
Johnson, M. 15, 36, 107, 134, 145, 181,
     275
Joseph, B. 93
Kabata, K. 105
Katz, J. 36
Kemmer, S. 171, 172
Keogh, A. xvi
Killingley, S-Y. 279
Kimball, G. 19
Kisseberth, C. 75, 80
Kövecses, Z. 146
Kretschmer, P. 58, 278
Kroeber, P. 171
Kuteva, T. xv
Lakoff, G. xii, 3-4, 15, 36, 107, 134,
     138, 145, 146, 171, 172, 275, 277
Langacker, R. xii, xiii, 35, 38, 43, 49,
     59, 66, 74, 81-82, 83-84, 104,
     123, 163, 202, 284
Lewis, M. 279

Li, C. 197, 213, 214, 247, 248
Liang, J. 199-200, 215, 283
Lichtenberk, F. 75, 135, 270-271
Liem, N. 217
Lincoln, N. 111
Lindner, S. 36, 135, 148
Lodge, D. 65
Lodge, G. 106-107
Lord, C. 211, 246, 248
Loveday, L. 23
Matisoff, J. 218
Mester, A. 202
Newman, J. xiv, 272, 283
Nguyen Dang Liem (*see* Liem)
O'Grady, W. 280
Oates, L. 177-178, 283
Ogden, C. 13-14, 32
Ogo, P. 19, 21, 116
Omar, A. 90-92, 96, 103, 281
Patrick, J. xv
Paul, H. 229
Pawley, A. 9
Perlmutter, D. xiii, xiv
Peterson, K. 171
Petterson, R. xv
Peyraube, A. 271
Philippaki-Warburton, I. 93
Pulleyblank, D. 213, 215
Reddy, M. 138
Rice, S. xv, xvi, 82, 105, 205, 278
Roberts, J. 17-18
Rosch, E. 3
Rubba, J. 284
Rude, N. 74, 221
Rudzka-Ostyn, B. ix, xii, 84, 86, 116,
     278, 280

Rumsey, A. 210

Salomao, M. 150, 164, 170-171, 207, 227, 238, 239, 268

Sandra, D. 82

Schachter, P. 218

Schanen, F. 169, 282

Schaub, W. 106, 108

Scott, N. 90-91, 103, 281

Serzisko, F. 23

Shadily, H. 189

Shakespeare, W. 239

Shibatani, M. 13, 171, 173, 283

Smith, M. 85, 86, 163

Sperlich, W. 70

Stahlke, H. 247

Starks, D. xv, 29

Stein, G. 203

Stubbs, M. 8, 16

Sukcharoen, S. 180

Sweetser, E. xii, 182, 275, 284

Talmy, L. xii, 40, 171, 172, 182, 282-283

Tarring, C. 230

Thomas, D. 96

Thompson, S. 64, 65-66, 197, 205, 213, 214, 247, 248

Tomasello, M. 7, 97, 100

Topping, D. 19-21, 116

Tuggy, D. xiii, 109, 178

Turner, M. 36, 134, 275

Vaid, K. 230

Verhagen, A. 171, 172

Vilgelminina, A. 229

Wahrmann, P. 58, 278

Wang, W. xvi

Weir, E. 74

West, M. 3

Whitman, W. 189-190

Wierzbicka, A. 12-13, 14, 85, 86

Wlaschim, K. 278

Woodbury, A. 71-72

Xu, D. 283

Yoshikawa, M. 1

Zhang, S. 215

Index of subjects

Ablative 89, 106-107, 118

Absolutive 109-110, 113-114

Abstract setting 163, 168

Accusative 62, 85, 93, 128, 161
   See also Object

Active zone 42-46
   See also Representation

Adessive 89

Adposition 81, 247, 280
   source for verb affix 73-74, 279

Adversative 51-52

Agent
   AGENT-PATIENT interaction 61-64, 66, 259
   See also Trajector

Allative 71, 72, 89-94 passim, 113, 118
   compared with dative 89
   compared with locative 93-95
   for RECIPIENT 90, 119-120
   form cognate with "come" and "go" 90-92, 111-112
   See also Goal

Applicative 30-31

Argument Transfer 202

Auxiliary 230-231, 282

Base 37-59 passim, 152
   See also Cognitive Grammar; Frame; Profile

Basic English 13-14, 254-255
   See also Basic vocabulary

Basic level category 3-4, 138, 277

Basic vocabulary 7-14, 192, 254-255, 258, 266, 274-275

as a source for extensions 258
   body parts 275
   semantic primitives 12, 13
   Swadesh Word List 8
   See also Basic English

Benefactive 51-52, 81, 95-97, 130, 194, 199, 205, 211-212, 217-223, 250, 261, 281
   Cantonese *béi* 219-220
   Hokkien *hɔ* 220-221
   See also Polysemy; Representation

Beneficiary 152-153, 211, 219, 223
   See also Benefactive

Body parts 239-240, 275, 284

C-command x

Case xiv, 52, 81, 111, 280
   See also Ablative; Absolutive; Accusative; Adessive; Allative; Benefactive; Comitative; Dative; Elative; Ergative; Genitive; Illative; Inessive; Instrumental; Locative; Nominative; Object; Schematic network; Subject

Causation 145, 234, 249, 263
   causative suffix 135
   compared with enablement 171
   different types of 171-173, 283
   manipulation type 173-175
   part of ditransitive *give* 130
   part of GIVE 13, 19, 34, 173, 257, 277

Causative (*see* Causation)

Cognitive Grammar 35-36, 56, 62, 81,
   122, 135, 163, 191, 202, 206, 284
   See also Base; Domain; Figure;
   Ground; Landmark; Profile;
   Representation; Schematic network;
   Trajector
Cognitive linguistics ix-xii, 36, 136,
   171, 253, 260, 262, 265, 275
   argumentation xii
   methodology xi
   paradigm ix-xii
   See also Experientialist approach;
   Metaphor; Polysemy
Comitative 107-109
Completedness (*see* Perfectivity)
Complex matrix 53-54, 59, 95, 185,
   191, 224
   See also Domain
Conduit metaphor 138
   See also Interpersonal
   communication
Construction Grammar 66
Control domain 46-48
Core Vocabulary (*see* Basic
   vocabulary)
Cross-linguistic approach 266
Dative 81, 82-87, 89, 126-128, 130-
   132, 213, 260, 280, 281
   dative of interest 84, 199
   double datives 112-114
   extended to benefactive 120
   for experiencer 117
   for malefactive 116
   for THING 112-114
   in Cognitive Grammar 126-128
   meaning of 82-87, 113

punctual vs. areal 85-86, 278
   with GIVE and TAKE 115-118
   See also Polysemy; Representation;
   Schematic network
Dative Shift 72, 73
   See also Ditransitive; Object
Derived forms of GIVE 268-270
Destinatory
   compared with donatory 129
Direct objectivity 62
Ditransitive
   with figurative GIVE 202
   with literal GIVE 21, 74-80, 99, 113,
   260, 267, 280
   with literal *give* 64-66, 74-75, 123,
   128-129
   See also Dative Shift; Object
Domain 37-54 passim, 135, 205, 234
   complex matrix 54, 135
   control 37, 46-48
   force-dynamics 37, 48-51, 60
   human interest 37, 51-52
   source domain 134
   spatio-temporal 37-46
   target domain 134
   See also Cognitive Grammar
Donatory 212, 217
   compared with destinatory 129
Double *gěi* construction 214-215
   See also Serial verb
Double object (*See* Ditransitive)
Elaboration site 54-56, 123
   unfilled 54-56
   See also Representation
Elative 89
Emergence 145-157, 249

See also Es gibt; Manifestation;
Representation
Empty category principle x
Enablement 181-194, 234, 249
  compared with causation 171
  compared with permission 188
  different types of 181
  negated restriction 182
  positive enablement 182
  See also Representation
Ergative 176
Es gibt 161-164, 166, 263
  compared with *es ist* 161-163
  origin of 163, 271-274
  See also Manifestation
Existential construction 271
  See also Es gibt; Manifestation;
  Representation
Experientialist approach xi, xiv, 191,
  254, 257, 275, 284
Figurative GIVE (*see* GIVE,
  figurative)
Figure x, xiii, 35, 38, 40
  See also Cognitive Grammar;
  Profile; Trajector
For
  with RECIPIENT 97
Frame ix, 37, 130, 153, 212, 247, 249
  See also Base
Generative paradigm xi
  See also Transformational Grammar
Genitive 283
  simple vs. general in Dyirbal 98-99,
  281
  See also Possession
GIVE, figurative xv, 133

__ "big stomach" 240
__ "concert" 142-143
__ "fruit" 151-152
__ "judgement" 141
__ "light" 149
__ "noise" 146-148
__ "people" 240-243
__ "permission" 182-185
__ "profit" 154
__ "tear" 145
__ "to think" 186-188
__ "word" 141
__ "young" 149-150
agentive preposition 135, 196-198
auxiliary use 230-231, 282
"become" 168-171
benefactive 211-212, 217-223, 263
causation 171-178, 263
causative suffix 135
compared with TAKE 243-248, 264-
265
completedness 228-231
emergence 144-156, 263, 273
emphatic in imperative 199-201
enablement 181-194
for birth 152-153
for growth 153
forming manner adverb 151
heterosemy 135-136, 270
hortative 194-195
impersonal 160-166, 237, 271-274
impersonal reflexive 237
in Oceanic benefactive 271
interpersonal communication 136-
144, 234, 263
intransitive 168

involving metonymy 238-240

manifestation 156-171, 263

meaning of 133

motion 170, 223-228, 263

movement away 225-227

movement into 227-228

object marker 248

passive 166-167

perfectivity 228-230, 231, 263

permission 234

polysemy 270

presentative 158-160, 167

purposive 135, 180-181

RECIPIENT marker 211-215, 263

reflexive 153, 158-160, 237

review of extensions 262-265

schematic interaction 201-210, 263

summary of figurative extensions
(diagrammatic) 233

"tell" 282

verbal affix 135

See also Ditransitive; Representation

Give, figurative

__ *a call* 148, 176-177

__ *a concert* 142-143

__ *a hand* 239

__ *advice* 136

__ *me to warble songs* 189, 192

__ *milk* 145

__ *on to* 226-227

__ *one's daughter in marriage* 240

__ *one's word* 141

__ *oneself out as* 160

__ *oneself to a man* 241

__ *oneself to God* 241

__ *permission* 183

__ *someone the boot* 238

__ *the ball a good throw* 204

__ *the ball a kick* 204

__ *the car a wash* 201-207

__ *the show a miss* 203

__ *to understand* 186-188

__ *way* 184-185

(I) __ you the Queen! 242

ditransitive 205-206

perfective 176, 202, 203, 205

what gives? 168

with *to* phrase 205-206

See also Representation

GIVE, literal xv, 61

alternative constructions 266

as a basic level category 3-21, 138,
254-256

as a complex matrix 54-55

as a source of extensions 258

as basic vocabulary xiv, xv, 30, 34,
254-256

as goal-oriented 23

as transfer of control 3

basic forms of 17-21, 257

causative as part of 19-21

choice of object 62

direct objectivity 63

directionality 22-23

exceptional forms of 21-31

force-dynamics 66

honorific variants 23-27

influence on TAKE 60

metaphorical extensions 15-16

passive 28-29

prototypical meaning 1-4, 34

reciprocity 1

review of constructions 259-262
role of hands in 42-46
semantic complexity xv, 33-34, 254, 256-257
summary of constructions (diagrammatic) 131
verb marking 68-74
with allative phrase 72
with benefactive phrase 95-97, 99, 267
with dative phrase 82-88
with goal phrase 88-93
with incorporated object 109-110
with instrumental phrase 105-109
with locative phrase 93-95
with possessor phrase 98-101, 267
with RECIPIENT as object 68-70
with RECIPIENT as primary object 75
with THING as object 70, 74
with THING as primary object 75-78
with two datives 112-114
with two oblique phrases 110-114
zero morph 17-19, 277
See also Representation
Give, literal 87
__ *me...* 4, 277
__ *me* compared with *give to* 128-129
__ *someone a book to read* 185
__ *to* 64, 66
compared with *take* 118
in children's comprehension 5-6
in children's production 6-7
in Cognitive Grammar 122-126
in language acquisition 4-7

in West's list 3
See also Representation
Goal 81, 89, 224, 261, 281
See also Allative
Grammaticalization xi, 135-136, 238, 262, 266, 270, 284
See also Heterosemy
Ground x
See also Figure
Have
used for *give* 100-101
Heterosemy 135-136, 181, 270
verb and preposition 211, 215, 218
See also Grammaticalization
Iconicity 17, 30
Illative 89
Impersonal GIVE 160-166
Incorporated object 109-110
Indirect object 84, 214
Inessive 89
Instrumental 72, 105-109, 111-112, 130, 261, 281
Interpersonal communication 134-144, 184, 188, 214, 249
See also Conduit metaphor; Representation
Intransitive GIVE 168
Invariance Hypothesis 134
Landmark (in Cognitive Grammar) 38-46 passim, 56, 74, 90, 92, 103, 114, 122-130 passim, 166, 196, 197, 206, 207, 219, 220, 227
two landmarks 74, 113-114
with emergent senses 138-154 passim

See also Cognitive Grammar;
Ground; Object; Trajector
Language acquisition 4-7, 274
  gimme 7
  have for *give* 100-101
  use of *for* with RECIPIENT 97
Light verbs 202
Literal GIVE (*see* GIVE, literal)
Locative 81, 93-95, 130, 261
  See also Ablative; Allative; Goal
Manifestation 156-171, 249
Manipulation 173-175
  See also Causation
Metaphor xi, 36, 121, 170, 227, 231,
  238, 240, 262, 267
  metaphorical productivity 16, 258,
  274
  See also Cognitive linguistics;
  Metonymy; Polysemy
Metonymy xi, 153, 238-240, 262
  See also Cognitive linguistics;
  Metaphor; Polysemy
Mirror Principle 279
Motion 170, 223-228 passim, 250
  abstract 225, 227-228
  as part of figurative GIVE 223
Motivation for extensions xiv, 264
  See also Polysemy
Natural path 49
Nominative 161
Nuclear verbs 11
Object
  higher and lower types 70
  incorporated 109-110
  primary vs. secondary 75-80, 123,
  280

subject-object organization 81
  See also Dative Shift; Ditransitive;
  Landmark
Oblique 105, 110, 113-114, 260, 261
  Japanese *ni* 103-105
Passive 77, 79-80, 245, 280
  passive GIVE 166-167
Perfectivity 176-177, 195, 202, 205,
  228-231, 246, 250
Permission 181-194
  compared with enablement 188
  See also Enablement; Representation
Polysemy xiv, 35, 133, 135, 237, 260,
  270, 273-274, 280
  agent and authority 200-201
  agent and benefactive 198
  allative 119-120
  allative and ablative 118
  allative and dative 94
  benefactive and malefactive 116-117
  benefactive and possessor 120-121
  benefactive and RECIPIENT 217
  complex types 101-105
  constructional xi, 68, 116
  dative 119, 280
  directionality of extensions 232, 281
  in grammatical categories 81
  instrumental and comitative 107-109
  Japanese *ni* 103-105, 115
  Kanuri *rò* 101-102
  locative and dative 94
  motivating extensions 234-237
  source and goal 92
  THING and RECIPIENT 113
  to 120

See also Heterosemy; Metaphor;
Metonymy; Schematic network
Possession 47-48, 81, 98-101, 130, 261
See also Genitive
Predicate 38
See also Base; Profile
Presentative 158-160, 167
See also Manifestation
Primary object 62, 75-80, 123, 280
primary objectivity 62
See also Object
Profile 38-59 passim, 141, 186, 191,
196, 215
See also Base; Cognitive Grammar;
Figure
Prototype xiii, 64, 82, 280
Prototypical meaning 47-48, 68, 82, 86,
88
in schematic network 120
Purposive 180-181
See also Causation; Enablement
Quantifier Shift 78-79
Receive 49-51, 244
See also Representation
RECIPIENT 250
complexity of 234
Reflexive GIVE 158-160
Relational Grammar xiii, 72, 73, 214
See also Mirror Principle
Representation (diagrammatic) of
AGENT-PATIENT model extended
to GIVE 67
base of GIVE-type predicates 39
CHANGE HANDS 45
clause structure associated with
literal GIVE 131

examples of emergence 155
examples of manifestation 165
extension to benefactive 222
extension to causative 179
extension to communication 139
extension to emergence 147
extension to enablement 193
extension to manifestation 157
extension to RECIPIENT 216
GIVE (control domain) 47
GIVE (force-dynamics domain) 50
GIVE (human interest domain) 52
GIVE (spatio-temporal domain) 39
GIVE (spatio-temporal domain,
alternative) 42
GIVE (with active zones) 44
GIVE (with RECIPIENT
unspecified) 57
give car a wash 209
give me money 124
give money to me 125
mir Geld geben 127
multiple motivations of "permit"
extension 236
overview of extensions 233
RECEIVE 50
TAKE 59
THROW 44
wash car 208
See also Schematic network
Schematic interaction 201-210, 228,
234, 250
Schematic meaning 10
See also Polysemy; Prototypical
meaning

Schematic network 81-82, 110, 133,
    261
  Babungo *nè* 109
  Chrau benefactive 97
  complex types 101-109
  Czech dative 117
  directionality of extensions 119-121
  Dyirbal simple genitive 99
  English *to* 90-91
  German dative 84-85, 117
  Kanuri *rò* 102
  Maori *ki* 95
  reversal of meaning 116-117
  Russian dative 82-86
  significance of 119-122
  West Greenlandic instrumental 107
  See also Polysemy; Representation;
    Schematic meaning
Secondary object 75-80
  See also Object; Primary object
Semantic complexity 33-34, 258
  as a source for extensions 258
  compared with basicness 34, 257
  See also Schematic network
Serial verb 211, 212, 263
  See also Double *gěi* construction
Subjacency x
Subject
  subject-object organization 61-62,
    66-68, 81
  See also Trajector
Swadesh Word List 8
  See also Basic vocabulary
TAKE 56-59, 264
  as source-oriented 23
  force-dynamics 58-59

influence on GIVE 58, 283
object marker 247-248
opposite of GIVE 243
with dative phrase 115-118
Take
  __ *a beating* 245
  __ *a message* 244
  __ *advice* 244
  __ *charge* 245
  __ *off* 243
  __ *oneself off* 225
  __ *permission* 183
  __ *the book to read* 247
Target domain 134
  interpersonal communication 138-
    140
  See also Domain
Time-stability scale 159
Topicworthiness 66
Trajector 38-46 passim, 56, 74, 122-130
    passim, 138, 140, 166, 197, 201, 207
  agentive trajector 278
  trajector-landmark with *give*
    122-127
  with emergent senses 145-156
  See also Cognitive Grammar;
    Figure; Landmark; Subject
Transformational Grammar 72, 73, 199-
    200
  See also C-command; Dative Shift;
    Generative paradigm; Quantifier
    Shift; Subjacency
Transitivity 205
Verb particle 135
Verbal communication (*See*
    Interpersonal communication)

West's list 3
Wh-questions 80
Word semantics 259
Zipf's Law 17

DATE DUE

AUG 1 9 1999			